DISPLACEMENT BEYOND CONFLICT

Displacement Beyond Conflict

Challenges for the 21st Century

Christopher McDowell and Gareth Morrell

Berghahn Books

New York • Oxford

Published in 2010 by

Berghahn Books

www.berghahnbooks.com

©2010 Christopher McDowell and Gareth Morrell

Library of Congress Cataloging-in-Publication Data

A C.I.P. record for this book is available from the Library of Congress.

British Library Cataloguing in Publication Data

A catalogue record for this book is available from the British Library
Printed in the United States on acid-free paper.

ISBN: 978-1-84545-772-3 (hardback)

Contents

List of Tables, Boxes and Figures

Tables

Boxes

Figure

Foreword

With more than twenty-six million people uprooted within their own country by conflicts and human rights violations, internal displacement is one of the great human tragedies of our time. While the international community has slowly come to acknowledge the scale of the problem, recognised the specific vulnerabilities of Internally Displaced Persons (IDPs) and improved its response to their needs, it has until recently mainly focused its attention on one specific category of displaced people – those fleeing conflicts and human rights violations. Over the last few years, it has been acknowledged that the causes of displacement are increasingly rooted in multiple, interlinked factors, from extreme deprivation and poverty, to environmental degradation and natural disasters, to conflict.

In the hope of bringing some clarity to the concepts and definitions used to describe and analyse the various experiences of displacement, the Internal Displacement Monitoring Centre (IDMC) commissioned Christopher McDowell, a political anthropologist specialising in population displacement, forced migration and involuntary resettlement to carry out a study in 2007 on non-conflict related displacement. The study provided the inspiration for this book. The IDMC is grateful to Christopher McDowell and Gareth Morrell for their much-needed and valuable clarification of the complex legal, political and humanitarian dimensions of forced displacement.

Kate Halff, Head of IDMC

Acknowledgements

The authors are indebted to Frederik Kok and the team at the IDMC in Geneva for their advice and guidance on all aspects of this study, and in particular for their topical input into Chapter Seven and critical commentary at various stages of the book's preparation. We are also grateful to Dr Ruwani Jayewardene whose expert advice on the national and international legal and policy frameworks governing development and displacement, and the weaknesses in those frameworks, contributed importantly to the preparation of Chapter Five in this report and shaped also the concluding comments. Chapter Five contains ideas presented in an unpublished proposal for further research on these issues prepared by McDowell and Jayewardene in 2007 and 2008. We are grateful to Professor John Pilgrim for allowing us to use material drawn from a research proposal prepared by McDowell and Pilgrim on multiple displacement in Cambodia in 2007. Brief sections from Christopher McDowell's article published in the *Australasian Journal of Trauma and Disaster Studies* (2002, Volume 2) are included in the Conclusion. The views expressed in this volume are those of the authors who take responsibility for any errors or omissions.

List of Abbreviations

ADB	Asian Development Bank
CHAP	Common Humanitarian Action Plan
CLSPI	China Land Survey and Planning Institute
COHRE	Centre on Housing Rights and Evictions
CRED	Centre for Research on the Epidemiology of Disasters
DDP	Development Displaced Person
EM-DAT	International Emergencies Database
HFA	Hyogo Framework for Action
IASC	Inter-Agency Standing Committee (on humanitarian assistance)
ICAR	Information Centre about Asylum and Refugees
ICCPR	International Covenant on Civil and Political Rights
ICRC	International Committee of the Red Cross
IFRC	International Federation of Red Cross and Red Crescent Societies
IDMC	Internal Displacement Monitoring Centre (Geneva)
IDP	Internally Displaced Person
IOM	International Organisation for Migration
IPCC	Intergovernmental Panel on Climate Change
IPRI	International Peace Research Institute
LAA	Land Acquisition Act (India)
MDC	Movement for Democratic Change
MEND	Movement for the Emancipation of the Niger Delta
MJN	Niger Movement for Justice
MPCI	Patriotic Movement for Côte d'Ivoire
NEZ	New Economic Zone
NHA	National Highways Act (India)

NPC	National People's Congress
NRC	Norwegian Refugee Council
OECD/DAC	Organisation for Economic Cooperation and Development/Development Assistance Committee
ODI	Overseas Development Institute, London
RETA	Regional Technical Assistance Programme
R2P	Responsibility to Protect
SEZ	Special Economic Zone
SPDC	State Peace and Development Council
UDHR	Universal Declaration of Human Rights
UN	United Nations
UNHCR	United Nations High Commission for Refugees
UNOCHA	United Nations Office for the Coordination of Humanitarian Affairs
WCS	Wildlife Conservation Society
WWF	World Wildlife Fund
ZANU-PF	Zimbabwe African National Union – Patriotic Front

CHAPTER ONE

Introduction

We have long been aware of refugee flight and asylum seeking in Western countries occurring against the backdrop of international armed conflict and civil war. The provision of humanitarian assistance and protection to displaced populations has been under constant scrutiny with a general acceptance that while the delivery and effectiveness of material aid is improving there remain serious gaps in on-the-ground protection combined with slow progress towards genuine conflict resolution and longer term rehabilitation. This situation is worsened by inconsistent funding and the politicisation of humanitarian aid that threatens to undermine the cooperation upon which it depends. By means of comparison with the 'non-conflict' humanitarian challenges discussed in this volume, we devote some time in the following chapters to assessing continuing efforts to reform the humanitarian system and to address those shortcomings through better institutional coordination and a genuine widening of responsibility to nongovernmental groups and organisations that are well positioned to assist in humanitarian work and to achieve better targeting of donor assistance.

While media coverage of humanitarian responses is fairly extensive, there is far less awareness of population displacement and the responses to it, occurring and largely remaining within the developing and fast industrialising world, but which is not a direct consequence of armed conflict. Such displacement, often misleadingly termed 'non-conflict displacement', is largely beyond the remit of the UN-led humanitarian reform process and its agencies except in those circumstances where streams of displacement, both conflict and non-conflict, intersect. An illustration of this is the so called asylum–migration nexus[1] which recognises that people fleeing persecution and conflict often share their flight and the vulnerabilities this entails with people who are traditionally termed economic migrants pursuing opportunities beyond the shores of their own countries. Most graphically, these mixed types of movements grasp media headlines where overcrowded boats make landfall on Mediterranean shores at the height of summer and thus assume the proportions of a humanitarian event. The United Nations High Commission for Refugees (UNHCR), under its High Commissioner Antonio Guterres, acknowledges that such movement poses difficult challenges to the world's refugee agency which has a narrow mandate to protect people fleeing persecution and that in order to fulfil that mandate the organisation must now confront the realities of globalisation and respond to the protection needs of 'people on the move' even where they include non-refugees.

This volume makes a contribution to better understanding this modern phenomenon – though Elizabeth Colson (2007) prefers to describe such movement as a 'process' rather than a phenomenon – of 'non-conflict displacement': in the context of state-led economic development and private development; as a result of environmental change and natural disasters; and that which is politically motivated. The term 'non-conflict' is used to describe displacement which occurs outside of formally declared armed conflict as recognised in international humanitarian law. The distinction is made because there is a fundamental difference in the way law provides protection for, and the international community through its international institutions responds to, complex forced displacement emergencies in formal conflicts as opposed to non-declared or non-recognised emergency situations, the clear inference being that in the latter there are protection and humanitarian needs that may be similar to armed conflict situations – effectively people find themselves in a refugee-like situation experiencing similar human rights violations – but which are not being adequately acknowledged or addressed. Furthermore, such displacement emergencies consistently avoid international scrutiny and leave populations dangerously exposed to the actions of states that hide behind the too rarely challenged veil of sovereignty. This point was most graphically illustrated in the aftermath of Cyclone Nargis in Burma in 2008 when the ruling junta refused to permit the delivery of essential international aid, citing claims to sovereignty and suspecting political motives on the part of Western governments with the effect of endangering the lives of many tens of thousands of people. The term 'non-conflict' may also be considered misleading because all displacement, whatever the underlying or proximate causes, is embedded in conflict: conflict between individuals and the state, between people and the environment, within displaced communities, and between displaced communities and with those among whom they settle. Displacement, at its most rudimentary, is principally a conflict between the powerful and the powerless and the inability of the law, the state and its institutions and, importantly, international bodies to protect the latter against the former and to address underlying structural inequalities and historical disputes.

For many it will be unsatisfactory to make such a generalisation about what are very divergent phenomena or processes. Displacement taking place as a result of natural disasters is very different to deliberate forced evictions by a political leadership determined to hang on to power at all costs. Creeping desertification and the resultant loss of productive land and other resources essential for building livelihoods generates population displacement that is very different to the forced relocation of people to make way for a mega dam or an urban highway. And in the case of climate change the displacement effects are only now being modelled and there are many uncertainties related to our technical ability to better manage, for example, sea level rise or resistance to erratic weather in order to avoid or minimise displacement. Where displacement is predicted as inevitable, such as following the submergence of low-lying islands or populated coastal strips, the feasibility of anticipatory population resettlement is only now being discussed.

While we acknowledge, therefore, that displacement takes many forms, as do the responses to it, this volume suggests there are significant similarities in these divergent displacement experiences to justify the intellectual task of examining them in the round. It is also argued that these similarities strongly support the case for strengthening ongoing efforts to firmly embed the UN Guiding Principles on Internal Displacement as the international standard to guide governments as well as international humanitarian and development agencies in providing humanitarian assistance and protection to displaced people with a minimum aim to at least match the levels of protection and international concern that in theory guide responses to armed conflict emergencies. This is a tall order because, as we later describe, there are states who are resistant and fearful of what they regard as yet more international intrusion into sovereign matters, and who would need to be persuaded of the value of human rights-based Guiding Principles which place the world's development, environment, natural disaster and political fiat-displaced on the same stage as conflict-displaced people. According to them the same levels of legal protection would recognise the common vulnerabilities that all displacement creates particularly for those most marginalised in society. Indeed, recent initiatives such as the African Union draft protocol on displacement and the Protocol on Protection and Assistance to

Internally Displaced Persons adopted by member states of the International Conference on the Great Lakes Region may yet serve to trigger the next stage in the acceptance of the Principles as a 'convention by any other name' by spawning new binding instruments that oblige states to incorporate the provisions of the Principles into their domestic law and which as a consequence would see states voluntarily giving up fractions of their sovereignty. There are, however, many obstacles which would need to be overcome in order for this position to be reached and we address these with a particular focus on the contentious challenge of development-created displacement and involuntary resettlement.

This study is aware of the conceptual and definitional difficulties that arise when trying to conceive of displacement as a single phenomenon. For this reason Chapter Two examines the unsatisfactory lexicon of terms used to describe people who have been forced against their will to abandon their homes and familiar surroundings and lose their source of livelihood as a result of external events over which they have insufficient control. Like others who have examined this mainly officially-derived set of terms, we note the very real human impacts of the political and administrative use of terms or labels when they serve to set limits on people's entitlements and set them apart as 'people of concern' not only to legally constituted agencies with mandates to help, but also in society where they are often perceived as a threat and a cause of instability. This is true both within their countries of origin as well as in a different country, as refugees or migrants are singled out for blame and, seen most starkly in South Africa in 2007 and 2008, for physical harm. This official and socially institutionalised labelling has developed over time as layers of policies, new laws and mandates embed difference and create distinct classes of citizens where displacement becomes an obstacle to the realisation of the full rights of citizenship. However, and related to the humanitarian reform process, a range of human rights initiatives mean the problems posed by rigid demarcations are being rethought. Increasingly it is acknowledged that displacement, while generating protection and humanitarian needs, is a symptom of deeper underlying structural problems. It is further acknowledged that a displacement-driven humanitarian focus is too narrow. The displaced may be the most visible victims, and may be the most accessible (but not always) and amenable to humanitarian aid, but there is more likely to be as much if not greater need among those who are not displaced but are rather trapped in situations of escalating violence. There are dangers, of course, that directing assistance on the basis of need, as the International Committee of the Red Cross (ICRC) advocates, rather than on the physical fact of displacement, may cause the pendulum to swing too far in the other direction at a time when the number of people internally displaced by conflict is rising and their situation is worsening. These are the kinds of discussions taking place in the corridors of the Palais des Nations in Geneva and shaping funding decisions of the main Western donors. The commonly understood definition of displacement as physical uprooting is also criticised for positing a botanic understanding of the human condition as rooted in one place and identifiable in that place as opposed to a more nomadic understanding acknowledging movement as a fundamentally human characteristic. From part of the displacement literature, specifically that dealing with involuntary resettlement studies, displacement is understood as being alienated from physical, social and cultural resources essential to maintain a life and livelihood of choice which may be the fate of people who remain in the same location as a result of actions taken by others to deny access to those resources and is not necessarily linked to relocation.

There will be further concern that the catch-all of 'non-conflict displacement' assumes equivalence between displacement events that is overly reliant on our experiences of refugee flight over the past sixty years and, in seeking solutions from the same shelf of operational and legal options that has governed the refugee regime, risks the replication of some of the same mistakes or watering down of the hard-won protections for refugee populations. There is a danger of contriving equivalence most notably in the journalistic shorthand of 'development refugees' and 'climate refugees'. For this reason, and throughout this volume, we go to some lengths to carefully prise apart the complex causalities that generate displacement in the separable domains of planned economic development, natural disasters, environmental change including climate change, and situations of unstable peace where instability does not reach the legal threshold of armed conflict. Through an examination of the literature we seek also to understand the similarities of outcomes for displaced populations. Further we examine the policy and legal frameworks within which people's rights and entitlements are defined and which govern the types and quality of assistance they can expect to receive.

Chapter Three develops further a theme of the volume which is the need for definitional clarity when discussing 'global displacement' by examining ongoing attempts at capturing and explaining its scale. We explain that achieving an accurate count of the worlds displaced is inherently difficult because populations are fluid, because circumstances are not conducive to robust and verifiable census methodologies and because governments, humanitarian agencies, civil society and the media will occasionally use numbers that best support a set of arguments or a funding call rather than striving for accuracy. The Internal Displacement Monitoring Centre (IDMC), which is part of the Norwegian Refugee Council (NRC) and based in Geneva, has made enormous strides in the rigorous collection, collation and presentation of the scale of internal displacement in conflict situations and has successfully initiated a reconsideration of how UN agencies define and count displacement for their own purposes. However, based on this chapter's survey of existing data sources for displacement in the domains that principally concern this study – development, political instability, natural disasters and environmental change – definitional confusion remains coupled with politicised data gathering and alarmist presentation producing unreliable statistics that cloud rather than clarify policy making and public understanding. The chapter picks its way through available data sets and seeks to explain discrepancies including both underestimations of the scale of displacement (common to planned development schemes and forced evictions) and overestimations (which is an emerging problem with the climate change literature). It is argued that there is a need for the more systematic monitoring and analysis of these fast changing non-conflict displacement domains.

The governance and management of 'non-conflict displacement' is discussed in Chapter Four with a focus on the evolution of the Guiding Principles on Internal Displacement. We explore the process around the Principles spearheaded by the Brookings Institution and the Special Representative of the UN Secretary General on the Human Rights of IDPs and their role as the springboard for regional and national legislation of aimed at addressing the so called protection deficit: that is, a deficit in existing laws to prevent displacement and protect internally displaced persons, as well as a deficit in actual practice to deliver protection and humanitarian assistance. The human rights foundations and scope of the Principles are described and their implications for national governments and for global agencies charged with upholding international agreements on protection are also considered. The provisions of the Principles are compared with other displacement management policies, specifically those advanced by the World Bank and the Asian Development Bank (ADB) (and incorporated by the Western Development Assistance Countries) in their own operational directives governing the uprooting and resettling of people as a result of development-justified land acquisition financed with Bank loans and grants. This comparison is returned to in the Conclusion where ideas are presented for incorporating some of those Principles into new laws governing land acquisition and involuntary resettlement to radically improve the protection of individuals and communities displaced through development interventions. The Chapter further examines the evolving cluster approach as one aspect of ongoing humanitarian reform and considers what the new approaches might mean for non-conflict displaced people by assessing the challenges such reforms seek to overcome. An important element of this is the reworking of the basis upon which international agencies work with national governments and how any reframing of that relationship may open the door to a broader engagement on displacement issues. It is not suggested, as discussed in the concluding chapter, that a UN humanitarian-led approach is necessarily the best approach for all displacement challenges. However, it is clear that climate change, if predictions are correct, demands unprecedented levels of international cooperation (as well as regional cooperation) to 'manage' its migration and displacement impacts and the current reform process, though very modest, may be a step towards a shared vision and the means of achieving it.

Chapter Five focuses on the deliberate and planned displacement of populations occurring as a result of political and economic decisions designed to accelerate modernisation and industrialisation. It concentrates on India and China, both fast-industrialising countries where the respective governments are acquiring or permitting the private sector to acquire vast areas of rural and large areas of urban land for development and economic projects requiring the involuntary resettlement of many millions of people annually. The chapter describes the different ways in which land is acquired and resettlement is governed and managed in India and China by drawing on a recent ADB technical assistance project in which McDowell participated. It describes the challenges involved in acquiring land and resettling and compensating individuals, households and communities; the complexity of the challenges often proves too great for policy makers and administrators resulting in the impoverishment and social and political marginalisation of those resettled. This analysis is important because it is in the domain of development-created displacement, the authors would argue, that we best understand important aspects of the politics of displacement in non-conflict settings, and the huge socio-cultural and economic impacts displacement and resettlement have on all populations affected, but particularly on vulnerable and minority populations. It is also the domain in which non-binding but widely accepted guidance on displacement and resettlement, and national laws governing resettlement are at their most sophisticated. That is not to say they are always effective or well implemented: they are not and this is discussed further in the Conclusion, but technical issues relevant to displacement and resettlement in other domains (related to climate change or natural disasters for example) around asset valuation, compensation, prior informed consultation, cultural heritage loss and other important issues are being researched and thought through in policy making and accountability procedures such as the Inspection Panel of the World Bank with considerable relevance to the overall population-displacement challenge.

In Chapter Six we turn our attention to environmental and climatic change creating conditions that are widely predicted to lead to changes in human settlement including increases in human displacement, migration and relocation. The Chapter explores the literature that debates observed or predicted linkages between changes in the environment and displacement outcomes, specifically drawing on environmental migration research which cautions against making direct causal connections between complex change events (desertification, land degradation, drying rivers or natural disasters) and a human or societal response. It is found that environmental change is never a single event but rather occurs as a result of numerous factors and processes (environmental and economic) over many time scales, while the individual or household response is varied and shaped by a range of economic and ecological circumstances, not to mention support from governments to overcome external shocks. The findings of the Intergovernmental Panel on Climate Change (IPCC) are considered in the context of this knowledge as is the scope for avoiding or mitigating the worst human impacts of change. The possibility of the large-scale resettlement of populations from uninhabitable areas is also raised.

Chapter Seven explores displacement taking place in those 'grey zones' of political violence that do not (yet) reach the threshold of armed conflict as recognised in international law. It is in this domain that the 'non-conflict' label hangs most uncomfortably. The point being made, however, is that in the situations we describe, such as in Zimbabwe from 2005 to 2008, ongoing clan-based violence in East Africa's Karamajong or the clearance of entire villages in Burma for economic and political gain, such violence and the displacement it creates is a core human rights and development priority (and increasingly a security priority) but one that consistently evades international scrutiny or meaningful intervention, leaving its victims prone to human rights violations and continuing state repression. The chapter links these instances of political violence and societal instability to the processes of environmental change discussed in Chapter Six to examine the correlation of risks related to the impacts of climate change to conflict and forced displacement. It further considers, by drawing on the situation in Cambodia, the coming together and increasing severity of different types of displacement and the detrimental cumulative impact on livelihoods and aspects of human security, particularly for the rural poor. In this way it opens an analysis of the structural processes that contribute to rural insecurity as both contributing causes and consequences of increased displacement and vulnerability to future displacement. Evidence would suggest that displaced people enter a cruel cycle in which an ability to resist multiple and sequential displacement is reversed with the result that the same people at different times may become conflict IDPs, international refugees, returnees, only to become displacees once again, development evictees, and then homeless as a result of natural disasters or land degradation. Researchers working among Zimbabweans displaced by local violence against migrants in mid-2008 for example found that some were earlier victims of Operation Murambatsvina and for whom a future of displacement looked certain as their vulnerabilities and inequalities increased.

In the final chapter of the volume we bring out the main findings of the study which are clustered around impoverishment as a shared outcome of the displacement types we have examined and, related to this, the human rights vulnerabilities that displaced people confront. We then make some policy and operational recommendations to elevate levels of protection and improved responses to the needs of the rising number of so called 'non-conflict' displaced people with a particular focus on development-created displacement for the reasons previously discussed in this introduction.

Notes

1. It is not clear where this term was first used, yet it has since been employed and tested regularly (Castles and Loughna 2002, van Hear 2004, Papadopolou 2005, UNHCR 2006).

CHAPTER TWO

Displacement: Conceptual Difficulties

An extensive body of academic literature seeks to define, categorise and create new typologies of human displacement, forced migration and involuntary resettlement. Definitions are important because they underpin labels which have direct implications for policy and operational practice shaping the protection and assistance individuals receive in emergency, disaster, transition and post-emergency situations. There are clear limitations to the robustness of definitions which often over simplify and take highly complex issues out of historical and immediate human and cultural contexts. It is this complexity that makes arriving at broadly agreed definitions associated with displacement and forced migration problematic. In addition, states and others with vested interests, the requirements of policy makers and the structures within which they work, impose further constraints. Against such a background, this chapter examines the origin and accuracy of existing terminology relevant to the subsequent chapters, identifying overlap between apparently distinct definitions and providing an interpretation of how definitions are currently understood in policy and practice. This is important for the overall aim of this book because at present, through the UN reform process and the evolving cluster approaches (discussed in Chapter Four), states and agencies are reconsidering the scope of their responsibilities towards displaced persons and those considerations are not always grounded in the consistent and shared use of terms.

Categories and Definitions of Displacement and Forced Migration

Usages of 'Forced Migration' and 'Displacement'

The term 'forced migration' tends to be used to describe different types of displacement, population movement, resettlement, migration and individual journeys and also, increasingly, diasporas. The complexities of causation, experience and outcome involved complicate the task of definition-making. Muggah (2003a, 2003b) and Turton (2003a) are critical about the imprecise use of terms, an imprecision which emerges in part out of legal frameworks and institutional mandates but also out of self-imposed boundaries of interest. Media reporting on forced migration, for example, is consistently inconsistent in the use of terms contributing to public confusion and misunderstanding (ICAR 2004, 2006, 2007). Helton and Jacobs (2006) trace the evolution of this terminology from the refugee protection regime and its associated policy making which includes the imperative to create new categories and new terms to fill the protection gaps in the existing legal framework (see also Black 2001, Muggah 2003b).[1] There is evidence that such taxonomy will remain a feature of future humanitarian reform processes including the emerging cluster approach and other reform measures which we discuss later in this volume. In researching this book a number of interviews were conducted with stakeholders in and around the UN humanitarian sector, in which respondents expressed their concerns about the broadening of the IDP definition with the danger that it may be rendered meaningless or at a minimum less efficacious.

A number of academics have sought to bring clarity to the bureaucratic and academic language and forestall the somewhat ad hoc evolution of terms (Muggah 2003a, Turton 2003a, Cernea 2006, Helton and Jacobs 2006). While this sort of analytical separation is crucial in creating a discourse in which all stakeholders are 'speaking the same language', there remains concern to ensure that essential linkages, overlaps and blurring between different kinds of forced migration are not lost in any attempt at definitional clarification. Indeed, the now waning asylum–migration nexus argument, while capturing the nature of mixed flows of people, and mixed motivations, may counter-intuitively have served to focus minds on the need to disentangle degrees of coerciveness in migration. What follows is a review of definitions and categories currently in use, noting where there is cross-over between or debates about specific categories or definitions.

First, it is useful to highlight the distinction between displacement and migration. In the literature, displacement is always characterised as 'forced', as an external event or a process to which an individual or group is subjected that is enacted with a specific purpose or intent. To be displaced usually describes a situation where people have been uprooted from their home through acts that endanger them and pose ongoing risks. Conversely, migration, as Turton (2003a) reminds us, 'is something we do, not something that is done to us'. Following from this, some form of displacement is likely to have occurred at the outset of any forced migration episode – it is simply the 'forced' element of forced migration. This does not make forced migration oxymoronic, rather the 'migration' element recovers the definition from denying agency to forced migrants. Displacement, over which the subject has little or no control, is what sets in motion a forced migration, which subsequently is directed by individual and group agency where people are faced with (limited) options and make constrained choices about route, mode and destination. McDowell (1996a), writing about the movement of Sri Lankan Tamils to Western Europe in the mid-1990s, favoured the term 'asylum-migration' to capture precisely this dynamic in movement and constrained decision-making. While this offers a clear conceptual distinction between displacement and forced migration, in policy and practice the boundaries of both are blurred.

Defining Displacement

Population displacement is likely to occur as a result of a complex set of interrelated factors and, according to a number of commentators, common among situations of displacement is that they involve 'coercion', physical uprooting and some measure of 'de-territorialisation' (Muggah 2003a). Coercion can derive from fear of or actual persecution and a lack of security in times of conflict, or from a physical change in the local environment as occurs in displacement arising as a result of environmental degradation or disaster. Elsewhere it is argued that land acquisition by the state, resulting in mandatory involuntary resettlement without the opportunity to return home, or to remain in situ but with a diminished status, may also be considered a form of displacement (though this may more accurately be described as involuntary resettlement). The displaced are subjected to this uprooting and can be characterised as having 'no choice to remain'. The de-territorialisation element of displacement is conventionally divided between that which takes place 'within the confines of a state or across an internationally recognised border' (Muggah 2003a). Such a distinction is not only geographic but also legal. Those displaced across an international border are legally defined as refugees subject to meeting certain criteria laid out in the Refugee Convention and 1967 Protocol in terms of the causes of their displacement while those displaced within internationally recognised borders have no such international legal status, but take the definition of internally displaced persons (IDPs). In many crisis and conflict situations people may move between these 'legal statuses' and consequently are subject to changing bureaucratic definitions, labels and entitlements.

In parallel, as suggested above, the literature reflects a growing debate, and one that informs this study, taking place over a broadening of the definition of 'displacement' beyond physical uprooting and homelessness. Such arguments suggest that displacement should also encompass 'occupational and economic dislocation not necessarily accompanied by the physical (geographic) relocation of the local users' (Cernea 2006). An example of this can be found in the literature on so-called development-induced displacement and resettlement and also in the literature on the human impacts of conservation projects, where partial asset loss or loss of access to assets or resources (both privately and commonly owned) as a result of external actions in the absence of forced physical removal may also be considered displacement. Indeed this broadened definition has already been accepted by the World Bank in their recently revised environmental policies which recognise 'restricted access to certain natural resources as a form of involuntary displacement without actual relocation'. This extension, if widely applied, would have significant implications in terms of who is entitled to protection, humanitarian assistance and/or compensation as a result of 'being displaced' and on future directions in development assistance strategies. Another possible extension of the definition of displacement has implications for agencies providing protection to those displaced internally. In developing its policy on IDPs, UNHCR suggests that the cluster approach to providing protection in times of armed conflict should cover populations who are 'affected by internal displacement but who are not necessarily displaced themselves' (including those who host displaced populations) and also include those who are 'at risk of displacement' (UNHCR 2007).

In addition to these debates around broadening the definition of displacement, there is also discussion about when displacement should be deemed to have ended (Mooney 2005). According to Mooney (ibid.) there is currently no agreement on when to stop counting an individual as displaced: does it require a full reversal of displacement, something not possible for some of those displaced by development projects that permanently change land use? This is discussed further below and in Chapter Three.

Defining Forced Migration

Academic research suggests that migration is the consequence of a complex set of economic, political, social, environmental, cultural and indeed personal factors triggering decisions at different stages of migration and involving varying levels of choice and compulsion. There is no simple dichotomy between voluntary and involuntary, forced and 'unforced', such that the use of these terms can actually be misleading

(Turton 2003a, 2003b). Even those fleeing conflict or persecution, considered a type of forced migrant, may 'have the latitude to decide where to go and ... whether to flee at all' (McDowell 1996a; see also UNHCR 2006). Not all people in situations of danger flee elsewhere: some remain (Castles 2003), and relative socio-economic standing and other factors will to some degree determine who is able to leave a situation of danger and at what point, to where and for what duration (van Hear 2006). To address the complex causality involved in migration there have been attempts to develop a continuum of migration (Richmond 1994, van Hear 1998). These devices are helpful in that they are indicative of the many reasons why people migrate and illustrate elements of compulsion and choice in each decision made along the way; they do, however, have heuristic limitations. There is a danger in 'lumping together people in categories' (Turton 2003a), as it can have the effect of obscuring the widely diverging experiences of individuals within a given category. This consolidating of particular social groups can have methodological implications for research in this area. Furthermore, a migration continuum is likely to imply that those at the 'forced', 'reactive' or 'involuntary' end of the scale have little or no opportunity to exercise their agency. This 'dehumanising effect of language' can seep into policy making and the practice of those responsible for responding to 'forced migration' (ibid.) and importantly shape public perceptions and media representation.

Realities on the ground also suggest that it is becoming increasingly difficult to separate forced migration from what is conventionally understood as economic migration (Castles 2003, Borjas and Crisp 2005). The asylum–migration nexus is used to illustrate the reality that in the contemporary world, asylum seekers and economic migrants may come from the same region and country, may use the same migration routes and may have similar experiences, vulnerabilities and protection needs en route, in transit and in host countries. It is also the case that one individual may go through phases of being considered, and may indeed maintain such a dual identity, as an asylum seeker and/or an economic migrant at different stages of migration. However, some academics would argue strongly for the maintenance of the legal sanctity and specificity of 'refugeehood' and for it not to be subsumed under a wider migration or displacement rubric (Hathaway 2007).

Despite the difficulty in defining whether someone should be considered a forced migrant or otherwise, Turton (2003a, 2003b) is clear that such categorisation is unavoidable for three reasons: firstly, while the homogenous refugee experience does not exist, different types of forced migrants in different situations can have distinctive needs; secondly, the magnitude of forced migration and the risks associated with it are on the increase; and, finally, the way we respond to forced migration requires us to consider what sort of moral community we wish to live in. 'Forced migration' today is an umbrella term that covers the broad causation, experiences and outcomes emerging out of different types of displacement. It is an experience that is initially imposed upon people by the structural forces of displacement within which people make restricted choices that are embedded in existing social structures. The body of literature assembled on forced migration discusses blurred and overlapping 'types' of forced migrants, including asylum seekers and refugees, people displaced internally by conflict, and in the name of development and conservation projects, social engineering, environmental degradation and disasters. What follows in this chapter are definitions and examples of the different categories of IDPs and some further consideration of where these categories overlap or impact upon one other.

Definitions of Internally Displaced Persons (Conflict)

Individuals or groups displaced as a consequence of conflict or persecution that remain inside their country of origin are considered to be IDPs. They are not refugees and enjoy none of the protection benefits afforded to that legal category. Instead, as they remain inside their own borders, the responsibility to protect remains with their own state. They are, therefore, 'coerced' into relocating and de-territorialised (in line with the above definition of displacement – within and not across internationally recognised borders).[2] In broad legal terms, it appears a relatively straightforward definition, but it is one that becomes less clear when tested by the reality of actual complex displacement emergencies and the operational aspects of humanitarian assistance programmes and funding lines.

Sustaining the idea that someone is displaced or has migrated internally as an exclusive consequence of conflict can be problematic. For reasons similar to those detailed above regarding the asylum–migration nexus, the causes of migration and displacement are complex and varied and therefore difficult to disentangle, and it is difficult to assign a particular episode of conflict as the trigger of displacement. It is certainly the case that most displacement occurs as a result of first-order consequences of conflict, yet it is also likely that conflict has a knock-on effect on other spheres, such as the economy, security and civil society, which subsequently lead to displacement or force people into a situation where their best course of action is to move away from their preferred location. It is also the case that triggers of displacement can emerge from pre-existing underlying structural conflicts that either contribute to outright violence, are exploited through violence or are inadvertently intensified by violence (see Chapter 6 for further discussion of climate change and "stress"). Underlying structural conflicts that feed into IDP movements would include, in the case of southern Sudan for example, undermined livelihood strategies as a major cause for disputes and conflict in rural areas between different groups (i.e. reduced access to natural resources, degraded resource base, curtailed pastoralist mobility) that flare up and contribute to wider, frequently, nation-wide conflicts (see in particular De Wit and Hatcher 2006, and COHRE 2006a).

Secondly, the definition of IDPs turns crucially on the definition of conflict and a clear understanding of its direct impact on those displaced in and around zones of conflict. International humanitarian law distinguishes between international armed conflicts and non-international armed conflicts, but contains no definition of these terms. Whether an armed conflict can be said to exist in a particular situation is essentially a question of fact depending on the surrounding circumstances. However, guidance for assessing whether a non-international armed conflict exists can be found in Additional Protocol II to the Geneva Conventions, which deals with the Protection of Victims of Non-international Armed Conflicts (ICRC 2010). Protocol II applies to conflicts between the forces of a state and 'dissident armed forces or other organised armed groups which, under responsible command, exercise control over part of the state's territory to enable them to carry out sustained and concerted military operations'. The Protocol adds that 'situations of internal disturbances and tensions, such as riots, isolated and sporadic acts of violence and other acts of a similar nature' do not constitute armed conflict.

A number of definitions of conflict, including of civil war, have been proposed by academics, primarily as the basis for statistical analysis of the incidence and effect of conflicts. Government aid and defence departments will often benchmark their achievements in conflict situations based on data produced by, for example, the Stockholm International Peace Research Institute (IPRI) or the International Institute for Strategic Studies (IISS), both of which use a definition of 'major armed conflict', referring to the use of armed force resulting in more than one thousand battle-related deaths in a year. However, these statistical measurements are mostly thought unhelpful in determining the success of policies.

Populations of IDPs in and around areas of conflict can usually be identified, yet it is often unclear whether a particular displacement episode is a direct result of that conflict. This is reflected in the evolution of the UN Guiding Principles on Internal Displacement and its definition of IDPs:

> Persons or groups of persons who have been forced or obliged to flee or to leave their homes or places of habitual residence, in particular as a result of or in order to avoid the effects' of armed conflict, situations of generalized violence, violations of human rights or natural or human-made disasters, and who have not crossed an international border (UNOCHA 2004).

This description contains a number of concessions to a broadening of the original working definition. Firstly, 'places of habitual residence' was inserted alongside homes to cover non-citizens who have lived in a country for many years and reflects also the fact that nomadic peoples may have a specific vulnerability to displacement. Secondly, 'or in order to avoid the effects of' was added to account for those who made decisions to move as potential for conflict was building and not just those physically and directly displaced or evicted by fighting or persecution. This reflects the fact that many civil wars or territorial conflicts increasingly involve the strategic targeting of civilians or civilian areas (UN Security Council 2006). Thirdly, while the definition refers to a number of possible causes of displacement, the phrase 'in particular' is inserted so as not to render the Guiding Principles inapplicable to displacement for any other reason.

Despite the definitional problems, the Guiding Principles have proved administratively meaningful, have widespread support[3] and are widely adopted (Cohen 2004). There is a large body of research evidence which argues that IDPs in areas of conflict have greater and more specific needs than either legally defined refugees or those displaced by non-conflict causes (Singh Juss 2006). It is important to consider that 'IDP' is not a legal category like refugee, but a descriptive, operational definition (Mooney 2005) and there are as yet no overarching and binding international laws protecting IDPs. As many commentators have argued, this is problematic because in times of conflict it is frequently the case that the state itself, charged with protecting IDPs, may be unwilling or unable to offer protection to a particular group of IDPs (Turton 2003a) or may indeed be responsible for their uprooting. Within the international system, the UNHCR recognises the protection needs of these individuals as 'persons of concern', has historically intervened in situations of internal displacement and (for example in Sri Lanka) is currently further developing its strategy with respect to IDPs (see the discussion of the cluster approach in Chapter Four). The humanitarian reform process is built, in part, on the continuing need to maintain a definition of conflict-induced internal displacement based on clear assessments of needs and numbers.

In addition to the problems of defining whether displacement is caused by conflict or by other factors, there is also debate over who is an IDP and when someone stops being an IDP (Muggah 2003a, Mooney 2005, Singh Juss 2006, Cohen 2007). As discussed above, recent discussions within UNHCR about which persons should be covered by the cluster approach for providing IDP protection suggest that there appears to be interest in including those at risk of displacement and those affected by displacement, such as communities hosting IDPs (though the UN can expect strong resistance to this 'mandate creep' from a number of member states). Furthermore, as Cernea (2006) discusses in terms of conservation projects, there is growing support from academics and some development agencies to broaden the definition of displacement to include those suffering economic dislocation. Again, this is perhaps less of a definitional issue than one of who should legitimately expect compensation for the impact of conservation or development projects.

As discussed above, it is unrealistic to suggest that displacement can only be considered to have ended once the processes that are responsible for displacement have been reversed as vulnerability, insecurity, human rights violations and impoverishment may persist or even intensify after return. Safe return is not always possible in times of conflict and sustained return may be elusive where instability (political and economic) persists beyond the cessation of hostilities. For Singh Juss (2006) the lack of grounding in international law renders the definition of IDPs open to wide interpretation in terms of when displacement ends. Unlike in the case of refugees, whose status ends when they are able return to their country of origin or find a durable solution elsewhere, the situation is less clear for IDPs. Roberta Cohen (2004) describes the situation:

> Does internal displacement end when the displaced return home? What if their homes are occupied by others? Does it end when they integrate into other areas? What if they continue to want to return home, as many Greek Cypriots or Bosnians do, despite their integration elsewhere? Does it end when the situation causing displacement has seized to exist? In the absence of guidelines, calculations are made on a case-by-case basis and are arbitrary.

Mooney (2005) suggests that the end of displacement should be dependent upon (durable) solutions. Whether the solution is return or resettlement it should happen voluntarily, safely and with dignity. The ICRC (2007) describes a similar cycle of displacement, with the final phase being described as either 'return to and reintegration in a place of origin' or 'final resettlement in a place other than original home'. Following this argument, displacement ends once IDPs no longer have distinct needs linked specifically to the cause of their displacement that distinguished them from the rest of the population (Cohen 2007). However, the criteria being used to draw a line under a displacement situation are based on official definitions and priorities which are unlikely to reflect displacees' own understanding of their situation.

The term 'conflict-induced internal displacement' has a specific meaning and is clear in what it describes. As demonstrated, however, it is difficult to separate out factors directly causing displacement. In addition there is not clarity over what actually constitutes conflict for the purposes of its effect on displacement and it is not always clear who is considered a conflict-related IDP at what time. Finally, there is a debate about the extent of the operational usefulness of the IDP concept in providing on-the-ground protection. Some argue that the fact that someone has or has not crossed a border should not determine the level of international protection they receive (Singh Juss 2006). To eliminate the distinction of internal displacement for conflict displacees would, however, increase the likelihood of states absolving their responsibility for upholding the rights of persons within their borders (UNHCR 2006).

Definitions of Resettlement/Involuntary Resettlement

If displacement is what sets in motion a forced migration, resettlement can represent the end of this process to the extent that it offers an acceptable solution to those displaced. The subject of resettlement has often been on the periphery of forced migration studies (Muggah 2003a), perhaps reflecting that arguably more of a moral and normative challenge is presented by those forced migrants without access to a pre-determined solution, as is the case in many resettlement schemes. Defining what is voluntary or involuntary encounters similar difficulties as distinguishing forced migration from other forms of migration. Despite this, the term 'involuntary resettlement' covers a whole range of causes, experiences and outcomes.

There are important dissimilarities between displacement and resettlement whether the latter is as a consequence of state acquisition of land, urban upgrading, disaster risk reduction or the pursuit of environmental conservation. In many instances of involuntary resettlement any 'choice to remain' is removed (Muggah 2003b) due to the exercise of the state's right of eminent domain or because of the physical nature of a public works project, for example, leading to the inundation of settled land to create a reservoir. It follows that many resettlers have no prospect of return. Unlike those displaced by conflict who may entertain some hope (however distant) of returning to their former places of residence, those resettled as a consequence of particularly non-linear large-scale development projects such as dams or reservoirs or attempts to conserve the local environment are physically unable to return to their former homes: either the landscape has gone through an irreversible physical change or it has been made illegal to inhabit certain areas.

The resettlement process and its outcomes vary enormously. Resettlement should, both in theory and in compliance with some national laws, hold out the prospect of 'development' and improvement whereas displacement does not. However, while there remains the potential for a better outcome for resettlers compared to conflict displacees, too frequently international standards for resettlement are not reached, protective frameworks are weak and associated policies are poor. In such cases involuntary resettlement creates deepened impoverishment, may contribute to new conflicts and may increase vulnerability to further displacement at some point in the future (Cernea and McDowell 2000). There is an acute and particular vulnerability to impoverishment and human rights violations for people displaced as a result of development projects who do not enjoy legal title to land and who do not receive legal protection or economic assistance. It is worth repeating, however, that most resettlement is carried out legally with the intention of providing a positive development outcome for the society at large and a 'solution' for those resettled, although, as we will later describe, in actual practice satisfactory outcomes are only rarely achieved.

There also remains debate about the usefulness of the terms 'voluntary' and 'involuntary' to describe resettlement. The ADB offers the following definition of involuntary resettlement:

> 'Involuntary resettlement' addresses social and economic impacts that are permanent or temporary and are caused by: i. acquisition of land and other fixed assets, ii. change in the use of land, or iii. restrictions imposed on land as a result of an ADB operation.[4]

A number of academics have taken issue with the use of the term 'involuntary' and the voluntary/involuntary dichotomy itself. Firstly, as

Muggah (2003b) explains, the distinction turns on the individual's 'choice to remain'. In planning for large-scale resettlement, communities may be given different options to resettle before the project commences. While 'choices' may therefore be offered during the planning phase, making resettlement appear 'voluntary', with no ultimate 'choice to remain' the resettlement is 'involuntary' in practice. Muggah also points to the potential for coercion and violence to be used during both 'voluntary' and 'involuntary' schemes. Secondly, the range of experiences involved in any large-scale resettlement precludes the use of any blanket description of 'voluntary' or 'involuntary'. Experiences and outcomes are often family-specific with some having their circumstances improved as a consequence of resettlement while others see their circumstances worsen. Furthermore, even resettlement that is seen as involuntary may include 'opportunists' who seize a chance to improve their socio-economic situations (Muggah 2003b). The experiences of resettlers are the subject of a World Bank study to assess the efficacy of their organisational procedure (Cernea and McDowell 2000).

Given the lack of clarity this dichotomy offers, some see 'voluntary' and 'involuntary' as unsuitable terms to describe resettlement. Turton (2003a) explains the difficulty of using the term 'involuntary' to describe human action. 'An act is involuntary', he suggests, 'when it is done without thinking, without deliberation'. In a separate article, Turton (2003b) proposes the term 'forced resettlers' to describe those 'resettled by government sponsored programmes which use resettlement as a technique of rural development and political control', in order to avoid using the legal idiom 'refugee' or other terms that 'depersonalise' the individuals affected. Muggah (2003a), on the other hand, argues that we should avoid preoccupation with the involuntary/voluntary dichotomy as there is no 'natural category' for resettlement. Instead, he suggests we should focus on what are the clear 'boundaries of the debate': the planned and controlled movement of a section of the population.

So far, this section has concentrated upon 'resettlement as relocation'. However, as suggested above, resettlement, as used in the literature and in policies, does not have to involve physical relocation. While resettlement schemes often involve total loss of land and relocation to another place, they can also involve the loss of only a portion of landholding or other assets not requiring relocation – it is unclear what portion of those often described as development displacees have been fully relocated or have lost some assets. Numbers of the latter are greater in linear projects such as road building than in water projects involving inundation. The idea that neither resettlement nor displacement necessarily involves migration has not only conceptual implications for academic work on the subject, but also policy implications in terms of which agencies are responsible for the displaced and the resettled and who, on this basis, should be eligible for protection and assistance.

Considering the discussion in this section it is difficult to place refugee resettlement in the context of discussions about voluntary/involuntary or resettlement and relocation. Refugee resettlement is never about a resettlement of land or livelihood but always about an often distant relocation to a third country rather than relocation within the country of origin. Furthermore, while the initial displacement and subsequent migration of these individuals is likely to be involuntary or, more accurately, forced, their actual resettlement would be voluntary, such that they would have had 'choice to remain', most likely in a refugee camp (though not all would have 'choice to leave').

Development Resettlement

The sheer scale of what is considered development resettlement has led to an explosion of recent academic research on the causes, experiences and outcomes of this phenomenon in developing countries (Cernea 2006) – though far less attention has been paid to compulsory land purchase and so called 'willing buyer willing seller' arrangements in the developed world.[5] Development, in this instance, is defined and justified on the basis of 'national interest' and the 'development' of the nation. This has significant implications for who retains responsibility for compensating those affected by such development processes: if it is in the national interest then the nation-state must have primary responsibility. Consequently, there has been little international involvement, beyond a fairly detached 'ombudsman' or oversight role, in the protection of those affected by development, despite international involvement in funding, resettlement standard setting, and construction. Susan Martin (1999) suggests that if the state in question is unwilling or unable to protect and assist development displacees (presumably through resettlement) then they could become of concern to the international community and an international response may be warranted. It is extremely unlikely that states would permit what would likely be deemed as interference in national development policies that are regarded as a purely sovereign matter. Yet, deciding upon what constitutes arbitrary displacement or resettlement and adequate protection or assistance is also likely to be considered within the jurisdiction of the state. Chapter Four discusses the implications of international involvement in development resettlement.

Planned Infrastructure Projects

As discussed above, large-scale projects with the aim of developing a nation's infrastructure are considered the largest cause of involuntary resettlement in the developing world. According to Cernea (2005) the construction of roads, dams or ports result in the uprooting of over fifteen million people a year. Recent projects contributing significantly to this total include the Three Gorges Dam in China and the Nam Theun 2 Dam in Laos. The study of this type of development-created involuntary resettlement has a comparatively long history. The inescapable dilemma of the unintended consequences and anti-development effects of development projects has been recognised since the 1950s (Muggah 2003a and 2003b; see also Chambers 1969, Colson 1971 and Scudder 1973). While donor agencies are involved in a number of development projects and strategies that generate displacement, they do not offer a definition of displacement; rather they define asset loss and relocation collectively as resettlement. Operational policy for the World Bank, for example, dictates that resettlement is provided for those displaced by World Bank projects – these people are therefore referred to as 'resettlers' in recognition of the differences between the process and experience of displacement and resettlement discussed above.

This categorisation is relevant in terms of sheer numbers, as the displacement of millions of people can often be traced directly back to a single project. Studying the impact of such projects can provide important lessons for similar future projects and other resettlement schemes, improving safeguards and livelihood restoration.

Government Resettlement Schemes

There are a number of historical examples of government resettlement schemes that may not be justified on the basis of any physical construction in the region but are argued as necessary for a variety of social, environmental and economic reasons. Similar to the previous categories, these schemes tend to form part of wider political economic strategies often justified in 'development' terms. Planned settlements of varying sizes have been described as acts of economic and political organisation particularly in the wake of a nation's independence and attempts to become economically self-sufficient (Turton 2003a). In the 1970s, Villagisation in Tanzania epitomised the policy of many sub-Saharan African nations to create small organised settlements. In Indonesia the policy of Transmigrasi – one of the largest resettlement programs in the world – has been much criticised (Toussaint 2004). Supporters point to the safe and orderly resettlement of millions of people, alleviating pressure on land in inner islands and contributing significantly to the development of the outer islands. Conversely, detractors argue that considerable resources have been wasted in settling people who have not been able to move beyond subsistence level, with negative effects including extensive damage to the environment, the displacement of tribal people and ensuing conflict. These examples of resettlement involve varying degrees of planning, legal precedence and consultation with affected populations. Common amongst them is that a series of development outcomes (such as the reduction of poverty, combating demographic pressures, or a more organised market economy) were cited as justification for the schemes.

Conservation Resettlement

A further form of resettlement arises not necessarily as a result of degradation of the environment but rather as a result of policies and projects that attempt to conserve it. Geisler and De Sousa (2001) define this process as exclusionary conservation in which areas of natural beauty or fragility are taken into the hands of state authorities and those living on the land are displaced from it and often excluded from utilising its resources. Those displaced by this process are defined by Geisler and De Sousa as 'other environmental refugees' (the next section discusses why this term is problematic). Such uprooting and dislocation is often experienced by small communities that have lived off the land in question, mostly common property resources, for generations. Research on the coexistence dilemmas of 'people and parks' and 'people and wildlife' suggest that those affected are rarely given realistic alternatives in terms of residence or livelihood, resulting in significant negative impoverishment outcomes and loss of cultural identity (Geisler 2003b, Kaimowitz et al. 2003, Cernea 2006).

It is in instances of conservation resettlement that arguments for a widened definition of whom should be considered displaced are most loudly heard. This subsequently affects considerations about whom should be resettled. Cernea (2006) charts how successive development banks have begun to change the definition of displacement used in conservation and protected areas schemes to include 'restriction of access' to certain resources. This means that to be entitled to resettlement assistance in light of displacement does not require the physical relocation of individuals or communities. Impoverishment risks from exclusionary conservation are a consequence not only of being forced to leave a place of habitual residence but also of suffering from restricted access to means of subsistence and resources previously utilised to sustain an economic livelihood. This could have implications not only for those displaced and/or affected by conservation projects, but also for those whose livelihoods, if not homes, have been taken away as a result of development projects, environmental degradation and other causes of displacement and resettlement.

Non-conflict Displacement

For the purposes of this section, non-conflict displacement is divided into the following categories: structural development, disaster and environmental displacement. Politically-motivated displacement in situations that do not reach the threshold of armed conflict is addressed in Chapter Seven. While we recognise that a focus on causes of displacement may lead to the construction of potentially de-humanising categorisations, this typology acknowledges that such definitions have considerable currency with policy-makers and advocates. In fact, this section will also illustrate some blurring, overlaps and causal links between these types of displacement: for example, the apparent impacts of climate change are likely to increase the frequency of natural disasters and erratic weather patterns (IPCC 2007). Further, it has been argued that those displaced by environmental degradation could be considered development displacees when environmental effects are compounded by state mismanagement or incompetence. And elsewhere, it has been suggested that all population movements are a consequence of or heavily impacted upon by unequal global social relations and the hegemony of neo-liberal economic and development policy (Castles 2003).

These definitional debates are crucial in apportioning responsibility for the protection and compensation of affected persons to particular states and agencies, rather than pinning the blame on the actions of the poor and marginalised or citing 'the environment' as the cause of displacement to diminish the culpability of states.

Structural Development Displacement

In addition to the planned involuntary resettlement of populations as a result of state land acquisition and public works construction, other state policies and strategies of development can lead to the displacement of large numbers of people over time and are unlikely to be followed by a state-sponsored resettlement scheme. These situations result from more incremental processes such as modernising the agricultural sector of a developing economy from small-scale and often subsistence production to mechanised procedures and commercial outputs. The phenomenon is often characterised by the consolidation of small agricultural plots and the displacement of former owners, typically subsistence farmers, from rural areas. Examples of this kind of displacement are a prevalent aspect of the unprecedented economic growth currently being achieved by China and India. Recalling the broadening definitions from previous sections, this form of development displacement often results in a loss of economic livelihood or a reconstitution of land ownership that is not always accompanied by relocation.

Scott Leckie (2008) has argued for greater recognition of those people forcibly evicted in non-conflict situations and better identification of which groups of victims of human rights violations could be considered as IDPs and for whom the rights regime could be strengthened. He points to those who are forced to permanently vacate their homes as a result of ostensibly development-mandated projects including slum clearance operations, urban renewal and redevelopment measures, city 'beautification' schemes, compulsory purchase orders, arbitrary land acquisition and land disputes. Leckie argues that 'development' evictees suffer very much in the same way as persons traditionally classified as IDPs. Elsewhere described as 'development cleansing', this involves 'direct or indirect violence, the loss of homes, lands and property due to circumstances beyond the owner's control, severe declines in their living standards and appalling housing and living conditions during their displacement'. For Leckie, such evictions result in the violation of people's economic, social and cultural rights as well as civil and political rights where evictees 'are often prevented from organising resistance, are specifically targeted by those wishing to take over their homes or lands and, most importantly of all, are almost never able to claim, let alone exercise, restitution rights to the housing or land from which they were evicted'.

The issues identified by Leckie came to a head in Zimbabwe in May 2005 when the government initiated a campaign of forced evictions and demolitions resulting in the internal displacement of an estimated 570,000 people most of whom, as we discuss in Chapter Seven, remain without a durable solution at the time of writing this book (see IDMC 2008). According to the IDMC, the campaign, known as Operation Murambatsvina, targeted informal settlements and business structures in urban areas throughout the country. Those evicted received little if any notice of impending evictions which were characterised by violence and brutality – twenty thousand vendors were reportedly arrested and, through bulldozing, smashing and burning, homes were first destroyed in shanty towns in high-density suburbs and subsequently the operation was extended to settlements on farms in peri-urban and rural areas. As we later discuss, the motivations behind the operation were unclear, according to the IDMC report. The government sought to justify the evictions as 'cleaning up' urban areas. Others have argued that the operation was aimed at retribution against those who voted for the opposition, that it was initiated through general concern over chaos and congestion in the cities or that it was intended to deter a popular uprising and force people to move to rural areas.

The UN Special Envoy on Human Settlements Issues in Zimbabwe, Anna Kajumulo Tibaijuka, produced a powerful report following a fact-finding mission to Zimbabwe to assess the scope and impact of Operation Murambatsvina conducted in the period following the evictions. The report described extensive human rights violations and accused the government of conducting the operation in an 'indiscriminate and unjustified manner, with indifference to human suffering and, in repeated cases, with disregard to several provisions of national and international legal frameworks'. Several follow-up reports, in particular from Human Rights Watch (2005), detailed further violations and abuses.

In many countries, including those in southern Africa, one of the first challenges to face nascent governments following historic political transitions to either independence or democratic majority rule has been to address the inequitable distribution of land. A legacy of settler colonisation has been to dispossess many native and tribal communities of land. Land tenure reform policies have aimed to redress this balance and implement strategies to secure a fairer agreement of land rights. Tenure reform has to contend with issues of antecedent overcrowding in common areas and overlapping land rights that are often a result of complex and ineffective colonial laws (Adams et al 1999). These schemes can not only instigate initial resettlement in terms of a reconfiguration of land rights but can also, if not handled properly, generate subsequent displacement pressures if new land rights are not clear or adequately protected. Alberts et al. (1996) outline a number of individual and group needs that must be satisfied to avoid further displacement, such as assurances not to be evicted without compensation, protection of inheritance and access to local utilities and infrastructure.

In South Africa, following the 1994 election of the ANC, the government embarked on a land redistribution scheme that offered subsidies to purchase land in former white areas. In this case, it was necessary to repeal 'the many and complex apartheid laws relating to land administration' by reforming land tenure law to reflect the spirit of the new South African constitution (Adams et al 1999). In this respect the scheme did involve some displacement, in as much as it reconfigured land ownership, yet it is perhaps better described as a resettlement scheme in principle. In most quarters it has been seen as a success in terms of 'managing displacement and resettlement', though there have also been some negative effects that have in fact generated further displacement, such as lack of security and documentation for new land owners. It has also been argued that the scheme has not been a success in development terms as it has failed to overcome 'agrarian dualism' (Hall 2007).

Disaster Displacement

Natural and human-made disasters uproot and make people homeless in a variety of ways and with varying degrees of severity – it is frequently stated that for every one person displaced by conflict, seven are displaced by natural disasters (though as discussed in Chapter Three, the evidence for actual numbers of 'displaced' as opposed to 'affected' people is open to dispute). In recent decades the frequency of disasters has increased with numbers of people affected reaching an estimated 250 million a year (IFRC 2007). Unlike the categories of development displacement above, 'disaster displacement' is included as a specified cause of internal displacement in the Guiding Principles definition of IDPs. Definitions of this type of displacement turn on how disaster is defined and how affected persons are defined. In terms of causation and knock-on effects, disaster displacement also links and overlaps with other forms of displacement. It should be noted, however, that the use of the term 'disaster displacement' is contested. If, as is argued in the literature, displacement requires a deliberate act on the part of the state or a non-state party in pursuit of other aims or where displacement is the intention then the forced relocation of people as a consequence of an Act of God for believers or natural forces for non-believers may not be considered displacement. Government neglect or mismanagement in permitting people to settle on land prone to disasters and in structures that are ill-suited to providing protection would not in itself seem to constitute 'intention'.

The UN defines natural and human-made disasters as 'a serious disruption of the functioning of a society, causing widespread human, material, or environmental losses which exceed the ability of the affected society to cope using its own resources' (quoted in IDMC 2009). Robinson (2003) offers a typology of such disasters: natural disasters are divided into sudden impact disasters (such as floods, earthquakes, landslides), slow-onset disasters (including drought, famine, desertification) and epidemic diseases (for example cholera, malaria); human-made disasters are divided into industrial or technological disasters (such as pollution, hazardous spills or explosions) and what are labelled 'complex emergencies' generated by multiple contributing factors such as war, internal conflict and natural disaster.

Defining who is considered to have been displaced by such disasters poses the same difficulties discussed in previous sections about what counts as displacement and when displacement ends. Disasters present a wide range of protection risks (see Kälin 2005a) from loss of documents and economic dislocation to the complete loss of homes and families. Given that the Guiding Principles include disasters in their definition of IDPs, the broad definition of displacement is relevant for use in the case of displaced disaster victims. This includes, therefore, people who have been forced to leave their homes (or places of habitual residence) to avoid 'the effects' of disasters. It is less clear when displacement, and therefore assistance, ends in this case. Some disasters may cause such severe physical destruction that return is not a feasible option in the short- or medium-term, or even permanently. On the other hand, those whose homes have been damaged less severely may be able to return immediately and some may not have to relocate at all. Yet can they still be considered displaced? Many may still require assistance to re-build their homes or become self-sufficient again as a result of economic dislocation. Kälin's report (2005a) compiled on a working visit to areas affected by the 2004 Asian tsunami for the Brookings Institute illustrates some of the difficulties in defining return and resettlement and also the implications of this for continued assistance.

It is clear that the above typology and the lack of clarity over who is considered an affected person suggest that disaster is not always the exclusive cause of displacement. There are a number of ways in which this form of displacement overlaps analytically with development displacement. Firstly, the extent of the impact of a disaster can often be dependent on how developed the affected region is in terms of preventing damage and being able to provide an efficient and immediate response. In aggregation, a reduction in the level of risk seems to have taken place in terms of deaths from disasters. As mentioned, while the frequency of disasters has increased in recent decades the number of deaths has decreased (IFRC 2005). However, the number of persons affected (many of whom may be defined as displaced) has actually risen. Where the response to a disaster is poor, displacement can be exacerbated and lengthened, often making the displaced vulnerable to further displacement. There is a clear differential between developed and developing countries in terms of the impacts of disasters, with developing countries accounting for 96 per cent of all deaths occurring from natural disasters (Singh Juss 2006; see also Castles 2002). Some may argue that in these cases, where prevention or warning mechanisms are poor, housing codes are breached or, in the case of industrial accidents, industry regulations are not met, displacement resulting from disasters should actually be considered as development displacement, ensuring the responsibility to protect (and prevent) falls on the state. It should also be noted that according to the European Court of Human Rights case-law, failing to take feasible measures that would have prevented or mitigated the consequences of foreseeable disasters amounts to a violation of the right to life and therefore incurs the responsibility of the state under international law.[6] Secondly, disasters can present 'development opportunities' for governments. This is particularly common when disasters strike areas already experiencing internal conflict. In these instances, humanitarian responses become politicised in terms of distribution of aid, the right to return home or to continue fishing water or farming land. The 2004 Asian tsunami again provides stark examples of this, most notably in Sri Lanka and Indonesia.

There is in addition a link between disaster displacement and environmental displacement. The effects of environmental degradation and changes in the global climate are considered as partly responsible for the recent increase in natural disasters. Major studies into the future of the earth's climate suggest that this situation is only likely to be exacerbated by an increasingly variable climate: both the Stern Review (HM Treasury 2006) and reports by the IPCC (2007) present a number of scenarios where climate change will increase the risk of flooding, drought, famine and extreme weather patterns. This is discussed further below and in Chapter Six; however, in terms of the definition of disaster displacement, there may be future discussion about incorporating those displaced by the effects of natural disasters within environmental or climate change displacement.

Environmental Displacement

The literature does not provide a single agreed definition of environmental displacement. There are significant problems, first and as we have already seen in regards to other 'categories' of displacement, in isolating environmental factors as exclusive or even primary causes of displacement, and second, in assessing the number of individuals that can be said to have suffered displacement as a result. In addition, there are arguments that suggest that many situations commonly considered as environmental displacement should more accurately be considered as the impact of development or disasters. Finally, there is much controversy over what these individuals should actually be called: displacees, refugees or migrants. What follows is an illustration of these difficulties through a brief analysis of some of the types of environmental displacement most commonly identified.

Environmental Degradation and Climate Change

A number of studies have attempted to produce typologies of causation for displacement related to environmental degradation. Often there is distinct overlap between this category and disaster displacement with some typologies including disasters at one end of a continuum that has climate changes at the other (see Black 2001). The International Organisation for Migration (IOM) and the Refugee Policy Group (RPG) (1992) produced a simpler distinction between emergency and slow-onset movements, with disasters in the emergency category. This section will concentrate on the slow-onset movements, such as deforestation, desertification, rising sea levels and water and air degradation, that are often said to create 'environmental refugees'. Myers and Kent (1995) describe environmental refugees as 'persons who no longer gain a secure livelihood in their traditional homelands because of what are primarily environmental factors of unusual scope'. A number of studies have suggested that millions of 'environmental refugees' originate from, for example, Bangladesh (Homer-Dixon 1994), sub-Saharan Africa (Jacobson 1988) and northeast Brazil (Sanders 1990–1991). Myers (1997) has calculated that there were at least twenty-five million people displaced worldwide in the mid-1990s as a direct result of environmental degradation or by subsequent and linked conflicts and impoverishment, with the IFRC more recently estimating a similar figure of people moving from areas of environmental degradation (Traufetter 2007). In 1994, the Ditchley Conference Report suggested that 'environmental refugee' was a suitable term only in situations where environmental disaster or degradation was 'compounded by crass political failure' (quoted in Singh Juss 2006). This addendum does not necessarily seem to be present in the above calculations, where as others may argue that such state failure is an issue of development or politics rather than the environment.

Richard Black (2001), in a paper prepared for the UNHCR, illustrates a number of problems with such definitions and calculations. Firstly, he describes how several of the causes themselves, particularly desertification, are not straightforward phenomena. Secondly, he suggests that it is misleading to claim that 'millions' of people are displaced exclusively by environmental causes. Numerous other factors, Black argues, need to be taken into account to understand the complex causal patterns of displacement and seasonal migration in these instances. Interconnected political, economic and social factors often play an equal if not more significant role in this displacement; disaggregating and prioritising these factors becomes a difficult task (Lee 2001, Castles 2002). In fact, it is often the case that environmental degradation is a consequence of development failure, general mismanagement or even direct political actions rather than uncontrollable natural forces. Examples of famine, drought or diminishing arable land often represent an unequal distribution or mismanagement of resources by state apparatus rather than an absolute shortage (Black 2001, Lee 2001).

In this respect it becomes problematic to describe those displaced as refugees, which invokes a number of legal connotations and would necessarily mean that these individuals have crossed an international border and warrant formal international protection in line with the 1951 Geneva Convention on Refugees. Black (2001) suggests that for the environmental refugee definition to be conceptually sound, there needs to be demonstrable evidence that migration has increased dramatically at times of degradation – something there is little evidence for in most cases (Castles 2002). In many harsh environments, migration can actually be part of a structural coping strategy or an active response to degradation rather than something to which these individuals are subjected. Research on responses to famine (Pottier 1993) and drought (Turton and Turton 1984) and the importance of remittances to the communities in these regions backs up this argument (Condé and Diagne 1986).

The above does not suggest that environmental degradation is never a factor or even the primary factor in some instances of displacement. A recent IPCC report (2007) provides a gloomy prognosis of the numbers of people that may be displaced by climate disaster in the future (Traufetter 2007). The report suggests that 'many millions more are projected to be flooded every year by the 2080s' and predicts more landslides, glacier melt and unpredictable weather patterns. In suggesting that recent temperature change is 'very likely due to the observed increase in anthropogenic greenhouse gas concentrations' the report is putting the responsibility for responding to 'environmental refugees' onto high energy consuming countries, corporations and individuals. Additionally, in definitional terms there are significant overlaps with disaster displacement that are provided by research on climate change that suggests the warming of the earth's atmosphere is contributing to increasingly turbulent and unpredictable weather patterns (HM Treasury 2006, IPCC 2007).

Given the confusion and complexity surrounding causes of displacement, it is perhaps appropriate to suggest that 'environmental refugees' would more accurately be described as environmental migrants, moving for a number of associated political and economic reasons and with varying degrees of compulsion or choice. It is important to note that divergent definitions of this form of displacement are probably the result of both methodological and political concerns. Castles (2002) argues that those using the term 'environmental refugees' look for global patterns presenting causal links, rather than the opponents who look at complex local contexts. In political terms, it has been argued that the term 'environmental refugees' may also serve a variety of agenda wishing to link security and the environment, widen the applicability of the refugee convention or contain asylum flows within their region of origin (Black 2001, Singh Juss 2006). All of these issues are discussed at length in Chapter Six.

Climate Change, Security and Displacement

Despite these academic misgivings, growing attention within Northern states is being paid to the security and displacement dimension of energy and climate change. John Ashton, adviser to the UK Government on climate change, is critical about current discussions on the causes of conflict – including the academic discussion – for focusing too much on the debate about whether particular drivers lie at the heart of conflict. Rather than focusing on choices between possible single predominant causes (is the conflict fundamentally a political problem; a clash of ideologies; to what extent is religion or other cultural drivers dominant?) he believes we should instead concentrate on the relationship between climate change and security. Conflict, Ashton argued in a 2006 paper, almost always arises from:

> an interplay of different drivers some of them human, some of them related to the environment, to resources, and sometimes it's the interplay rather than the individual drivers themselves that provide the triggers that lead to violence, lead to political stress and take societies beyond the system conditions within which they can develop peacefully, stably and offer their people a prospect of prosperity.

For Ashton, therefore, it is necessary to take a much more systemic view of the problem of conflict and link it to climate change by asking in what way will existing stresses be extended by climate change and subsequently make conflict more likely or more difficult to prevent? It is in this relationship that human displacement (IDPs in particular) is a potentially critical factor. The case of the Government of India's recent decision to build a 4,500–kilometre long barbed wire fence around Bangladesh, presumably on security grounds, is often cited as an example to illustrate the climate–security nexus. Extreme weather conditions in Bangladesh were said to have triggered a migration of several thousand people across the border into India in 2000, and immediately as a response to that migration there was violence. Those who migrated came into conflict with the people on the other side of the border who did not welcome their arrival in India. It has been widely predicted that one consequence of climate change is likely to be the inundation of a large part of Bangladesh and, therefore, displacement, both within that country and potentially beyond its borders, of much larger numbers of people than were displaced in 2000. The consequences of water scarcity, particularly in Africa, is also used to illustrate the nexus particularly in those parts where there is existing violence in relation to scarcity of water, land and other resources (the Darfur crisis may be analysed in this way, see De Waal 2007). Other less obvious but nonetheless significant stresses are thought to be increasingly evident where there is a growing scarcity in productive land and where climate change may exacerbate livelihood-based conflict. Such analysis tends also to point to the complexity and unpredictability of these processes and the policy challenges they present.

Summary

The lack of clarity over definitions associated with forced migration and displacement is primarily a consequence of the reality of complex and overlapping issues. It is notable that the discussion around definitions is based on what causes displacement and, as demonstrated, the difficulty in isolating the exclusive cause of a particular displacement situation is partly responsible for the lack of clarity of distinction between 'types' of forced migration. An alternative approach might involve categorising displacement according to outcomes (impoverishment, accountability, protection needs) rather than by causation. The differences that exist among agencies and political institutions on definitions are in many cases a consequence of vested political and institutional interests and the rigid logic of policy making that often requires simplified categories in order to function. These difficulties have been illustrated throughout this section. The complex mix of legal guidelines and policy frameworks is discussed in Chapter Four. In the next chapter, it is shown how definitions also impact upon how we count displacement, who does the counting and how accurate are the figures used.

Notes

1. A UN agency official interviewed for this study made a very similar point in arguing that the current humanitarian approach demands the creation of labels or categories to frame issues to which are fixed a series of outcomes experienced by communities but the process is a false one that forces causalities that in reality do not exist.
2. See the IDMC definitions page at: http://www.internal-displacement.org/idp.
3. A number of governments – including those of Angola, Burundi, Colombia, Georgia, Liberia, Peru, Sri Lanka, Turkey and Uganda – have been incorporating the Principles into their domestic laws and policies because they see IDPs as a category that needs to be addressed in their countries (Wyndham 2006). At the regional level, the African Union is in the process of developing a binding instrument based on the Guiding Principles, while at the sub-regional level, the member states of the International Conference on the Great Lakes Region have already adopted a Protocol on Protection and Assistance to Internally Displaced Persons – a binding instrument, that obliges states to accept the Guiding Principles by incorporating them into domestic law. At the international level, UN human rights treaty bodies have been regularly invoking the Principles when addressing situations of internal displacement. Ultimately, all these efforts may well lead to a universal convention on the protection of IDPs or to recognition of them as an expression of international customary law (Cohen 2007).
4. www.adb.org.
5. COHRE's monitoring of infrastructure development in Olympic cities is an exception.
6. Two judgments of relevance: European Court of Human Rights, *Öneryildiz v. Turkey*, Application 48939/99, judgment of 30 November 2004, and European Court of Human Rights, *Budayeva and others v. Russia*, Applications nos. 15339/02, 21166/02, 20058/02, 11673/02 and 15343/02, judgment of 20 March 2008.

CHAPTER THREE

Counting the Displaced

Introduction

Counting the number of people displaced for reasons other than conflict is not an easy task. Identifying, collecting and collating accurate data on the number of people uprooted, displaced, relocated or subsequently returned to their place of origin as a result of conflict and non-conflict situations, presents an enormous challenge. As discussed in Chapter Two, there remain disagreements over definitions of who should be counted as displaced and how, the types or categories of impact of displacement, and when that impact has ended. The situation is further complicated by the fact that on the ground and in organisations' headquarters where statistics and other data are analysed and presented, numerous, often parallel, agencies collect similar statistics but use different criteria and timeframes, produce often significantly varying figures and do not share data sets. In extreme cases some statistics are produced and creatively presented in pursuit of funding, political or academic agenda and certain media coverage. Statistics, however, are important: 'displacement' numbers are often used to mobilise advocacy and policy to address issues of impoverishment and human rights violations.[1] Maintaining global interest in and funding for this response is reliant upon statistics to help convey the scale of displacement or resettlement.

UNHCR figures suggest there are nearly twenty-one million 'persons of concern' including nearly seven million 'conflict' IDPs to whom they provide assistance, while IDMC (2008) estimate that overall there are currently around twenty-six million conflict IDPs in the world. Currently there is no overarching organisation collecting or collating statistics on the numbers of people displaced by natural disasters, development interventions, situations of political instability that do not reach the threshold of armed conflict, or as a result of climate change. However, official and academic reports are frequently published estimating the universal population of the world's displaced and migrating normally running into several hundred million each year.

This chapter will take these forms of resettlement and displacement in turn and review available statistics. This will address the actors and agenda involved, the methods used and results obtained, and the difficulties and limitations encountered in counting the numbers affected. To do so, the following questions are addressed for each category:

- Who is counting the displacement or resettlement?
- What figures have been published?
- Who is using these figures?
- How accurate are the figures?
- What are the difficulties in collecting, counting and monitoring?
- What are the limitations of the existing statistics?

Addressing these issues provides an overview of what statistics exist on different forms of non-conflict displacement and involuntary displacement and offers a critical assessment of the validity of these figures and how they are used.

Counting Development Resettlement and Displacement

Planned Infrastructure Projects

The World Bank and the ADB collect statistics on the numbers of people resettled as a consequence of the projects they fund (in part or whole). They also estimate from time to time the number of so called development displaced persons (DDPs) created by similar projects funded and executed by other organisations in the countries within which they operate. Governments in neither the industrialised nor the developing world routinely collect statistics on the extent of mandatory resettlement or other forms of uprooting as a result of state or private sector land acquisition. Tables 3.1 and 3.2 show a regional breakdown and figures by project type for DDPs from World Bank sponsored projects from 1993.

As the figures demonstrate, World Bank sponsored projects, dams and infrastructure projects account for a significant majority of DDPs and the overwhelming amount of development resettlement takes place in Asia. The latter is unsurprising given that China and India combined accounted for nearly three-quarters of resettlement from these projects. Given the acceleration of economic growth in both of these countries in the last decade, the impact of development on displacement in Asia is likely to be significantly greater than these

Table 3.1. World Bank Projects Active in 1993 with Resettlement, Including Number of People Displaced.

Region	Projects	Percentage	People	Percentage
Africa	34	23.3	113,000	5.8
South Asia	29	19.9	1,024,000	52.1
East Asia	58	39.7	588,000	30.0
Europe/Central Asia	5	3.4	27,000	1.4
Middle East/North Africa	7	4.8	32,000	1.6
Latin America	13	8.9	180,000	9.1
Total	**146**	**100**	**1,964,000**	**100**

Source: WBED 1996.

Table 3.2. Distribution of Displacees by Cause of Displacement in World Bank Projects (Active in 1993) with Resettlement.

Cause	Projects	Percentage	People	Percentage
Dams, irrigation, canals	46	31.5	1,304,000	66.4
Urban infrastructure, water supply, sewerage, transportation	66	45.2	443,000	22.6
Thermal (including mining)	15	10.3	94,000	4.8
Other	19	13.0	122,000	6.2
Total	**146**	**100**	**1,963,000**	**100**

Source: WBED 1996.

figures suggest, yet no equivalent study exists to confirm this. It can be useful, therefore, to look beyond these absolute figures. According to Cernea (2006) development projects in Africa, for example, tend to affect a greater proportion of the population and territory than equivalent projects in Asia.

The World Bank figures have proven useful and influential, bringing to the attention of a wide audience the scale of displacement taking place in the developmental process. These figures are ten years out of date and it appears unlikely that the study led by Michael Cernea will be repeated by the World Bank. Cernea has confirmed in personal correspondence that for the purpose of this World Bank review a small working group was convened to estimate world-wide displacement caused by development projects. This was a difficult task since governments either do not keep statistics or, when they do, they tend not to publish the aggregate data on either internationally assisted projects or domestic projects. Furthermore, as discussed below, deliberate under-reporting of the numbers of persons actually displaced is a consistent practice on the part of governments. Nonetheless, the 1996 World Bank informal group (which consisted of an urban specialist, an infrastructure specialist and Michael Cernea) reached an estimate based on data from Bank projects and data from national investments in urban transport infrastructure. Proceeding with caution, the team adopted a conservative stance to avoid any inflation of the figures and attempted to apply correctives to the calculations made. The result published at the time, and which became widely accepted, was a ten million cohort of new DDPs in the developing world each year.

The estimate reached in 1996 had two major caveats: it included displacement in only three sectors of the economy and was also primarily based on data about displacement under public-sector projects so therefore excluded projects undertaken by the private sector. It is Cernea's view that the widespread use of this figure has been inadequate, and in particular it is essential to take account of the very rapid growth in displacement in India and China and under-recorded displacement in the private sector, particularly in urban settings. Based on these considerations and taking into account the methodology that produced the initial estimates, Cernea has concluded that a more accurate figure for today's annual displacement would be at least fifteen million people per year – though once again Cernea, and many would agree with him, believes this estimate to be conservative.

In addition to the statistics collected by the major development agencies and states involved in organising resettlement, a number of specific research and project assessments can shed further light on the potential scale of resettlement as a result of individual projects. The Three Gorges Dam project in China's Yangtze River basin has already displaced in the region of 1.3 million people according to the Chinese Government while other research suggests this figure could be short by up to 700,000 (Dai 1998). This kind of discrepancy is indicative of two issues commonly associated with counting displacement of this kind: first, various stake-holders engaged in the land acquisition and development process are likely to produce lower-end estimates of the numbers of people affected; second, such conservative estimates are unlikely to take into account the indirect effects of development projects where people are not physically relocated. It also further reveals a surprising lack of accurate demographic statistics held by governments in these instances.

Official statistics on the human impacts of development are, as Cernea has pointed out, likely to be underestimates for several additional reasons. First, the statistics themselves are incomplete and, with the focus on 'large-scale' development resettlement, tend to undercount the patchwork of fractured displacement from innumerable small-scale projects. Second, government figures, particularly from India and China, tend to count only 'official resettlers' rather than others who may be displaced or otherwise affected. A Chinese study cited by the World Bank estimates that only a third of those resettled by dam projects over thirty years now live in a socio-economic situation that is equal to that from which they were uprooted (Stein 1998). It is a definitional question as to whether the remaining two-thirds are still considered as displaced; a similar rate of resettlement success in the Three Gorges project could leave hundreds of thousands displaced for decades, something that is a distinct possibility given the bureaucratic constraints of such a large-scale project (Steil and Yuefang 2002). As discussed in Chapter Two, however, it may be misleading to define these people as displaced, given the difference between them and other displaced persons in terms of access to remedies. The fact that a development project may have been initiated through legal land acquisition offers those affected by the project a legal avenue to claim assistance and compensation, however limited or unsuitable this may be (McDowell and Morrell 2007).

Furthermore, resettlement is often only offered to those directly affected and in requirement of physical relocation. Government figures are therefore likely to exclude those indirectly affected by the project including people subsequently displaced through project side-effects and those who suffer 'economic dislocation' or land reconfiguration if not physical displacement. Dams, for example, can initiate soil erosion, landslides and spread of disease causing displacement years after the project has been completed (Stanley n.d.). In Nigeria, the development of oil resources has contributed to environmental degradation and conflict in the region, both causes of further displacement. Furthermore, examples abound in which the livelihoods of populations that remain close to development projects are severely disrupted: in Thailand, the Pak Mun Dam not only generated initial resettlement but also contributed to further displacement by contributing to a dramatic decline in the catch of local fisherman (Robinson 2002). A recent study in India (ADB 2006c) found that indirect causes of displacement of this nature had not been factored into calculations of displacement and resettlement across the last fifty-five years. The report claims that the frequently reproduced figure of fifty to sixty million displaced in post-Independence India significantly underestimates the numbers affected by development projects. This finding is based on secondary data, which suggests that estimates made near to the completion date of a development project are always likely to understate the scale of displacement ultimately caused.

The literature points to more direct attempts at underestimating displacement caused by planned development projects. Linked perhaps to political expedience, Table 3.3 illustrates significant discrepancies cited by Cernea (2006) between the numbers of people estimated to require resettlement during a project appraisal and the revised estimates during implementation in a number of high-profile projects. There is, therefore, substantial evidence to suggest that government authorities, lenders and construction companies consistently understate the extent of development-created displacement and resettlement. Many academics as well as officials in the development banks and in the NGO sector argue for far greater transparency and professionalism in the collection of statistics and the need for those who use the current data to do so with caution.

Table 3.3. Underestimates of the Extent of Displacement Caused by Significant Development Projects.

Development project	Underestimate
Congo, Ruzizi II Power	99%
India, Singrauli I and II Mining	100%
India, Farakka	100%
Turkey, Izmir Water Supply	71%
Colombia, Guavio Hydroelectric Dam	99%
Cameroon Second Urban Project	48%

Cernea (2006).

Government Resettlement Schemes

As with development impacts, there is no supranational or independent organisation that monitors and presents data on populations affected by government resettlement schemes and international involvement in such schemes is extremely uncommon as states regard them as internal and sovereign matters. The controversial nature of many government resettlement schemes means that policies, operational decisions, outcomes and, critically, numbers are extremely politically sensitive. Schemes usually take place over a number of years to enable a gradual population transfer and there are genuine difficulties in assessing accurately the numbers affected at any one time; it is also difficult to exclude the possibility of other factors causing further displacement for the duration of the scheme.

For some resettlement programmes, such as Transmigrasi in Indonesia where external agencies provided funding and expertise, partial though generally unreliable statistics have become available. Estimates of the numbers resettled by the Transmigrasi programme are indicative of difficulties in assessing such a large-scale and ambitious human migration programme across an extended period of time. The Indonesian Government planned to move hundreds of thousands of people in three five-year plans: 1974–1979 – 250,000 families; 1979–1983 – 500,000 families; and 1983–1988 – 750,000 families (Castles 2002). However, the Indonesian Government did not reach its targets and a number of those resettled participated in the scheme voluntarily identifying opportunities for improved social and economic circumstances (Tirtosudarmo 2001). Although they claimed to have 'relocated 6.4 million people between 1950 and 1994' (Robinson 2003), it is difficult to accurately gauge the numbers of people within that total whose migration was not a direct consequence of the Transmigrasi policy. It has also been argued that additional displacement was caused by the arrival of resettlers in the new locations: ethnic tensions, negative impacts on the local environment and economic competition are all thought to have contributed to new displacement from these host societies.

A further example that illustrates the political sensitivity of figures for these programmes is the 'Return to the Village' scheme embarked upon in Vietnam following the end of the war. As the name suggests, this scheme worked on the premise of returning people that had been forced into urban areas during the conflict back to the land. There is debate over the 'voluntary' nature of this scheme (Robinson 2003), though it is clear that large numbers of people returned either to their land or moved into the state-constructed New Economic Zones (NEZs). One estimate calculated that by 1977, 700,000 people had moved from Ho Chi Minh City (formerly Saigon) and another suggests that around 1.5 million had been moved to NEZs by 1980 (see Desbarats 1987). There is disagreement, though no real controversy, over the absolute numbers moved under this scheme; the contention is over whether these people should be considered as resettled, displaced, returnees or voluntary migrants. In initiating the scheme, the Vietnamese Government was responding to legitimate concerns over its population distribution and certainly encouraged voluntary resettlement. It is clear, however, that there was a level of discrimination involved in the resettlement, with disproportionately high numbers of Chinese and families of political prisoners being moved into the NEZs (Robinson 2003). It is a contentious issue as to whether this can be seen as mandatory resettlement for development purposes or a voluntary resettlement programme and the different figures that exist for this scheme may reflect these divergent opinions.

Conservation Resettlement

Occupying one side of the environment–security nexus is the phenomenon of conservation displacement. Environmental degradation, particularly where exacerbated by climate change, can be a cause of displacement yet actions to conserve and protect parts of the environment can also have resettlement consequences. Those affected by conservation resettlement have, as we have previously discussed, been defined as 'other environmental refugees'. There is, however, heated debate over the extent of this phenomenon and how the issue is conceptualised and defined, as discussed in Chapter Two. It has been estimated that more than ten million people have been resettled by acts that aim to conserve the immediate environment. According to Schmidt-Soltau (2007), in twelve protected areas in six central African countries, around 5 per cent of the rural population (120,000 people) have been uprooted since 1990, with a further 170,000 people at risk of displacement from World Wildlife Fund (WWF) proposals. As identified in Chapter Two, academics and advocates concerned with conservation resettlement are at the forefront of a widened definition of displacement (and its effects) to incorporate those affected by the physical migration of the displaced and those economically affected if not physically relocated (Cernea 2006). Incorporating such a wide definition of displacement would see the numbers of displaced rise further, with 250,000 people becoming 'hosts' for the displaced (Schmidt-Soltau 2007). Criticisms of these figures come from conservationists who question the accuracy of the methods used to generate them (Redford and Fearn 2007) and argue that the issue of displacement has not been ignored by conservation organisations (Maisels et al. 2007).

Geisler and de Sousa (2001) discuss three methods that have been used to calculate a total of 'millions' resettled and displaced by conservation projects in Africa. The first relates directly to the area of protected land and the average population density of that area. Such a method has been applied to Africa calculating that 778,484 people live in and around conservation areas. This approach relies heavily on officially protected land and ignores much private conservation currently being carried out. However, the population figure effectively equates to a 'population at risk of displacement' rather than those actually resettled and such a calculation requires more specific investigation of individual protected areas. A second method involves extrapolating an estimation of the number of resettled and displaced persons within one country to a region or a continent. This is considered to be more accurate in terms of estimating the population densities of a region but tends to significantly increase the numbers 'displaced' by conservation by estimating the potential population density where Africa's conservation areas were 'opened to multiple economic uses' (Geisler and De Sousa 2001). A final method is the case study, focusing on particular occurrences of resettlement and displacement and not attempting to extrapolate or estimate a 'global outlook'. Table 3.4 provides examples of the numbers uprooted from particular parks in Africa. These estimates use different definitions of conservation resettlement and displacement, yet as Geisler and De Sousa note, the figures suggest that 'conservation may have damaged hundreds and thousands of African lives'.

Table 3.4. Studies of Conservation Resettlement and Displacement in Selected African Countries.

Country	Park Name	Area (ha)	OERs	Reference
Botswana	Central Kalahari Game Reserve	5,180,000	39,000	Kelso (1993)
Madagascar	Mananara Biosphere Project	23,000	35,000	Ghimire (1994)
South Africa	Kruger Park	1,948,528	250,000	Ellis (1994)
Tanzania	Selous Game	5,000,000	40,000	Yeager and Miller Reserve (1986)
Uganda	Kibale Forest Reserve and Game Corridor	33,915	30,000	Colchester (1994)

Source: Geisler and de Sousa 2001.

These assertions are supported by case studies from other central African parks that use the Impoverishment Risks and Reconstruction Model developed by Cernea to address the impact of those resettled by development projects (Schmidt-Soltau 2003, Cernea and Schmidt-Soltau 2006). These studies offer what the authors consider to be a conservative estimate of the numbers displaced by the establishment of parks in Africa at 120,000–150,000. It is in these figures that conservationists find most to disagree with. An extensive working paper from the Wildlife Conservation Society (WCS) compiles these criticisms (Redford and Fearn 2007). Conservationists question not only the assumptions inherent in applying the population densities used to calculate those 'at risk of displacement' from conservation, but also the evidence that any forcible, physical displacement has taken place in many of the areas cited in the above studies and those by Cernea and Schmidt-Soltau (Maisels et al. 2007). Schmidt-Soltau in particular is criticised for data collection methods that could only lead to claims of 'rough estimates'; the conservationists argue that it is misleading to draw firm conclusions on the impact of park establishment on the basis of such figures. Taking each of the examples quoted by Cernea and Schmidt-Soltau in turn, Maisels et al. (2007) provide alternative interpretations of the impact of these conservation projects, in the creation of some parks suggesting that 'not a single individual' has been displaced.

Once again, this controversy illustrates the difficulty in isolating causes of displacement, defining displacement and collecting data on the displaced. Yet despite inconsistencies, controversies and gaps in the statistics on conservation resettlement, they have been used in conjunction with development theory to illustrate the relationship between human and environmental security (Geisler and De Sousa 2001). Additionally, these estimates have been instrumental in attempting to lobby organisations, such as the WWF, to develop policies on involuntary resettlement in line with international donors and development agencies (Schmidt-Soltau 2007; see also Cernea 2006). Conservationists would argue that their organisations have been grappling for years with issues such as displacement that emerge out of the fundamental spatiality of conservation (Redford and Fearn 2007). Chapter Four discusses further the progress that has been made on suitable policies and guidelines.

There is potential for further conflict between groups advocating on behalf of the resettled and environmental lobby groups in relation to conservation resettlement. While it was posited that predictions of climate change displacement could be used to make a case for implementing green policies it is also clear that some conservation schemes with comparable aims may actually contribute to resettlement and displacement. Statistics would most likely feature prominently in this developing debate. In fact, this is already proving the case with respect to Western-based carbon off-setting schemes: a reforestation scheme organised by the UK-based Co-operative Bank has been accused of causing displacement and exacerbating local conflict in the forests of Kibale, Uganda (FERN 2007), which have experienced forced relocation over many years.

Planned Evictions/Displacement

Research, advocacy and policy making addressing the problem of displacement arising as a direct result of forced evictions benefit from a more comprehensive attempt of data collection. The *Global Survey on Forced Evictions*, compiled by the Centre on Housing Rights and Evictions (COHRE 2006a) estimates the number of reported evictions across a three-year period. Table 3.5, reproduced from the *Global Survey*, shows the regional breakdown of the 4.2 million reported forced evictions between 2003 and 2006. There are a number of qualifications to make about this headline figure. First, as a global survey, the estimates are based entirely on evictions reported by 'a global network of contacts, including individuals, grassroots groups and organisations'. The report's authors suggest, therefore, that the actual number of forced evictions is much higher than the total of 4.2 million presented in the latest report, while states tend to respond that the figures are inflated and misleading (the Chinese Government in particular reacted strongly to COHRE's claim that 1.5 million people were displaced and inadequately consulted or compensated to make way for the 2008 Olympic Games). Governments of states that make up this total would contend that such figures are likely to be impressionistic rather than scientific. The data received is not always specific and estimates are constructed using a number of equivalences. For example, one family was considered to equal five persons, one apartment building one hundred persons or one community two hundred persons. There are obviously severe limitations with using this method, which is not as such a criticism of the report but an acknowledgement of the vast and complex task that collecting these statistics presents.

Most of all, however, the definition here is crucial: 'The term "forced eviction" refers to the removal of people from their homes or lands against their will, directly or indirectly attributable to the State' (COHRE 2006a). This does not mirror the narrow definition for *planned* evictions discussed in Chapter Two. In fact, further to this definition the report provides a non-exhaustive list of causes of forced

Table 3.5. Estimated Numbers of Reported Forced Evictions by Region: 2003–2006.

Continent	Persons
Africa	1,967,486
Europe	16,266
The Americas	152,949
Asia and the Pacific	2,140,906
Total	**4,277,607**

Source: COHRE 2006.

evictions that includes: development and infrastructure projects, urban redevelopment and 'beautification' initiatives, political conflict, ethnic cleansing, and war. The COHRE definition, therefore, is a definition of eviction that almost equates to resettlement *and* displacement. What reins this definition in, however, is that it refers only to evictions that can 'be attributed to specific decisions, legislation or policies of States, or to the failure of States to intervene to halt forced evictions by third parties'. In effect, therefore, COHRE's definition cuts across a number of the other definitions of displacement and resettlement outlined in Chapter Two. The global total it arrives at is, therefore, of little comparative use, particularly given that it is based only on evictions reported to the authors of the report. COHRE uses the headline figures as a lobbying tool to show the extent of what it perceives to be state malpractice leading to evictions. The report is more useful, however, in the extensive detail it provides on specific cases of evictions and displacement in many countries around the world.

It is useful to explore further some specific examples of planned, authoritarian eviction that fit with the definition given to planned evictions in Chapter Two and review available estimates of the numbers displaced. Authoritarian and repressive governments are often involved in systematic programmes of evictions which are frequently part of wider strategies of maintaining political power over ethnic, religious or other minorities. Despite this, such actions tend to be couched in broadly developmental rhetoric. In Zimbabwe, as elsewhere discussed in this volume, President Mugabe's Operation Murambatsvina provides a recent and vivid example of the sheer scale of displacement. The effects of this policy were wide-ranging and exacerbated by Zimbabwe's economic and political isolation. Many people in the path of Operation

Murambatsvina fled prior to the government forces reaching their homes as have many people in surrounding areas – as many as four million people in total are thought to have fled their homes (Johnson 2007). The Zimbabwean case presents an example of just how difficult it is for humanitarian and advocacy agencies to keep track and monitor the number of people displaced and the extent of human rights abuses occurring across a wide geographical area. Gaining entry into affected areas and making contact with individuals is a significant problem for national and international agencies alike, while threats to physical security are a particular problem for Zimbabwean nationals engaged in human rights work. In addition there is the analytical challenge of isolating the causes of displacement in situations which are highly unstable. Operation Murambatsvina was by no means the only example of displacement caused directly by the policies and actions of the Government of Zimbabwe. Other Zimbabweans who have been displaced as a result of the government's actions include farm workers displaced as a result of the fast-track land reform programme, and mine workers who were displaced by Operation Chikorokoza Chapera. In any academic analysis or human rights reporting it is essential to highlight all of these Operations and their human costs, while at the same time not ignoring the more generalised hardships that confront many millions of Zimbabweans in rural and urban areas. The situation in Zimbabwe has been one of almost total breakdown, with state repression vying with health problems, land insecurity and famine to cause widespread displacement.

Elsewhere Robinson (2003) discusses less 'structured' or 'formal' interventions by states that are couched in developmental rationale but in all appearances could be described as forced evictions. Examples cited include:

- Brazil, May 2000: 2,000 squatters evicted from their homes in Sao Paulo.
- Burma, 1988–1994: an estimated 500,000 residents of Rangoon removed from their homes.
- Bangladesh, May 1999: 20,000 households lost their homes and belongings in a forced eviction with no prior written warning.

The numbers of people displaced in Rangoon were calculated by the US State Department and would likely be used by activists lobbying the UN to take action in response to the activities of the government run State Peace and Development Council (SPDC). While the validity of these figures is likely to be challenged by the Burma/Myanmar

Box 3.1. Development and Displacement Monitoring: Cambodia.

There is no systematic or centralised collection, presentation and analysis of data about population displacement and resettlement created by development projects and development processes in Cambodia. Many of the points below are indicative of a general lack of coherence in data collection on non-conflict IDPs.

- External lenders, principally the ADB, track the numbers of households and individuals directly affected by construction projects it has funded or part-funded.
- Within the Royal Cambodia Government, the Inter-Ministerial Resettlement Committee (IRC) chaired by the Ministry of Economics and Finance, through its technical wing, the Resettlement Unit, maintains a database of Resettlement Plans for all government-funded projects that involve land acquisition and resettlement. The plans include a detailed measurement survey, subsequently approved by the IRC and any external funding agency, which includes a count of affected households. The surveys are normally conducted by external consultants and NGOs. The data are not updated once approval has been given.
- The Cambodian media, in particular the English-language Cambodian Daily Press, monitors and regularly reports on 'land grabbing' and local land disputes, as well as legal land acquisition.
- A European Commission-funded project has recently commissioned an assessment of displacement arising out of twenty small-scale water projects (canals and drains) which showed that three thousand households were affected and lost assets (unpublished).
- The Cambodian NGO Forum has a functioning Resettlement Network but undertakes no independent monitoring.

There are considerable gaps in the Cambodian data on development-created displacement both as a result of legal land acquisition, 'land grabbing' and indirect displacement. The data is spotty in terms of its quality and coverage and there is a lack of transparency in how data is used in policy and operational decision-making.

Source: McDowell and Pilgrim 2007.

Government, their verification is also problematic given the closed nature of the state. This particular example is indicative of the difficulty of obtaining accurate and verified figures in displacement situations that are politically contested. It also points to the political use of statistics on both sides of the development–human rights nexus.

Land Redistribution Schemes

Counting the numbers affected by land redistribution schemes may not suffer from some of the difficulties of other categories in terms of definitional questions or isolating the particular cause of displacement, though it is likely to be a highly politicised practice. In the case of South Africa, by 1999 the land redistribution scheme had given more than 35,000 households rural land tenure in former areas of white control. The Land Rights Bill of 1998 was expected to benefit four to five million black households by transferring of property rights from the state to the de facto owners (ODI 1999). Many of these schemes are still under way.

Counting Disaster-created Displacement

Millions of people lose their homes and other assets as a result of natural and human-made disasters each year, either directly though the destruction of their property or as a consequence of being evacuated from affected areas for their own safety or to allow emergency relief operations to be carried out in full. Obtaining precise numbers of people displaced in this way is problematic as a consequence of the lack of clarity over who can be considered displaced in this way and when displacement comes to an end.

The primary international organisation responsible for providing emergency humanitarian assistance in natural disasters is the International Federation of Red Cross and Red Crescent Societies (IFRC) and the organisation's World Report (IFRC 2007) estimates the number of disasters each year and the number of people affected by such events. It uses a number of different international disaster databases to compile these figures and the IFRC's own Disaster Management Information System comprising many thousands of reports submitted by its field offices feeds into the Emergency Events Database (EM-DAT) at the Centre for Research on the Epidemiology of Disasters (CRED), based at University of Louvain, Belgium. EM-DAT is the most complete, up-to-date and accessible database that records the frequency and impact of disasters. There are limitations to the collection methods employed by CRED: EM-DAT suffers from a lack of systematic and standardised local collection of data and an inability to identify sub-national trends. It is estimated, for example, that the Iranian authorities respond to around 3,500 emergencies each year, though data from very few enter available databases.

Two privately run databases, acting largely for insurance clients, also collect similar information: NatCat and Sigma, managed by Munich Re and Swiss Re respectively. These databases measure losses in currency and therefore have limited data on countries with a low insurance density. The DesInventar database is an alternative method of 'bottom up' counting that has been developed, initially by the Latin American Network for the Social Study of Disaster Prevention, to monitor highly localised impacts of disasters. The figures it generates are built up through anecdotal evidence and local press reports and attempt to capture the effects of disasters that do not appear on those databases offering a 'global' picture. IFRC (2007) demonstrates, however, that while this method can be invaluable for recording small disasters and picking up localised nuances, it suffers from problems of data quality, reliability, verifiability and duplication. In addition to these databases, the Asian Disaster Reduction Centre produces daily updates on the immediate impacts of disasters across the continent as well as country profiles.

According to the IFRC figures, in 2006 there were 724 reported disasters. It appears clear that the frequency of disasters has increased in recent years: the IFRC (2007) report charts an increase from an average of 424 disasters a year between 1987 and 1996 to an average of 681 between 1997 and 2006. This increase can partly be attributed to better reporting of smaller disasters. What is perhaps of more significance, particularly with respect to the discussion of the relationship between climate change and an increase in the severity of weather patterns that generate many natural disasters, is the observed increase in severe disasters (ibid.; see also Ferris 2007). The collection of statistical information becomes more difficult when assessing the number of people actually displaced by disasters. The IFRC collates figures for the number of people killed by disasters and also the number of 'affected persons'. While the frequency of disasters is on the increase, available statistics suggest that the number of people killed by disasters has fallen across the last decade until 2003 and 2004 when major disasters, such as the Asian tsunami, saw a huge increase in disaster-related deaths. The number of affected persons, however, also appears to be on the increase, with an average of more than 260 million people per year affected by disasters between 1997 and 2006. Asia, by any of these measures, remains the continent worst hit by disasters as shown in Table 3.6. Significantly, while a large proportion of disasters do occur in Asia, an even larger proportion of the people killed or affected by disasters live in the continent. This is also the case for the proportion of people killed or affected in all developing countries. It is important to bear in mind the limitations of this kind of data collation. As the IFRC acknowledges, there is a lack of standardisation of definitions and methods among disaster databases.

The IFRC does not make specific estimates about the number of affected persons that could be considered displaced, but it does offer broad assessments of the total number of people who are affected in any one year by 'floods, droughts, earthquakes and displacement': the figure for 2007 was thirty-four million. The proportion of all the affected persons who could be considered disaster displacees depends upon the definition of displacement used. For example, natural disasters routinely deprive people of their homes and directly cause displacement yet they also contribute to economic dislocation, destruction of physical property and local infrastructure responsible for loss of livelihood. If the latter definition of displacement is preferred, then the overall figure of disaster displacement would be extremely high (see Christian Aid 2007). In the 2007 World Report the IFRC details a new methodology to clarify the criteria used to capture the effects of 'slow-onset' disasters, though it is unclear at this stage how this might affect the publicised headline figure.

Table 3.6. Selected Disaster-related Statistics, 1997–2006 (IFRC 2007).

	Global Total	Developed Countries*	Developing Countries*	Asia
Number of reported disasters	6,806	1,645 (24.2%)	5,161 (75.8%)	2,823 (41.5%)
Number of people killed by disasters	1,209,002	100,977 (8.4%)	1,108,025 (91.6%)	966,797 (80.0%)
Number affected by disasters (in thousands)	2,679,151	38,518 (1.3%)	2,640,633 (98.7%)	2,287,325 (85.4%)

Developed countries refers to those countries described as 'high' on the human development index; developing countries refers to those described as 'medium' or 'low'.

Recalling the discussion in Chapter Two, some argue that those displaced by disasters should be considered purely as a category requiring humanitarian assistance rather than be seen as a form of displacement requiring a specific displacement response. If this argument holds any weight, then it is reflected in the fact that disaster agencies themselves, though responding to the needs of displacees through general humanitarian assistance mechanisms, do not disaggregate the numbers of displaced people from the total of affected persons. Additionally, with increasing evidence for anthropogenic warming of the earth's temperature contributing to greater uncertainty and fluctuations of weather patterns, there are arguments that suggest disaster displacement is a form of environmental displacement. This parallels the difficulty in defining the effects of slow-onset disasters like drought (IFRC 2007).

Beyond the definitional challenges there are additional obstacles to accurately counting the number of people displaced by natural disasters. Humanitarian responses to disasters are by their very nature emergency responses. Estimating the number of people affected or displaced by any one disaster becomes increasingly difficult in unsafe and highly complex humanitarian episodes. Disasters can often be contributing factors in the causation of other disasters, creating 'disaster cascades'. Furthermore, disasters often take place in areas that already generate displacement through conflict, development or environmental degradation. As we have seen throughout this chapter, this makes isolating causes of displacement a difficult task and presents an obstacle to the collection of data on numbers of people displaced by an exclusive cause. It can also be difficult to interpret when displacement ends in these cases. Similarly, as discussed in Chapter Two, there are some disaster situations in which failures of development exacerbate the displacement caused through poor preventative measures or building and construction guidelines. In this respect politics may come to the fore in influencing the counting of disaster displacement. Finally, the IFRC (2007) suggests that a significant number of people are affected by smaller unreported disasters that are not incorporated into headline totals, to which the development of the DesInventar database attests.

Nevertheless, statistics are collected for the numbers of people affected and displaced by some individual natural and human-made disasters opening the possibility for case study or incident-specific assessments and analysis arguably vital for planning humanitarian responses at the time and for future operations (see Aleskerov et al. 2005). Figures are used by international agencies in encouraging donor states to increase their funding, as well as generating donations from individual members of the public. This was notably the case in the aftermath of the 2004 Asian tsunami: as the numbers killed, affected and displaced continued to rise to unprecedented levels for a single disaster, so did the charitable response from the rest of the world. A final use for these figures is to illustrate the impact of development on disaster responses. Table 3.6 shows that although over three-quarters of all disasters occur in the developing world, nearly 99 per cent of all affected persons are from the developing world. The situation in Asia is even more pronounced with only 23 per cent of disasters occurring in Asia, yet the continent is home to 88 per cent of the persons affected by disasters (ICRC 2006). More specifically, Castles (2002) explains how although the Kobe earthquake in Japan initially displaced around 300,000 people, after three months only 50,000 were still displaced. He contrasts this with those displaced by the Mount Pinatubo eruption in the Philippines, many of whom remain in 'temporary' camps several years after the event.

Counting Environmental Displacement

Counting environmental displacement is the most challenging of all the categories of displacement discussed in this chapter. Several disagreements and controversies over definitions converge here in terms of type and cause of displacement, which consequently generates a series of contested figures. Furthermore, much of this displacement can be seen as being caused by slow-onset factors across long periods of time, meaning that causes of displacement become tangled and complex. Finally, the increasing politicisation of climate change science, statistics and advocacy provides more opportunities for less robust and reliable predictions of displacement to be produced (see Christian Aid 2007).

Environmental Degradation and Climate Change

Counting displacement from environmental degradation is a complex and controversial task. Many of the definitional debates reviewed in Chapter Two can be replicated here to explain the lack of consensus on the number of environmental migrants or displacees. As noted earlier, Norman Myers' work on estimating the scale of environmental displacement has received much attention. The IFRC has estimated that as many as twenty-five million people have moved from areas affected by environmental degradation (Traufetter 2007), termed 'environmental refugees' by Myers and others. Statistics on particular instances of environmental displacement also exist, with specific research studies claiming that 4.1 and 4.7 million environmental refugees were displaced in northeast Brazil in the 1960s and 1970s respectively (Sanders 1990–1991), and that 'environmental scarcity' led to the displacement of between twelve and seventeen million Bangladeshis across the last forty years (Homer-Dixon 1994).

We have previously reviewed the scepticism about the use of estimating the extent of displacement arising directly out of environmental or climate change. The term 'environmental refugees' and the methodologies involved in counting these individuals has caused concern. Black (2001) taks issue with both parts of the term environmental refugee: 'environmental' is problematic because it assumes that the migrants in question have moved primarily as a consequence of 'environmental factors of unusual scope' (Myers and Kent 1995); 'refugee' is problematic because it is legally inaccurate and suggests that the migration was embarked upon under coercion. As Chapter Two illustrates, those often identified as environmental refugees are likely to have migrated for a number of factors and their decision to do so is likely to have involved elements of both compulsion and choice (Black 2001, Castles 2002). Consequently, estimates of the numbers of environmental migrants are problematic on the basis of the definition of what they are counting. But there are also methodological problems in the examples above that are exposed by Black. The statistics for northeast Brazil and Bangladesh do not account for other factors that may have contributed to displacement and merely correlate environmental degradation with out-migration in a particular area.

Those who are critical of these statistics do not, however, offer alternative statistics of the number of environmental migrants or the human displacement cost of environmental degradation. The criticisms made of the statistics preclude any such alternative set of figures and suggest that the causes of displacement in areas of environmental degredation are often too complex to attempt disaggregation. Conversely, the methodology of those collecting statistics on environmental refugees has a more global outlook. The acceleration of research into climate change has a similar global outlook and is increasingly visible in literature on displacement and migration associated with environmental degradation. In this respect, the term environmental migrant is often associated with predictions about the effects of the warming of the earth's temperature. The recent IPCC (2007) Climate Change Report forecast significant temperature change across the next fifty years, with the impact felt disproportionately by the section of the population in the developing world with the fewest resources to mobilise in response. Rising temperatures, the report suggests, are likely to contribute to lower crop yields, famine and drought as well as increasing the potential for natural disasters associated with inconsistent and often violent weather patterns. The Stern Review (HM Treasury 2006) also assesses the impacts of temperature rises, offering estimates for the number of people affected by additional rises in the earth's temperature of one degree Celsius. The current rate of warming would see the earth's temperature rise by five to six degrees Celsius, which would cause, it is predicted, flooding affecting between seven million and three hundred million additional people each year, reducing crop yields by up to 35 per cent in Africa. Taking such evidence into account the report suggests that the number of environmental refugees (or migrants) may reach two hundred million in the next fifty years.

In addition to the difficulties of defining the people affected by climate change, critics of these predictions suggest they are problematic as they represent an unrealistic worst-case scenario. The estimates of climate change displacement take the scientific predictions at face-value and, similar to the above calculation on Bangladesh, correlate potential flooding with actual displacement. Castles suggests that more consideration needs to be given to the way in which people respond to the impacts of climate change rather than assuming that all will make the constrained choice to migrate;[2] nor is it certain that individuals will be forced without agency to do so. More concern needs to be given to and more research conducted into ameliorative measures in response to climate change and the possibility that communities and/or governments may be able to adapt to the effects of climate change. One such strategy may be circular economic migration to relieve population pressure in the affected area and increase the diversity of income sources (see Black 2001). This is not to downplay the importance of climate change or the potential severity of its effects; rather it is crucial to incorporate sociological and anthropological understandings of decision-making in situations that cause displacement into estimates of the potential human costs of a warming climate, as discussed further in Chapter Six. In situations of conflict, disaster and environmental displacement it is often a minority that 'forcibly migrate', which compels forced migration academics to ask why most people faced with the same circumstances do not migrate (Castles 2003). This body of work needs to be incorporated into estimates about the extent of future climate change displacement.

Politics also has a role to play in arriving at definitions of 'environmental migrant or refugee' and, therefore, in the collection of associated statistics. Black (2001) has suggested that much of the desire to categorise those displaced in an often ill-fitting manner derives from the 'bureaucratic logic' of policy makers. For planning budgets and distributing responsibility, it is often easier for policy makers to categorise in this manner and statistics are collected accordingly. Statistics for environmental displacement can also be used to illustrate or bolster political arguments that are more about the environment and energy policy than the displaced. Advocacy groups and governments that are attempting to affect a change in attitude towards energy use and sustainable living, predominantly in the West, may use the prospect of millions being displaced by climate change to help make this argument, without fully appreciating or acknowledging the possibilities that may exist to avoid such displacement. In this respect, environmental displacement is no different to any of the other categories in that it needs to be understood alongside the numerous and complex political contexts that it straddles.

Summary

This chapter has outlined some of the headline figures that are collected on non-conflict displacement and identified some of the principle actors. What it illustrates is that there are only estimates with a wide margin of error for the total number of people displaced in each of the above categories. Where there is an overarching mechanism of statistical collection, it tends to suffer from other problems of defining those it should and should not be counting. Agencies involved in advocating for the displaced and responding to displacement situations are often tied into some understanding of the definitions discussed in Chapter Two that relate to how they are funded or how their mandate is devised. Consequently, the incentive and opportunity for pooling resources on statistical collection are limited. In this sense it is also perhaps not clear what such a 'global total' of the displaced would add academically or in practice. Given what has been illustrated throughout this book about the difficulty in isolating individual causes of displacement and the significance of local contexts in responding to displacement situations, statistical collection may be of more relevance if targeted to particular situations and contexts rather than engaging in attempts to produce a global overview.

Notes

1. See Christian Aid (2007) and see: http://www.icar.org.uk/?lid=8733 for a critique.
2. Quoted in Traufetter 2007.

CHAPTER FOUR

Governance and Management of Non-conflict Displacement

Legislating for Protection and Assistance

The discussion of definitions in Chapter Two and their importance illustrates the rigid categorisation that structures the international humanitarian system of protection for forced migrants. The system privileges those who cross international borders for whom there is a relatively robust regime defining legal entitlement and state responsibilities backed up by international structures; but it offers far less to those displaced within the borders of their own countries where the regime is far weaker. Other legal, policy and operational frameworks adopt their own categorisations of displacees, both international and internal, the result of which is a set of standards and practices that are not sufficiently agile or comprehensive to respond to the fluidity of contemporary forced displacement and consequently, a significant number of the world's displaced suffer a protection deficit. While it has become clear that the current international framework provides inadequate protection for the majority of forced migrants (Martin et al. 2006), legal and policy instruments to fill the gaps in protection have been developed in an ad hoc fashion. This section outlines a number of these hard law, soft law, policy and voluntary responses, from the Guiding Principles grounded in international human rights and humanitarian law to domestic state policies and development agencies' operational guidelines, which are expanded in the following chapter with a specific focus on the situation in China and India where the largest flows of development-related displacement and migration are taking place. The drafters of these different frameworks have divergent priorities and legal imperatives that are reflected in the standards they adhere to on human rights, development and sovereignty. Although the evolution of these frameworks can be seen as an attempt to address the complexity of contemporary forced displacement, it is that very complexity – the multitude of national and supra-national social structures, political agendas and institutional frameworks it spans – that will make it particularly difficult to harmonise standards and achieve adequate coverage to provide effective protection for all the displaced persons discussed in this volume. Such harmonisation will be a major challenge for the UN system in the immediate period; a theme discussed further in the second part of this chapter.

It has long been recognised that the failure to respond to the challenge of internal displacement is one of the more serious gaps in the existing international protection for displaced populations. The Guiding Principles constitute the most significant step forward in providing a standardised and coherent legal framework for providing protection and assistance to IDPs. This section assesses the feasibility of this aim given the multiple contexts of law and jurisdiction within which displacement occurs. While the law in which the Guiding Principles are grounded is international, the responsibility for IDPs remains that of the sovereign state. Furthermore, economic development strategies, conservation policies and climate change prevention measures, which have international support and could not have been fully predicted at the time the Principles were drafted, present new challenges to the effectiveness of the Guiding Principles. Providing protection and assistance to the displaced also needs to be understood in the wider context of, *inter alia,* the security–development nexus and the development–migration nexus. The developing role of the UNHCR is apparent with a number of recent documents and policy statements setting out an expanded role in protecting IDPs and in the provision of material assistance for other non-conflict displaced populations (see Guterres 2008).

Three main concerns arise in relation to new approaches to protection and the standardisation of guidelines for IDPs. First, there is concern about so called 'mandate creep' on the part of the UNHCR, particularly where the organisation includes in its remit people at risk of displacement as well as people in areas affected by displacement. Such an extension of the UNHCR role in conflict situations would see it taking on by default the functions of a High Commission for Forced Migrants, something that has been proposed by academics (Martin et al. 2006), but is likely to be widely opposed by states, international agencies and NGOs. In fact it could be argued that by including those in areas affected by displacement, it may even be considered as a High Commission for Protection. Singh Juss (2006) suggests that the work of the ICRC in disaster response and the UNHCR in responding to conflict and human rights violations should be merged, forming one agency to respond to all situations and events that generate (risk of) displacement, impoverishment and persecution. The potential for mandate creep leads on to two other concerns: the dilution of legal refugee protection and the potential for what might be perceived as interference in the internal affairs of sovereign states. Some academics and refugee advocates have suggested that by widening its remit the UNHCR risks diluting the principles upon which existing refugee protection is currently built. Additionally, some G77 states have expressed concern about the proposal that the UNHCR become more involved in internal displacement in their country, seeing conflict-related IDPs as the thin edge of the displacement wedge permitting international involvement in a range of domestic decisions.

All these concerns are underpinned by explicit legal and conceptual differences between the categories of displacement already discussed. Though many of the impoverishment effects and experiences of different forms of displacement may be similar (and we discuss this in the final chapter), there are apparent differences between types of displacement in terms of cause, legality and responsible agent. While it could be argued that monitoring and strategies for dealing with the potential negative effects of displacement may benefit from the pooling of resources, the legal structures and political structures that types of displacement interact with are conceptually and qualitatively different.

The Guiding Principles and Human Rights Conventions

The Legal Basis of the Guiding Principles

As a central contribution to the evolving normative framework, the Guiding Principles on Internal Displacement 'highlight the descriptive and non-legal nature of the term "internally displaced persons"' (Kälin 2000) and provide a re-description of how existing humanitarian and human rights law should apply in situations of internal displacement. Norms of international law already prohibit a number of the negative consequences of displacement. In international human rights law, for example, the Handbook for Applying the Guiding Principles (UNOCHA 1999) states that 'protection against arbitrary displacement is a fundamental human right'. Article 12 and Article 17 of the Universal Declaration of Human Rights (UDHR) proscribe arbitrary interference with an individual's home and being arbitrarily deprived of property respectively. Further, the Guiding Principles also look to minimise or mitigate negative impacts associated with displacement, many of which can be characterised as human rights violations, from the most basic human rights concerned with personal security to social and political rights concerned with standard of living and equal recognition before the law. These rights are, once again, enshrined in the UDHR and also the International Covenant on Civil and Political Rights (ICCPR).

What the Guiding Principles recognise, however, is that in practice the unique needs of IDPs are not fully articulated by the existing body of law. The so called Compilation and Analysis team of the UN representative for IDPs identified seventeen areas of insufficient protection and eight areas of clear gaps in the law on the protection of IDPs (Cohen 2004). In these cases, it was considered that the norms of international law required a particular articulation to make them specific to IDPs and this was to be the role of the Guiding Principles. From the outset, the authors made clear that the Guiding Principles were not to be considered legal instruments but rather their role was to reinforce and strengthen existing provisions of already sufficient international law (ibid.). It was not the case that a specific legal status equivalent to that of the refugee was required for IDPs. Not only was existing law sufficient to protect IDPs, but to suggest a legal status comparable to refugees would, it was argued, have implications for who is actually responsible for IDPs. The Guiding Principles acknowledge that in crisis, conflict and emergency situations, IDPs have technically not lost the protection of their state and the primary responsibility for their protection remains with the state. This position is reiterated throughout the Guiding Principles and their associated documents and statements.

The Guiding Principles, therefore, are grounded in norms of international humanitarian and human rights law and strengthen these norms by articulating the particular ways in which they can and should be applied in situations of internal displacement. Kälin (2000) sums up this position in the annotations to the Guiding Principles, 'as human beings who are in a situation of vulnerability they [IDPs] are entitled to the enjoyment of all relevant guarantees of human rights and humanitarian law, including those that are of special importance to them'. In this respect, the Guiding Principles are regarded as an acceptable interpretation of international law. While there is no explicit mention of 'displacement' in any of the articles of the UDHR, the negative consequences of many displacement situations are covered by a combination of articles that serve as a legal grounding for the Guiding Principles.

Development, the Guiding Principles and Human Rights

The evolution of the Guiding Principles saw the definition of IDPs broadened on a number of occasions, culminating in the following definition:

> Persons or groups of persons who have been forced or obliged to flee or to leave their homes or places of habitual residence, in particular as a result of or in order to avoid the effects of armed conflict, situations of generalized violence, violations of human rights or natural or human-made disasters, and who have not crossed an international border (UNOCHA 2004).

This revised definition was notable for the phrase *in particular*, added before the list of situations that may be likely to cause internal displacement, indicating as Robinson (2003) notes, that the 'listed examples are not exhaustive'. Despite this, it is perhaps notable that development displacement, though responsible for a large proportion of all displacement annually, is *not* one of the listed examples contained in the definition despite its scale. Furthermore, throughout the remainder of the Principles, clauses can be identified that refer specifically and exclusively to development and displacement, most notably in Part c. of the second paragraph of Principle 6, which states that the prohibition of arbitrary displacement includes displacement 'in cases of large-scale development projects that are not justified by compelling and overriding public interest' (UNOCHA 2004). It is perhaps an anomaly of the Guiding Principles that development as a cause of displacement is not explicitly included in the initial IDP definition while large sections are devoted to it in the main document and annotations by Kälin (2000). It is possible that this reflects the greater political controversy and sensitivity over the application of the Principles to displacement generated through development projects – how the Guiding Principles will be applied to development displacement in practice is still under discussion. Alternatively, it may reflect the fact that 'development induced displacement' was only highlighted as a significant issue of concern from 1998 onwards and as such was brought to the attention of the Representative of the Secretary-General following academic research and policy review by the major development banks.

Firstly, however, it is important to note that the Guiding Principles do not prohibit *all* displacement for development purposes. Principle 6 makes clear that prohibited displacement is that which is considered to be 'arbitrary'. While humanitarian and human rights law prohibits the 'forced movement' of persons, it does acknowledge specific circumstances where this may be justified. The Guiding Principles do not, however, take these exceptions lightly and suggest that displacement should only be accepted as a last resort having explored all possible alternatives. Kälin (2000) explains, 'forced displacement of persons may be allowed in certain circumstances but ... these exceptions from protection against displacement are restricted to cases of ultima ratio which shall be resorted to only if there are no alternatives'.

In times of conflict or disaster it may be more apparent what should or should not be considered arbitrary: the removal of civilians to places of safety in conflict situations, for example, is unlikely to be considered arbitrary and indeed is perfectly legal. In the case of development and involuntary resettlement, on the other hand, there will inevitably be protracted debate and disagreement between states, development agencies, civil society, affected populations and lawyers over what constitutes 'arbitrariness', 'public interest', 'certain circumstances' and suitable 'alternatives'. In the annotations, Kälin lays out the circumstances to which the Guiding Principles refer. Article 12 of the ICCPR, for example, declares that everyone should have the right to choose their residence, a right that should be subject to no restrictions 'except those which are provided by law, are necessary to protect national security, public order (*ordre public*), public health or morals or the rights and freedoms of others, and are consistent with the other rights recognised in the present Covenant'. What the Guiding Principles are attempting to prohibit is 'arbitrary' displacement that does not qualify for one of the above exemptions. Kälin (2000), drawing on legal annotations of the ICCPR, defines an 'arbitrary' act as one that 'contains elements of injustice, unpredictability and unreasonableness' (proportionality) or 'suggests a violation by state organs'. With respect to involuntary resettlement to make way for development projects the key phrases in these excerpts are 'provided by law', 'rights and freedoms of others', 'arbitrary' and 'reasonableness'. The Guiding Principles may have little impact upon a particular state wishing to legislate to initiate a development project that may displace some of its own population. The state in question is likely to justify such legislation as being in the 'overriding public interest'.

The Guiding Principles may be seen as presenting a justification for international involvement in situations of displacement that are 'arbitrary' or 'unreasonable'. Countries such as India, Egypt and Bangladesh have been critical of the development of the principles and keen to point out that they are not legally binding (Cohen 2004). In fact, it is on the issue of development displacement that the application of the Guiding Principles is most equivocal and least consensual. India, for example, is reluctant to bow to an international body on this issue or to principles produced entirely by non-governmental organisations (ibid.). India has already experienced huge population movements associated directly and indirectly with development and has consequently developed an extensive body of law and variously binding policies on the issue, most notably on private land acquisition. The larger and more rapidly developing nations may consider that *they* are in the best position to judge the 'arbitrariness' of a particular displacement or whether it is in the 'overriding public interest' and regard this as a national rather than international matter subject to an internal democratic test (for example through election processes) rather than to be tested in the international courts. It should be noted, however, that India, China, Cambodia, Sri Lanka and The Philippines have cooperated closely with the ADB in the development of national policies and laws that go some way towards matching international standards.

In response to sovereignty claims the Guiding Principles develop the concept of 'sovereignty as responsibility', explained further in the Annotations as an attempt to ensure that 'development cannot be used as an argument to disguise discrimination or any other human rights violations'. Cernea (2006) argues that the concept of sovereignty is consistently 'misused and misconstrued as a shield for denying the rights of development-displacees'. These states consider sovereignty as absolute jurisdiction over their own legislation and the effects of that legislation. In *Masses in Flight*, Roberta Cohen and Francis Deng (1998b) offer an alternative interpretation of the concept. Sovereignty, they argue, is not only about the *right* to legislate within internationally recognised borders but must also incorporate the *responsibility* to protect all people within those boundaries: 'a state should not be able to claim the prerogatives of sovereignty unless it carries out its internationally recognised responsibilities to its citizens'. Internationally recognised responsibilities would include the protection of fundamental human rights. In order to encourage greater usage and implementation of the recommendations that the Guiding Principles provide, the Representative to the Secretary General developed a Legislator's Manual, which was formally presented in October 2008, to provide guidance for national lawmakers to translate the abstract principles of international law into concrete national policy.

It remains the case, however, that states that are not signatories of international human rights conventions or that consistently act in a manner contrary to the legislation are unlikely to consider the Guiding

Principles with any greater attention. In Burma, politically motivated displacement is commonplace as a consequence of conflict and persecution, state programmes and poverty (South 2007), yet access to international agencies has consistently been restricted to areas near the Thai border, while the concept of effective protection is not part of the government strategy for providing suitable outcomes for displacees. Other countries, furthermore, consistently flout the norms that international human rights law represents. However, most development-created involuntary resettlement takes place in countries that do engage with the international community and have incorporated aspects of human rights law and elements of international standards into their domestic policy and legal frameworks. At the same time, development projects that involve private land acquisition or change of use of state-owned land are initiated through domestic legislation.

Despite the potential shortcomings in the Guiding Principles for overcoming sovereignty and other obstacles in the path of providing meaningful protection for people displaced by economic development in non-conflict settings, it is significant that the legal protection they promise extends to all displaced people; places in the international political arena guidance on how authorities should treat those displaced; and provides the basis for a new rights-based approach to development and displacement. It is significant also that the 'rolling out' of the Guiding Principles has helped trigger other policy initiatives including an African Union draft protocol on displacement which was expected to be presented for endorsement at the time of writing this volume; and the Protocol on Protection and Assistance to Internally Displaced Persons adopted by member states of the International Conference on the Great Lakes Region, a binding instrument that obliges states to accept the Guiding Principles by incorporating them into domestic law. Together these are important openings for further domestic legislation on development caused displacement, and opportunities to further build on the Guiding Principles.

Outcomes of Development and Human Rights

The Guiding Principles are not simply instruments that aim to prevent displacement but also offer guidance in situations where displacement is considered justified or is unavoidable or spontaneous. Guiding Principles 10 to 23 address issues of protection *during* displacement. As previously discussed, many developing states would argue that democratically elected governments have a legitimate responsibility to judge what is in the national interest and take often difficult political and economic decisions about the risks and benefits of a particular project. Industrial and infrastructure development over the past twenty years in China and India are seen to be key drivers for economic success and the reduction of poverty, achieved in part through projects that require land acquisition and involuntary resettlement. Governments acknowledge that rapid industrialisation and urbanisation coupled with a fast-growing population and increasing demands on natural resources may entail high social costs, threaten political instability and even generate unrest.

The development and industrialisation process, however, is unique in offering the potential to manage land and asset loss and relocation in a manner that promotes human development through a range of legal protections, entitlements and strengthened contracts between the state and affected communities. Despite such opportunities being seized too infrequently, recent studies of 'resettlement with development' approaches in China and new safeguards being developed in India and The Philippines (for urban squatter populations) would suggest that the risks of human rights violations are being acknowledged and partially addressed (ADB 2007). The Guiding Principles can play an important role in the further development and widespread acceptance of new laws and policies to protect and ensure assistance for 'displaced' populations. In a speech to the ADB in 2005, the Special Representative of the UN Secretary General on the Rights of IDPs outlined how a rights-based approach to development 'emphasises the complementarities of development and human rights goals'. In this respect, development is different to other causes of displacement as it is viewed as a positive in and of itself. Kälin (2005d) accepts, therefore, that being 'displaced by development may be considered essential for the greater good of the country'. Conceptually, this represents a stark difference between displacement as part of a resettlement project caused by development projects (into which you may incorporate conservation resettlement) and other forms of displacement. Conflict, disasters or environmental degradation are themselves seen as negative phenomena. If these causes can be prevented it may be possible to prevent displacement. Development, on the other hand, is not something to be prevented, though its negative consequences need to be anticipated and managed in the interests of those who are most likely to lose out in the process.

Additionally, there are practical differences between development and other forms of displacement that provide opportunities for mitigating human rights violations and creating alternative sustainable livelihoods for those affected. Large-scale development projects inevitably require extensive planning. The Guiding Principles suggest that this should include planning for the relocation, resettlement and rehabilitation (ultimately livelihood improvements) of those displaced by a project. One of the most effective ways to reach a suitable settlement for displaced people, they argue, is to involve them at every stage of the planning process (UNOCHA 2004). Principle 7 outlines some of the steps of informing and consultation:

> Adequate measures shall be taken to guarantee to those to be displaced full information on the reasons and procedures for their displacement and, where applicable, on compensation and relocation; the authorities concerned shall endeavour to involve those affected, particularly women, in the planning and management of their relocation (UNOCHA 1998).

The benefits of involving those at potential risk from a project are threefold: firstly, it is essential to fully assess the extent and personalisation of the risks that may arise from the project in order to make a better judgement on the justification for the project; secondly, if people are consulted early, have the justification for the project explained to them and are given assurances about future compensation they may move voluntarily (UNOCHA 2004); and, finally, planning and consultation provides the best mitigation against human rights violations during displacement and resettlement (Kälin 2005). This final point is crucial as there is significant risk of human rights violations in the development process particularly where assets are seized, where access to assets is fundamentally altered and where other risks of impoverishment present significant challenges to affected populations. Guiding Principles 10 to 23, however, are written to help avoid human rights violations during displacement. For agencies and governments involved in development projects they outline a clear standard to meet in order to avoid rights violations.

These principles are once again grounded in international conventions such as the UDHR and the ICCPR. Furthermore, they offer the displaced a framework for resistance. Cohen (2004) describes a number of cases where the displaced have themselves cited the Guiding Principles as part of their resistance to certain aspects of development projects and hold the authorities to account on guaranteeing and protecting their rights. Continuing to work with local civil society groups to improve their use of the Guiding Principles also appears to be a recent and future strategy for the Representative of the Secretary-General on human rights of IDPs, Walter Kälin, as his 2006 report to the Human Rights Council makes clear.

Box 4.1. The Human Rights Risks of Development-created Displacement – a Typology.

Balakrishnan Rajagopal (2000) of the Massachusetts Institute of Technology has distinguished five types of human rights challenge posed by development displacement:

- *Right to development and self-determination* – Rajagopal cites the UN General Assembly Declaration on the Right to Development which states that every human being has the right to 'participate in, contribute to and enjoy' all forms of development. It can be argued, therefore, that it is local communities with the right to development, not states. In opposition it could be argued that in many cases the state is in fact representative of non-local communities that also have a right to development.
- *Right to participation* – This should commence at the same time as the project is conceived and is grounded in the UDHR and the ICCPR. This is particularly the case for indigenous and tribal peoples who have the right to participation in the formulation, implementation and evaluation of all development plans that may affect them, as a consequence of an International Labour Organisation Convention on Indigenous People.
- *Right to life and livelihood* – This not only includes the right to life and to not be arbitrarily deprived of one's home but also the right to an adequate standard of living for the whole family. Furthermore, this also refers to protecting the sustainability of the local environment for current and future generations.
- *Rights of vulnerable groups* – There is growing evidence to suggest that development projects disproportionately affect those groups that are already vulnerable, such as women, children and ethnic and indigenous minorities. Principles of non-discrimination can be found in the UDHR (Article 2) and the ICCPR (Article 2).
- *Right to remedy* – It is often the case that development displacees have to react to decisions that have been taken without their consent. Therefore they require mechanisms not only to challenge these decisions but also to halt development while their appeal is heard. The UDHR (Article 8) and the ICCPR (Article 2) again provide the legal grounding.

This typology is largely reproduced from Robinson (2004).

Development Agencies and the Private Sector

A number of high profile development projects are carried out with full or partial funding of the multilateral development banks, such as the World Bank or the ADB, or more frequently directly by private corporations. In 2000, approximately three hundred projects that had support from the World Bank required some form of involuntary resettlement affecting around 2.6 million people. The ADB estimates that between 1994 and 1999, 130,000 people a year had been affected by its projects that involved resettlement (figures from Robinson 2004). There is general agreement that international organisations such as the regional development banks have legal personality under international law and should be held accountable for project-related human rights violations. Recent concerns have been expressed by the UN Special Rapporteur on the Right to Food, Jean Ziegler, regarding the role and legal obligations of multilateral organisations over the IFC-funded Newmont's Ahafo South gold mining project in Ghana, the Left Bank out-fall Drainage project in Pakistan, and the Nam Theun 2 Dam in Lao. At the same time, the development banks continue to maintain a close dialogue with their lenders over resettlement safeguards and there are indications of support that may lead to new guidelines and policies on rights-based approaches to project lending. These issues are addressed in greater detail in the next chapter.

Civil society groups nevertheless maintain that public financial institutions have an obligation to ensure that their clients meet international human rights standards; that International Financing Institutions (IFIs) are bound by general international law, including customary law, and international legal obligations take precedence over internal procedures; that human rights impact assessments need to be embodied in national and international normative and regulatory frameworks; and that clauses in host-government agreements that exempt the private sector from national laws and restrict access to justice for project-affected people should be prevented. These demands reflect the relatively weak 'legal and policy tools' available to those who seek to hold both IFIs and private sector companies accountable for their investments and activities in the development sector. It should be acknowledged, however, that the Inspection Panel reporting to the Board of the World Bank considers a number of controversial projects where complainants are mostly concerned with resettlement outcomes and Bank failure to comply with its own policies or to adequately monitor the implementation of the projects it funds. Despite often being recipients of large government grants to develop areas of certain countries, private companies are also often guilty of not adhering to official procedures and guidance. Patricia Feeney puts some of the responsibility for this on the state that does not define clearly enough in contracts the necessary requirements for protecting human rights in the region of development (quoted in Robinson 2004).

In such situations it can be argued that a development agency or private company should be subject to the same legal considerations regarding the human rights of affected populations as would the state. The International Law Commission has suggested that private entities that carry out core functions of the state take on a *de facto*, if limited, sovereignty. In terms of the Guiding Principles and the concept of sovereignty as responsibility this makes development agencies and private corporations responsible for the protection of those affected by the projects in which they are engaged and from which they profit. Development agencies certainly acknowledge the impact their projects have on local populations and in recent decades have attempted to make resettlement programmes a central, rather than peripheral, part of their project planning and implementation (Robinson 2004). The World Bank policy on involuntary resettlement accepts the potential for 'severe economic, social and environmental risks', 'impoverishment', loss of resources, lack of applicability of productive skills and the loss of 'community institutions or social networks'. For many more successful developing economies there is evidence that the environmental and social safeguards being imposed by the development banks are regarded as an increasing disincentive to taking on new loans when borrowing on capital markets is a less abrasive option. Many of the policy objectives of the development agencies are similar to those outlined in the Guiding Principles: for example, to avoid displacement where possible by exploring alternative project designs and promoting the participation of the displaced in planning and implementation. The ADB has also developed a specific Gender Checklist, which Kälin (2005d) has praised as acknowledging the particular needs and skills of certain groups relevant during displacement. In addition to the moral imperative of mitigating against human rights violations, both the World Bank and the ADB have also acknowledged that there are economic and development benefits from implementing suitable resettlement. The ADB judges that the negative effects of not applying an acceptable policy in development displacement 'almost invariably outweigh the investments that would have been needed to plan and execute an acceptable resettlement program' (Cernea 2006). Furthermore, the World Bank has proposed that those forcibly resettled should be able to 'share in project benefits'. Some have argued that this 'restoration language' is to some extent

Box 4.2. Private Corporations and Displacement – Three Examples.

Balfour Beatty in Lesotho and Ilisu – flouting of development guidelines and corruption
The Lesotho Highland Water Development Project was conceived in the 1980s and immediately caused concern for its method of financing. Additionally a number of sources claim that guidelines intended to protect local interests and the local environment have been systematically flouted (Hildyard 2000). In addition to these allegations the consortium of which Balfour Beatty has been part has been investigated for corruption (Earle and Turton 2005). In the case of the Ilisu Dam in Turkey, Balfour Beatty was the recipient of significant export credit guarantees from the British Government 'despite the absence of any government scrutiny of the resettlement plans' and the then impending case looking into corruption in Lesotho. The company pulled out of the Ilisu project in 2001 (Robinson 2004).

Oil in Nigeria – development displacement and potential conflict
A number of transnational oil companies have invested heavily in Nigeria's oil fields where revenues are estimated at $320 billion. This revenue has enriched a small Nigerian elite, while the majority of the population, not 'sharing in the development rewards', remain poor. Particular suffering, through displacement and industrial accidents, has been experienced by minority tribal groups, such as the Ogonis. The resistance organisation set up by this ethnic group was brutally repressed by the Nigerian authorities with the torture of thousands of activists and the execution of others across the early 1990s. This created significant political instability and insecurity in the area, a situation that could have generated conflict and did cause further displacement.

BP in West Papua – 'good intentions' vs. political instability
BP's involvement in West Papua is being seen as an important test case for the feasibility of private corporations making sufficient provision for protecting the human rights at risk from the effects of development projects. Irrespective of whether BP's motives are more associated with public relations, there is an appreciation that the company does have 'good intentions' (Robinson 2004). However, West Papua is a politically unstable region. The complex political economy of development presents a serious challenge for BP in order to carry out this project according to its original stated aims of providing a model for investing in the developing world. BP has incorporated the 'Voluntary Principles on Security and Human Rights' into its practices, a set of guidelines apparently distinct from any grounded in international law, yet according to a former Chief Executive, still not enough consideration is being given to local relations and prevention of human rights violations.

disingenuous given that the World Bank also proposes to 'improve the standards of living [of those displaced] or at least restore them'. The Centre for International and Environmental Law (2001) points out the potential for contradiction between these two statements: if the displaced are to enjoy the project benefits then their standard of living will need to improve, not merely be restored. However, it should be acknowledged that in practical terms livelihood improvements in a relatively short time period (typically Bank involvement in implementation of a funded project is between 5 and 7 years) and privileging one group over others in a relocation situation presents additional problems which are outside the scope of the Bank agreement and would fall to the government to address.

Much of this criticism has some justification when applied to policies across the last few decades, yet the development banks have shown a willingness since the mid-1990s to commit to further developing their guidelines on issues of displacement and involuntary resettlement (though a review of the ADB's policies on resettlement in early 2008 and the boycotting of public consultations by civil society in India suggest a wider concern that such commitment may now be waning under pressure from Chinese and Indian authorities). Those in receipt of World Bank funds are required to produce a resettlement plan covering a number of criteria guaranteeing the livelihoods of the displaced. The ADB requires from its debtors a plan that incorporates a statement of objectives, policies and strategies clarifying a number of areas that could potentially lead to human rights violations such as land tenure and ownership or the identification of alternative sites and locations (Robinson 2004). Many of the elements of the borrower guidelines chime with a number of aspects in the Guiding Principles. The World Bank's Operational Policy on involuntary resettlement states that displacement should be avoided if feasible through exploring alternative project designs, as called for in the Guiding Principles. Similarly, the ADB's implementation procedures call for community participation, valuation and compensation for lost assets and access to training, employment and credit, which echoes a number of the Guiding Principles from 10 to 23. Furthermore, the World Bank policy does not only consider those physically displaced but also those who suffer 'a loss of income sources or means of livelihood', something that arguably extends beyond the assistance of the Guiding Principles, which is afforded only to those physically relocated.

Despite this, development agencies have been reluctant to utilise the language and frameworks of international human rights law, and the policies of development agencies, Cernea and Mathur (2007) argue, 'insufficiently highlight the human rights dimensions embedded in development-caused displacements'. This is to say that where these operational policies differ from the Guiding Principles is that they are not grounded in international human rights law, but instead use their own assessment models and socio-economic indicators to judge the outcomes for affected persons. Cernea argues that this choice to 'eschew explicit human rights terminologies' represents a mistaken belief that to include them would politicise resettlement schemes and allow recipient governments to dismiss the guidelines on the basis of an infringement of sovereignty. There have been tentative signs, however, that the World Bank and ADB are assessing the viability of utilising a human rights framework within their operational policies. There is certainly willingness for further collaboration on the side of Walter Kälin, the Representative to the Secretary-General on IDPs, evidenced by his 2005 speech at the ADB to push this agenda.

As previously discussed, private corporations have less experience in developing guidelines or policies equivalent to the Guiding Principles and often lack the necessary skills to assess the social and environmental impact of their actions (Feeney 2000). It appears that there are several international standards and guidelines that could apply to promoting more responsible corporate behaviour. Robinson (2004) lists a number of codes and principles that may serve such a purpose and could be applied to private companies that have taken on core roles and, therefore, responsibilities of the state. However, and as we discuss in the Conclusion to this volume, what appear to be lacking are the mechanisms to enforce these guidelines. Feeney provides details of a number of examples where this is the case, with guidelines and lines of responsibility often not properly understood. Enforcement would be required to take place at the international level as in many circumstances the political economy of development is such that local authorities can be reticent about imposing too many conditions on private companies lest they lose the contracts. Yet the clamour for development can occasionally be so great for local and national leaders that projects are endorsed quite consciously at the expense of the rights of local citizens. It is simplistic to suggest that all private companies lack good intentions towards those affected by their projects, but it is necessary to understand the complex and unstable politics that often surround these developments.

Applying the Guiding Principles to situations of development displacement is clearly more complex than in other situations of displacement. Development continues to take place largely within national frameworks and under a national guise despite extensive involvement from supra-national agencies and third-party states.

Assessing the needs for protecting human rights in development projects can be characterised as a classic conundrum of global and domestic governance that is a feature of the contemporary global political economy. Although grounded in law, in many instances of development-created displacement the Guiding Principles may remain just that: guidance. The threat of justified international involvement in mitigating the consequences of a development project does not appear credible. As discussed above, it is the assertion of many states that their sovereignty as responsibility extends to being able to make a judgement about the overall cost-benefit analysis of a particular project. Furthermore, the Guiding Principles make it clear that some development-induced displacement is acceptable; evidence suggests, however, that the majority of development projects are likely to cause some human rights violations. Is it the case, therefore, that the Guiding Principles are effectively suggesting that there is a judgement to be made about the *acceptable extent* of human rights violations, acceptable in terms of proportionality to the benefits of the project?

The limitations of the Guiding Principles stem from their referral to international human rights law that in certain countries is either systematically ignored or not incorporated into domestic law. There is also concern that there has been no governmental involvement in their drafting and no convention of legal frameworks emerging from the principles. It may be a more effective strategy to use the Guiding Principles primarily for the mitigation of human rights violations during displacement rather than attempting to prohibit development projects that cause displacement. In this case the Guiding Principles can be used as a framework for domestic civil society groups and those displaced themselves to articulate their opposition to particular aspects of development projects. Furthermore the Legislator's Manual can play a key role in the drafting of new legislation. This may have an impact upon domestic governments being perceived as more legitimate opposition by those affected rather than international organisations advocating on behalf of those displaced, as developing countries may be suspicious about the motives of this 'interference' in their development affairs.

Managing Complex Forced Displacement Crises

Over the past five years the United Nations through its Humanitarian Response Review and the Humanitarian Reform process it triggered has responded to criticisms about the conduct and outcomes of international humanitarian operations in complex emergencies by seeking ways to enhance operational predictability and accountability. Much thought has gone into reforms necessary for improving protection and assistance for IDPs in conflict and crisis situations. The review and the process acknowledged that recent humanitarian responses to displacement failed to address the full range of protection and material needs of people uprooted by conflict. Initially the impetus for reform was the humanitarian challenges posed by conflict but in time the Asian tsunami and the Pakistan earthquake provided an additional focal point for reform considerations following reports detailing human rights violations suffered by those displaced in the successive phases of immediate post-tsunami relief, temporary shelter, relocation, and also on return. Institutional responsibilities for such emergencies were revisited and, most importantly, some clarity was reached in the role played by the UN's refugee agency, UNHCR, in taking the lead in the newly introduced 'cluster' arrangements for coordinating the provision of protection and coordinating the establishment and management of camps, and in the provision of emergency shelter in displacement situations not limited to camp situations. In parallel there is a process which sees the UNHCR 'mainstreaming' IDP response (in conflict situations) within all its mandated functions.

The cluster arrangements saw a grouping of UN agencies, NGOs and other international organisations around a sector or service provided during a humanitarian crisis. Each of the nine clusters had a designated agency that led (or convened) the cluster. There was a separate lead agency or convener in each of the two different humanitarian situations of conflict-related internal displacement and displacement through natural disasters in a number of the clusters. The approach was being developed simultaneously at two different levels. At the global level, the aim was to strengthen the so called system-wide preparedness and technical capacity to be able to respond to humanitarian crises. Global cluster leads were therefore given the task of ensuring 'predictable and effective' inter-agency responses within the cluster area. At the country level, the cluster approach aimed to strengthen coordination and mobilise a number of different in-country actors such as NGOs, UN agencies or non-UN organisations to assess and respond to gaps in the provision of basic humanitarian assistance. Overall, the new process was designed to give predictability and accountability to the humanitarian response system by making agencies and organisations responsible and accountable to the UN's Emergency Relief Coordinator.

An important aspect of the cluster approach, as suggested above, was the aim of increasing predictability and accountability for the provision of assistance and protection for IDPs by UNHCR in a number of key clusters. Darfur proved for many in the UN and NGO system that the current approaches failed those displaced within Darfur while greater levels of protection, albeit insufficient, were available to victims of the violence who fled across Sudan's borders. This inequity in which different categories of people receive different degrees of assistance and protection is widely condemned as all vulnerable people are entitled to receive the same levels of protection and assistance according to need, and any system should not discriminate between beneficiaries on the basis of whether they have crossed a national border. UNHCR argued convincingly through its corporate strategy that it was the best placed organisation to assist the internally displaced in conflict situations and the UN agencies and its donors agreed that the organisation should take a stronger role than it has in the past in addressing IDP crises.

At the global level the roles and responsibilities of the cluster, led by the global cluster lead agencies, included a series of practical measures: improving standard setting, monitoring and advocacy; establishing and strengthening surge capacity and standby rosters; training; establishing or improving stockpiles; and coordination. At the time of writing this book, NGO participation in the development of clusters was limited though increased efforts were being made in Geneva and New York to secure greater coordination between the UN and NGOs with both sides agreeing in public at least that NGO participation was vital if improvements in responding to humanitarian crises were to be made.

The cluster approach was officially piloted in four countries with conflict-generated internal displacement: Uganda, The Democratic Republic of Congo, Liberia and Somalia. It was also employed following the Pakistan earthquake in October 2005 marking the first time such an approach was used in response to a natural disaster; it was again used during the 2007 crisis in Lebanon. The arrangements also permitted UN country teams to choose to implement the cluster approach if it was thought by the Humanitarian Coordinator or Resident Coordinator that such an approach would 'add value'. Subsequently, in 2006, the cluster approach was introduced in Somalia and later in the same year in Colombia, while in April 2007 it was announced that Ethiopia would also become a participating 'cluster country' though whether on the basis of a new or existing emergency was unclear. It was intended that the new processes would also be applied to future large-scale disasters warranting an international response; though at the time of publication the definition of 'large-scale' was yet to be determined.

Senior officials involved in 'rolling out' the approach were content in the initial phases that managers were being flexible rather than dogmatic, taking into account different country conditions. Decisions on what number of clusters and which ones were needed and the lead agency or organisation for those clusters was agreed, on the ground, within the Inter-Agency Standing Committee on humanitarian assistance (IASC) country team. Inter-agency funding appeals (Consolidated Inter-agency Appeals and Common Humanitarian Action Plans (CHAPs)) were revised in the light of new agency responsibilities and plans in the four initial pilot countries.

At the end of 2006, the IASC conducted an 'Interim Self-Assessment' of the implementation of the cluster approach in the field, offering a progress report highlighting the main trends, themes and lessons from field experience. The self-assessment was an opportunity for field staff to contribute to policy discussions at the global level and the process was thought to have highlighted a number of practical challenges and emphasised the need for training of sector and cluster leads. Overall, however, it was generally felt that the cluster approach was demonstrating a *potential* to enhance the overall effectiveness of humanitarian response by improving predictability and response capacity (its principal objectives). Progress had been made in designating clear leads in former "gap" areas, and there were positive indications of a new atmosphere where partnership between UN and non-UN humanitarian organisations would become the norm. This was reflected in the authors' discussions with officials in the major UN agencies, though with some reservations (see below). In November 2006 the IASC Working Group agreed that the cluster approach should be used in all contingency planning for major new emergencies that involve multi-sectoral responses with the participation of a wide range of international humanitarian actors. It was also agreed that it should be introduced in all countries with Humanitarian Coordinators.

Reform Challenges

This volume is concerned with the types and scales of challenges posed to national governments and the international community by displacement occurring in non-conflict situations that traditionally have not warranted an international humanitarian response of the kind we see in conflict situations. The legal and policy framework is less comprehensive and the institutional structures are not in place for such a response. However, the UN Humanitarian Reform Review and the cluster approach which emerged from that review are one example of agencies (and their donor governments) recognising the realities of contemporary displacement dynamics and seeking ways to stretch and extend existing systems to address the gaps identified. It is, however, too early to assess the full impact of the cluster approach on the effectiveness of mutli-sectoral responses to population displacement in non-conflict situations. Population displacement, in the absence of formal, organised and legally sanctioned involuntary resettlement as an outcome of development processes, has not formed a significant part of the global or field policy discussions or on the ground evaluations. No humanitarian agency has thus far sought to develop specific procedures for identifying or responding to identified humanitarian or protection needs related to the human impacts of development projects or development processes.

At present there is an absence of firm evidence about the actual impact clusters are having in terms of improved humanitarian *outcomes* in relation to internal population displacement, rather than better *processes*. Donors, who were expected to provide close to one hundred million dollars during the formative years of the new system's establishment to build global capacity in support of clusters, will certainly demand more tangible evidence of impact before committing politically and financially to the new approach.

Areas in which there is a need for greater clarity include working relationships at the policy and operational levels within the cluster system. For example, the linkage between the global/headquarters level, the capacity-building effort and the delivery level through country teams remains unclear. As clusters roll out at field level, there is, according to some officials consulted for this book, evidence of an increasing resistance to the pace of their introduction from agency headquarters which would seem to contradict the more positive views coming from the field. According to some officials and donor representatives, this may have had much to do with a continued lack of agency 'buy-in' at headquarters level on the reform agenda. It may also be linked to the relatively low priority afforded to humanitarian programming within agency structures. There would appear to have been a sense among donors that until humanitarian reform gains proper traction within large agencies, such as UNICEF, there is likely to be 'continued dissonance' between the headquarters and the field, and patchy support to the field on issues like clusters. This has implications for any responses to the needs of displaced persons and may undo some of the good work envisioned in the original planning.

The gradual increase in the involvement of partners from civil society in clusters was regarded as a positive development, but there remained concerns that the high levels of funding being committed to cluster support by donors will actually not result in the breaking down of UN agency 'firewalls'. There is a view that greater capacity needs to be built across the cluster, improving the way they work through and with implementing partners and making improvements across their clusters, not just building their own agency capacity and thereby reinforcing the old firewalls that have led to such a fractured response in the past. In general, there is a sense of optimism that positive progress is being made, but caution for the need to maintain momentum and monitor how agencies actually build and maintain capacity within the cluster and embrace the reform agenda.

One important upshot of these rather wide-ranging and time-consuming reforms has been to cast new light on the need to address other non-conflict contexts of displacement and to map response and gaps in a similar fashion. Enthusiasm for such an exercise has not been universal with many in the UN system arguing that there is insufficient capacity to address the world's displacement problem in its entirety given institutional, financial and political constraints and the scale of the existing challenges they face.

There is however an acknowledgement that global displacement presents a genuine and wider challenge and one that humanitarian workers on the ground frequently witness as causes and consequences of displacement are intertwined, as are the populations they are trying to reach in their daily work. The High Commissioner for Refugees set out his agency's panoramic view on displacement in October 2007 (UNHCR 2007b):

> We see more and more people forced to move because of extreme deprivation, environmental degradation and climate change, and conflict and persecution.
>
> Many move simply to avoid dying of hunger. When leaving is not an option but a necessity, this is more than poverty. On the other hand, natural disasters occur more frequently and are of greater magnitude and devastating impact. Almost every model of the long-term effects of climate change predicts a continued expansion of desertification, to the point of destroying livelihood prospects in many parts of the globe. And for each centimeter the sea level rises, there will be one million more displaced. The international community seems no more adept at dealing with these new causes than it is at preventing conflict and persecution.
>
> I believe it is extremely important for us to examine the reasons, the scale and the trends of present-day forced displacement.
>
> Given these crushing pressures on populations who under normal circumstances live close to emergency thresholds, we expect the humanitarian

consequences to well exceed current and planned coping capacities – nationally and internationally. Burgeoning urban populations further expanded by displaced rural populations place enormous strains on existing services and capacities, leading to greater competition for limited resources. It is fairly easy to round the circle in demonstrating how these events lead in turn to conflict and subsequently more displacement, vulnerability and fewer opportunities for resolution.

The inevitability of tackling these new dynamics would seem to follow other related initiatives to address the protection needs of people caught up in so called mixed migration flows so visible in certain world regions, most notably West Africa and the Mediterranean. An unpublished internal UN document refers to:

climate change, industrial expansion, and changing urbanization patterns increasingly compounding humanitarian vulnerabilities arising from natural hazards. Challenging contexts such as politically-induced or development-induced forced displacement also require an expansion of the internal displacement causal paradigm.

Were humanitarian actors to collectively acknowledge their responsibility to address these changing dynamics both of cause and consequence, and to accept the wider humanitarian challenge, there would need to be, the document argues, 'a strategic re-examination of capacities and areas of intervention for the future'. The reform initiatives discussed above have initiated a process which identifies, in an ongoing way, gaps in IDP responses in given situations, and further the reforms are establishing procedures to put the right agencies in charge of any response. However, the political challenges of any re-examination and collective response remain formidable.

Protecting Environmental Migrants and Displacees – Legal and Political Challenges

Chapter Six demonstrates that the impact of environmental change on displacement has often been overstated. Despite this, it must be acknowledged that the effects of environmental climate change, mitigation and adaptation notwithstanding, are likely to have a significant impact on levels and types of displacement in countries that are politically unstable or economically underdeveloped. Displacement from areas vulnerable to the effects of climate change, particularly areas of political instability and economic underdevelopment, has the potential to generate human rights violations and increase impoverishment. The question arises, therefore, what type of regime could realistically be established to protect environmental displacees and reduce these risks. A corollary of *how* to protect is the question of responsibility, *who* should be responsible for the impacts of climate change? To address these issues, it is necessary to examine the capacity of existing legal and operational frameworks to provide protection for environmentally displaced persons and the issue of responsibility with respect to national sovereignty and the UN's Responsibility to Protect (R2P) doctrine.

Legal and Operational Frameworks

In Chapter Two we argue against the loose use of the terms 'environmental refugee' and 'climate refugee'. Proponents of this terminology view the plight of individuals who are denied the right to remain living in the location of their choosing because of environmental change as comparable to that of a refugee who has fled persecution or a lack of protection in their own country. The latter is specifically defined in international law by the 1951 Geneva Convention as a person fleeing persecution for one of five reasons: race, religion, nationality, membership of a particular social group or political opinion. These individuals have been forced to leave their country of nationality due to a lack of protection. It has been argued that the Convention definition should be redefined and expanded to incorporate climate refugees, affording those leaving their homes due to changing environmental circumstances the same legal protection as political refugees. There are a number of issues that require consideration if this argument is to be justified. The first is a question of definition. Chapter Six demonstrates that the likelihood of mass displacement purely as a consequence of climate change is limited. A more accurate proposition is that climate change will become a more prominent if rarely decisive factor in complex displacement situations, alongside numerous other economic and social factors also not present in the current definition of a refugee. In other words, how will a climate refugee be defined by the asylum systems of national governments? Incorporating this into asylum determination processes will make a decision already fraught with complications even more difficult to make. The likely effect of this move and of the proliferation of the term 'climate refugee', it is argued, would actually be to dilute overall protection for refugees. If the convention is amended to incorporate the effects of environmental change, it will be susceptible to arguments that demand that the refugee definition takes into account poverty, development or any other factor that could increase migratory pressures. Furthermore, the second part of the refugee definition is the stipulation that the individual be outside of their country of nationality and unable to avail themselves of the latter's protection. Evidence reviewed in Chapter Six suggests that where it can be discerned that environmental factors have contributed significantly to displacement, this has taken place predominantly within internationally recognised borders. Even if the definition of a refugee was reformed to incorporate environmental considerations, it would not, therefore, apply to the majority of environmental migrants.

A report for the NRC (Kolmannskog 2008) provides one possible exception to this analysis: the possibility of environmental persecution. In these cases states are responsible for knowingly degrading local environments and causing displacement as a result. While the legal position of these individuals is currently uncertain (Ferris 2007), there may be grounds for lodging a claim for asylum, particularly if the persecution took place along the lines of any of the five Convention reasons noted above. It is more difficult, however, to sustain an idea of climate persecution as identifying the persecutor presents some insurmountable challenges. It is not clear whether the state unable to provide protection from the effects of climate change or those states most responsible for climate change should be considered as the persecutor. If the latter, then it logically follows that an individual could be considered persecuted by the same state that offers him or her protection in the form of resettlement or financial or humanitarian assistance, representing a fundamentally different dynamic of persecution and protection than that with which the Convention is currently concerned or was originally conceived. It has been argued, however, that were an individual to arrive in an industrialised state and claim asylum on environmental grounds then while a positive decision may not be forthcoming, the right to *non-refoulement* may prevent the individual from being removed or returned. This instrument of international law prevents states from returning individuals to a situation where they are at risk of ill-treatment. It would almost certainly apply to individuals from small island states that become physically extinct. For others whose former community or livelihood has been decimated there is more room for legal debate, though the NRC report (Kolmannskog 2008) cites an example from British case law that illustrates the difficulty of returning people to a place where livelihoods are lost and quality of life has deteriorated.

Ultimately, all of these considerations suggest that any reformulation of the Convention definition of a refugee would not only be largely ineffective for protecting environmental migrants in particular but also counter-productive in providing protection for displaced people more generally (Ferris 2007, Piguet 2008). As noted previously, the majority of displacement and migration under consideration is likely to take place internally. In these circumstances, state institutions are responsible for providing protection and assistance for the displaced. In the case of IDPs displaced by conflict it is often the very state responsible for protection that is to blame for the initial displacement. This has generated a number of problems for IDPs in terms of human rights and impoverishment risks. The Guiding Principles emerged out of growing concern for IDPs in this predicament and their scope is conceptually wider than that of the Refugee Convention, incorporating displacement as a consequence of, *inter alia*, environmental change. Consequently, the Principles provide an existing framework for the protection of IDPs displaced by natural disasters or the impacts of climate change. Furthermore, the Representative of the Secretary-General for the human rights of IDPs has developed The Operational Guidelines on Human Rights and Natural Disasters (IASC 2006a) to protect persons affected by natural disasters and displacement. These guidelines may have the capacity to reduce human rights risks in instances of obvious mass displacement, but it is less clear how they apply to migrants moving within national borders partly as a consequence of slow-onset environmental change. These progressive departures will not be provided with co-ordinated humanitarian assistance or a network of camps. Some of their needs might be addressed by development agencies or state migration programmes but there is no overarching guidelines or strategic thinking on providing protection or the resources to diversify livelihood opportunities for this group of people. It has been argued that following the approach used to develop the Guiding Principles for those affected by environmental change could help cut across the conceptual distinctions of displacement and migration and the geographical distinction of internal and cross-border displacement (Kolmannskog 2008). The benefit of such an approach would be to prevent people with protection and assistance needs deriving from environmental change falling through the gaps in existing provision. Guidelines, however, do not provide legal protection and as we have seen with respect to other forms of displacement earlier in this chapter can be flouted or ignored by states.

Sovereignty and Responsibility

Two questions follow on from the above discussion: who is responsible for the changing climate and who bears responsibility for protecting vulnerable populations from its effects? Neither of these questions has a definitive answer but both need to be addressed by states, international institutions and others with a stake in limiting the human and financial costs of future environmental change. The questions have implications for how these costs are distributed and how aid and assistance are administered.

In terms of how costs are distributed two main issues arise: firstly, what are the principles under which costs are redistributed and secondly what are the methods for redistribution. The first issue is perhaps the more problematic as it requires not only effective measurement of the extent to which certain states are responsible for climate change but also international agreement over this measurement. A report for the NRC (Kolmannskog 2008) suggests that it is not necessary (as well as impossible) to identify who is directly responsible for each individual's displacement or particular displacement situations; rather there should be an acknowledgement that developed countries are primarily responsible for warming temperatures and therefore indirectly also bear responsibility for subsequent human impacts. Piguet (2008) argues that such agreements will require increased international co-operation, yet the lack of an effective institution of global governance may see attempts at such co-operation languishing in diplomatic circles. The proposal still requires agreement over the proportion of responsibility apportioned to and subsequent financial contribution required from each state. The global negotiations over trade arrangements provide an insight into the difficulty of achieving global consensus on issues that impact domestic populations in different ways. It remains up to the UN to attempt to provide a lead on this, but the past actions of major governments like those of the US and Australia with respect to the Kyoto Protocol reveal the difficulties confronting the UN in this role. The growing political power of India and China and their increasing confidence on the global stage is also likely to prove problematic for achieving an international agreement on burden-sharing. Measuring retrospectively developing states' contribution to climate change against the current and future impact of China and India will require a dynamic burden-sharing model requiring continual diplomatic negotiation.

Despite the difficulty of achieving an agreement on the principle of a burden-sharing arrangement, a number of methods can be used to attempt to achieve a more equitable distribution of the costs of climate change. Developed countries may seek support in the resettlement of populations vulnerable to the effects of climate change on their own soil, though this seems unlikely on a large scale. In the case of small island states under threat of extinction, the most likely scenario is that neighbouring developed states will agree progressive resettlement arrangements for the affected population as in the case of the Treaty agreed between New Zealand and the island of Tuvalu in the Pacific Ocean. Conversely, large-scale programmes resettling people in the developed world are likely to receive more popular resistance. Many developed countries already accept thousands of conflict refugees through resettlement programmes. Although these make only a small dent in the global refugee population, government targets for resettlement represent a balancing act of fulfilling international protection obligations without resettling a quantity of refugees unsettling to the domestic population. It is more likely, therefore, that the developing world and the international community will provide financial and managerial support for resettlement programmes within countries or regions of origin. A significant body of knowledge has been acquired through a number of in-country resettlement programmes, particularly in the wake of World Bank development projects (Cernea and McDowell 2000), the effects of which are discussed in detail in Chapter Five. Furthermore, research on programmes such as Transmigrasi and villagisation can provide important learning for governments looking to move people out of areas vulnerable to the impacts of climate change. In addition to providing resources for resettlement projects, developing states can also contribute to reducing the effects of climate change through investing in mitigation and adaptation programmes. More specifically, as explored in Chapter Six, there is a clear role for the developed world in engaging in technology and knowledge transfer to improve flood defences or building regulations in areas prone to natural disasters.

In some instances of natural disaster, however, it is not always straightforward for the international community to provide assistance and fulfil its international responsibility. The cyclone that devastated large parts of Burma in 2008 provides a stark illustration of this. The military regime in Burma delayed access to the country for international organisations, preventing humanitarian assistance, initially at least, from reaching those most in need. The British Foreign Secretary David Miliband argued at the time that in refusing international assistance, the Burmese Government failed in its responsibility to protect its citizens. In these situations the UN's R2P doctrine provides a theoretical justification for military intervention. Gareth Evans, former Australian Foreign Minister and central contributor to the early development of the R2P doctrine, has argued that military intervention is, in fact, a legal requirement of the international community in circumstances where states are forcing any form of disaster on their own people. On very few occasions, however, has this actually been acted upon. A clear consensus on the necessity and viability of R2P is yet to be reached at the UN. Opponents of the doctrine from developing countries argue that the threat of military intervention sets a dangerous precedent for the overriding of sovereignty in the global system. While the internationalism of the UN would suggest that it is the responsibility of the international community to protect those not protected by their own state, many developing countries see displacement within their own borders as an internal and sovereign issue. Alexander de Waal and Kinn (2008) argue that in complex situations such as Darfur, where it has also been suggested that the R2P doctrine should be invoked, intervention is more likely to cause further suffering and displacement. It is, they argue, impossible to make moral distinctions between the factions in the Darfur conflict, meaning that an internationally backed army would merely add another fighting faction to an already complex conflict. In situations like Burma, where a natural disaster takes place in a state isolated from the international community, threats of military intervention would more likely see the military junta close ranks and make accessing disaster victims even more difficult (ibid.). Despite these arguments against R2P, it retains support amongst important UN members, including the US, the UK and France. They argue that all states need to understand that the way they treat their own citizens has consequences beyond their own borders, providing other states, under the auspices of the UN, with the right to intervene. Countries opposing such intervention may, however, point to the poor government response to Hurricane Katrina as a case of double standards. Providing protection for those not protected from the impacts of climate change by their country of origin without encroaching on sovereignty is a key challenge for the twenty-first century.

CHAPTER FIVE

Displacement as an Economic and Development Dilemma

Chapter Four traced the evolution of the IDP Guiding Principles, policies and operational initiatives that emerge out of conflict situations, the refugee experience and humanitarian imperatives. In this chapter, and later in the Conclusion, direct parallels are drawn across the conflict and non-conflict domains with a focus on displacement occurring as a result of economic development. The internal thinking taking place in the UN humanitarian system through the rigours of the reform process are mirrored in the academic world where the benefits and drawbacks of stretching refugee studies to incorporate other displacement contexts is exercising the custodians of the discipline (see in particular a special issue of the Journal of Refugee Studies, Vol. 20, No. 3). On the part of resettlement specialists – those who research, administer and advise on compensation, relocation and rehabilitation for people displaced by development processes – there is a view that absorbing responsibility into the humanitarian agencies for population displacement occurring as a result of the acquisition of land by the state for public interest projects (leaving aside the issue of eminent domain acquisition for private profit-making investments) may not be a constructive way forward. Displacement occurring as a consequence of 'genuine' development investments by the state in peacetime is not routinely regarded as a 'humanitarian' issue in the context of how the UN may define a humanitarian emergency or disaster but rather has more to do with fundamental structural issues and the emerging development dilemma of absorbing several million displaced people in a given country where displacement has been caused by many factors – development being one facet shaped out of a complex set of political decisions.

In the following section the conceptual basis for defining the humanitarian dimensions of human displacement as an outcome of economic development is considered. The broad 'domain' and main issues associated with state land acquisition and involuntary resettlement as they would concern the humanitarian world are also set out.

Broadly, the development displacement issues that might inform any humanitarian-led discussions would include involuntary resettlement following state land acquisition for public interest purposes, for private investments and as transnational practice in a range of sectors (power, transport, environment, urban) and a complex and fast-evolving legal and policy framework. As we discuss in Chapters Two and Three, 'involuntary resettlement' as defined in multilateral development bank policies, national resettlement laws, multilateral (i.e. Organisation for Economic Cooperation and Development (OECD)/Development Assistance Committee (DAC)) guidelines, and voluntary codes governing the conduct of business includes both physical and economic displacement; as we have already discussed the term is not limited to physical relocation alone but conceives of displacement quite broadly in terms of impoverishment and asset loss as well as alienation from land and other resources vital for livelihoods and cultural life. Certainly, the process and management of involuntary resettlement holds within it many of the complexities that the humanitarian world confronts on a daily basis in its work in emergency situations. Some of these were described by Cernea and McDowell (2000) in their study of numerous displacement situations that compared the experiences of displacement, relocation and livelihood restoration (or decline) in development and conflict settings. Managing economic displacement from restoration to improvement poses major challenges and needs to be understood by considering multiple and complex factors that influence outcomes. To understand this complexity, involuntary resettlement like any humanitarian operation needs to be considered from a range of perspectives: legal, sectoral, financial, public, private, public–private partnership, institutional, land tenure and peoples rights, and also increasingly it is being considered from a security perspective.

This chapter focuses on involuntary resettlement as one stream of non-conflict displacement that is of interest to legislators and practitioners in the international law, development cooperation and humanitarian worlds. In the following section we will review the political economy of involuntary resettlement and then examine in some detail the situation in China and India, two countries experiencing the highest levels of land acquisition and which potentially have most to lose if the process is mismanaged. The humanitarian dimensions of failed land acquisition, displacement and resettlement are potentially at their sharpest in these two emerging economic superpowers.

Involuntary Resettlement in the Public Domain[1]

In theory, involuntary resettlement can only take place through the exercise of eminent domain powers where state land acquisition laws allow for expropriation for public purpose. The People's Republic of China is one of the few exceptions where public purpose is not defined and land is expropriated for both public and private development. Under this umbrella, the complexity stems from land acquisition laws, principally their failure to identify the impacts of compulsory acquisition, to address livelihood restoration and risk to affected persons or to provide compensation for legally certified assets. In most cases states apply the reparation standard (explicit, for example, in World Bank policies where the objective is to return people to their previous livelihood levels rather than to improve people's lives) rather than 'development' or improvement, which many believe should be the fundamental aim of any development underpinned, ostensibly at least, by human development objectives. The limited reparations objective for resettlement's harm coupled with archaic land laws – in many countries nineteenth century colonial land laws remain on the statute book – and their systemic problems in application lead to land and asset acquisition that undermines people's rights and leaves them vulnerable to impoverishment and cultural, social and political marginalisation with the added risk of political unrest.[2] The principal practical concerns over involuntary resettlement management lie with: insufficient or inappropriate compensation; delayed payments, often over several years late; and, importantly for the humanitarian debate, the exclusion of several categories of people affected by the exercise of eminent domain, in particular those who cannot prove legal title to their land and assets, thus risking livelihoods. These groups include indigenous people with usufruct rights and, in the urban context, several millions of 'informal dwellers' or those defined by states as 'squatters'. Not all states fall back on their compulsory land acquisition powers. Indonesia is a case in point, where the state has followed a negotiated purchase approach to state projects, but this process also presents dangers to displaced populations due to inherent problems with transparency, lack of sufficient and systematic valuation procedures and decentralised implementation.

Involuntary Resettlement in the Private Domain

The 'private' taking of land is based on negotiated purchase, usually described as a 'willing buyer willing seller' arrangement. In developing countries, however, the establishment of a level playing field and government regulatory frameworks for such land purchase is largely absent. The risks remain high, therefore, to those populations distanced from the centres of power, outside the national economy, and marginal in other ways such as indigenous populations and millions of land-dependent affected persons. The understandable temptation for displaced people to accept cash exchange increases the risk of impoverishment and the loss of sustainable land-based livelihoods for future generations. This is an important current issue in India for example where various states are using expropriation to establish special economic zones (SEZs) for private investment and are acquiring large tracts of land for major national road building. This raises a serious legal and moral question: should the state expropriate private land and displace populations for for-profit investments which may benefit the state through land lease or revenue and other profit sharing arrangements, but which may not benefit affected communities whose lands are expropriated? Furthermore, what role could or should international humanitarian agencies play in the matrix of private (market) and public (state) interests where rights violations have been identified and humanitarian needs emerge? And if not the humanitarian agencies then what other international provisions are there to address rights protection and material assistance needs of dispossessed individuals and communities?

The displacement situation in the private sphere is set to become yet more complicated as global processes, the rise of transnational corporations and public–private partnership development diffuse responsibility and jurisdictions. As we discuss further in the Conclusion, there are no binding regulations for global transnational corporations on involuntary resettlement and existing global standards (the policies of the International Financing Institutions, the Equator principles and OECD/DAC guidelines) are voluntary, subject to the pressure of bilateral political relations (in the case of DAC guidelines) and have never been independently evaluated. While one may argue that such standards are applicable to 75 per cent of global finance they are not, as we have said elsewhere in this volume, subject to legal scrutiny under domestic or international processes. In any event, it is unclear as to which laws would then apply and what recourse individuals might have under the ambit of international law and human rights standards as they apply to land acquisition. The question remains, should transnational companies have access to eminent domain powers? Examples of abuse or absence of due process range from Kelo vs. New London, in Connecticut, USA, which prompted several states to amend their laws of expropriation, to, in India, the fast growing use of expropriation for private development which is raising serious social concerns.

Displacement by Sectoral Development

A significant challenge to any future responses to development-created displacement is to understand the range of displacements that take place and the complexities of these types of displacement events. At one level these can be delineated by sector. Large-scale infrastructure in the extractive and hydro power sector not only requires acquisition of huge swathes of land but results in impacts that cannot be fully identified. Serious but often downstream and knock-on effects of such displacements on populations who do not live in the immediately affected area frequently remain unidentified and little understood but generate hidden additional displacement. Reservoir impoundment is more amenable to measurement but the unfortunate reality, as we outlined in Chapter Three, is that several more thousands of people are affected downstream of dam construction where relocation is not the key concern but impacts on fisheries, for example, which may result in loss of protein and critical livelihood resources, building pressures for indirect displacement. The figures for downstream impacts from the Nam Theun II Hydropower Project in Lao range from affecting 30,000 to 70,000 people and this uncertainty alone indicates risks of the 'unknown' but also warns of the inability to allocate adequate finance and institutional and technical capacity to respond to such risks, let alone legal protection. In the urban sector, mega city development affects large numbers of slum dwellers, drawn into the cities for employment and already vulnerable to the risks of a fluctuating labour market, lack of social protection and 'illegal' residence with no access to public services and basic needs of water, sanitation and shelter. Less is known about smaller-scale private operations whether they be domestic or transnational. However they potentially pose even greater risks to people as they remain hidden from the public eye.

The Development Challenge

Displacement as a result of economic development poses many practical challenges that when poorly handled increase the risk of impoverishment and loss of rights. The literature on resettlement (McDowell 1996b, Cernea and McDowell 2000) points to a generally poor record on restoring the livelihoods of affected people across the developing world. The institutional and financing constraints apply to both private and public sector projects due to either lack of funds or underassessment of real costs. Absence of institutional capacity is a very real problem in public sector projects, again linked to approaching resettlement as a matter for acquisition under expropriation laws and not in the context of social impact and social development. Large-scale infrastructure projects in the private sector are likely to be better financed and more likely to identify risks and plan for mitigation. Current research on involuntary resettlement calls for improvement not restoration of livelihoods and new approaches to land acquisition which consider land lease, land as equity and revenue sharing (Cernea and Mathur 2007). Such approaches may be conceptualised as attempts at 'distributive justice' though they are a long way from being adopted. Unless states incorporate such measures into law, they have little chance of being applied and even then require fundamental changes in thinking and resource allocation.

China and India: National, State Laws, Mechanisms and Procedures

In spite of very different land tenure and political systems, the two emerging economic superpowers are experiencing similar difficulties when attempting to acquire land to fuel rapid growth and are both developing new national and regional laws to manage the land acquisition and resettlement process. The remainder of this chapter examines some of those policies considering their efficacy in terms of enforcement and capacity.

The following analysis draws on ADB Regional Technical Assistance (RETA) documents prepared in collaboration with Chinese and Indian Ministries and international advisers between 2004 and 2006. The China study in particular is a significant landmark in terms of revealing a new willingness on the part of the Chinese Government to talk publicly about the scope of the land acquisition problem. The report shows that while China is rapidly responding with new laws, they have fundamental problems with land tenure and urban property ownership, with farmers remaining subject to expropriation by local governments with little recourse.

In general it can be argued that a normative framework has evolved quite rapidly over the past decade to manage rapid industrialisation and modernisation in both states. This evolution signals a new willingness on the part of the two governments to address the development and increasingly rights-based challenges that emerge in the management of conflicting interests in the development process. The ADB has played an important role in this policy development, as it has in Sri Lanka, Cambodia and The Philippines where similar policy reviews are underway. While new policies and laws are far more comprehensive than in the past and are accompanied by an increasingly open debate that engages civil society and has the potential to draw in wider rights – for example the range of civil and political as well as minority rights – and indeed is doing so in relation to land ownership, the implementation of policies is patchy, financial investments often deny full delivery of rights and entitlements and there is a lack of capacity to deliver at the level of local governments and in responsible agencies. However, in the absence of concerted international action to achieve protection for development affected populations in the developing world such national-level processes are constructive contributions to the evolution of new standards.

By means of a context for the analysis the policies of the two main development banks, the ADB and the World Bank will first be described. It is these banks' involuntary resettlement policies and operational directives which set the global standards and against which national practice is most frequently measured. Indeed part of the lending processes of these banks involves providing technical support to bridge the gap between local practice and international practice as set out in bank policies before money can be disbursed and construction can begin.

Setting International Standards

The development banks as major lenders for infrastructure development acknowledge that development investments frequently result in adverse environmental impacts, present social costs to third parties, and can deepen the marginalisation of vulnerable groups in society. In response to these risks the banks have adopted a series of safeguard policies that are designed to avoid, minimise or mitigate the harm that may result from development projects funded in full or in part through their loans. The three main safeguard policies are Involuntary Resettlement, Indigenous People, and the Environment. The development banks seek to ensure that these minimum standards are met through loan negotiations, ongoing monitoring and, more recently in the case of the ADB, through a series of RETA programmes with a number of Asian governments.

As we have sketched out previously, according to the development banks, the objectives of their involuntary resettlement safeguard policies are to avoid involuntary resettlement wherever feasible; minimise resettlement where population displacement is unavoidable by choosing alternative viable project options; and, in the cases where involuntary resettlement is unavoidable, to ensure that affected people receive assistance, preferably under the project, so that they will be *at least as well off* as they would have been in the absence of the project. Where involuntary resettlement is unavoidable, the Banks' policies are designed to internalise rather than externalise the costs of resettlement by ensuring that any resulting losses are included in project budgets. It is common, however, for some or all of the resettlement costs to be externalised, frequently resulting in a gross under-investment in resettlement, compensation and other forms of assistance. The policies seek to define involuntary resettlement as a development opportunity rather than merely as a cost of development that has to be ameliorated. In this way, through loan and technical assistance procedures including the preparation of resettlement plans in the project cycle, the banks encourage planners to identify and manage impoverishment risks and turn the people dispossessed or displaced into project beneficiaries, particularly the poor and vulnerable who may be disproportionately affected by resettlement.

The scope of the ADB's involuntary resettlement policy has three main elements: first, compensation to replace lost assets, livelihood, and income; second, assistance for relocation, including provision of relocation sites with appropriate facilities and services; and, third, assistance for livelihood rehabilitation to achieve at least the same level of well-being with the project as without it. Some or all of these elements may be present in a project involving involuntary resettlement.

For any ADB operation creating displacement and necessitating involuntary resettlement, resettlement planning is seen as an integral part of project design. The emphasis therefore is placed on the relocation and rehabilitation of affected populations and on livelihood re-establishment though not on livelihood enhancement. Clearly there are significant differences between, on the one hand, involuntary resettlement based on the legalised acquisition of land, the payment of compensation and increasingly on development-oriented relocation with legal safeguards, and on the other, conflict-created internal displacement where none of these apply. In ADB-funded projects the relocation of people in the way of national development projects is ideally conceived as a developmental process in its own right but such a policy objective is rarely fully realised.

Within those broad principles, both World Bank and ADB involuntary resettlement policies and operational guidelines seek also to ensure that each involuntary resettlement programme is conceived and executed as part of a development project or programme. In theory this should be achieved through a joint undertaking involving bank officials and so called executing agencies or project sponsors in the loan receiving country, to assess opportunities for affected people to share in the project's benefits. It is expected that the affected people would need to be provided with sufficient resources and opportunities to re-establish their livelihoods and homes as soon as possible, with time-bound action in coordination with the project construction. ADB policies, in particular, place a responsibility on the loan recipients, normally a government department with sectoral responsibility (such as a roads or water ministry), to put in place measures that guarantee that the affected people are fully informed and closely consulted on all aspects of resettlement including on compensation and resettlement options, relocation sites and socioeconomic rehabilitation. Pertinent resettlement information should be disclosed to the affected people at key points in the process and specific opportunities should be provided for them to participate in choosing planning and implementation options. The ADB insists that grievance redress mechanisms for affected people should also be established. Where adversely affected people are particularly vulnerable groups, resettlement planning decisions should be preceded by a social preparation phase to enhance their participation in negotiation, planning and implementation.

Policies of the ADB also make reference to the protection and support of the social and cultural institutions of affected populations and their hosts. This extends to making provisions to enable affected populations to integrate economically and socially into host communities so that adverse impacts on the host communities are minimised and social harmony is promoted. Special attention is also paid to the particular vulnerabilities of people without formal title who are disproportionately and negatively affected by resettlement. The policies state that indigenous groups, ethnic minorities, pastoralists, people who claim for such land without formal legal rights and others that may have usufruct or customary rights to affected land or other resources often have no formal legal title to their lands. The absence of a formal legal title to land is not a bar to ADB policy entitlements. For these entitlements to be effective the policy insists that involved parties in the civil project identify affected people as early as possible in order to establish their eligibility through a population record or census that serves as an eligibility cut-off date, preferably at the project identification stage, to prevent a subsequent influx of people that wish to take advantage of such benefits.

There is also an insistence that measures to protect affected people pay particular attention to the needs of the poorest affected people and vulnerable groups that may be at high risk of impoverishment. This may include those without legal title to land or other assets, households headed by females, the elderly, disabled people or indigenous peoples. Policies contain the direction that appropriate assistance should be provided to help them *improve* rather than merely restore their socio-economic status.

In terms of financing resettlement operations, bank policies require that the full resettlement costs are included in the presentation of project costs and benefits. This includes costs of compensation, relocation and rehabilitation, social preparation and livelihood programmes as well as the incremental benefits over the 'without-project' situation (i.e. assuming the development project had not gone ahead). The budget should also include costs for planning, management, supervision, monitoring and evaluation, land taxes, land fees, and physical and price contingencies. Where loans include sub-projects, components or investments prepared only after project approval and loans through financial intermediaries that are likely to cause involuntary resettlement, sufficient contingency allowance should be allocated for resettlement prior to approval of the loan. Similarly, resettlement plans should also reflect the timeframe for resettlement planning and implementation.

China: the Normative Framework for Land Acquisition[3] and Resettlement

With 7 per cent of the world's arable land, development demands rapidly consume available land in China removing an essential economic and subsistence base of the rural population. According to the China Land Survey and Planning Institute (CLSPI) from 1993 to 2003 the total amount of cultivated land acquired for construction amounted to 1.67 million hectares (ha) and the number of farmers affected by land acquisition over the same period numbered 36.4 million with an average of 3.31 million farmers affected annually. The estimate for the amount of land required for the period 2001 to 2010 is 1.23 million ha, affecting approximately 26.5 million farmers. The fate of these millions of people if not provided with rehabilitation opportunities is both an individual and a group risk. The CLSPI report further points out that based on available positions to employ labour at 5 to 6 million annually, China will face difficulties in appropriately resettling 2.6 million farmers per year by finding alternative employment opportunities. Official estimates of China's landless peasants are put at 70 million people.

Phenomenal economic growth in China has in part been achieved through this unprecedented scale of land acquisition and resettlement. This has been highly controversial within China though has attracted surprisingly little international attention. China's economic development has been largely state financed through a combination of government reserves, commercial loans (both domestic and international), new taxes and with the assistance of export credit guarantees and direct foreign investment including through the Chinese diaspora. World Bank or ADB loans form a relatively small element of international loans, limiting the oversight role of the development banks. However, the ADB in particular has played an important role not only through the loans it has made to China, but also through its RETA programmes to assist the Chinese in developing new resettlement policies, advising on resettlement implications of proposed laws and other operational guidance and also in bringing internal critical discussions of these issues to public attention.

Development-created involuntary resettlement in China over the past twenty years has exposed directly and indirectly affected rural and urban populations to an increased risk of asset loss, unemployment and impoverishment in an economic climate which is more uncertain. As in other countries, major risks arise due to the loss of land and other assets and insufficient compensation or quality replacement land that together adversely affect the ability of those displaced to achieve secure livelihoods, replacement productive land and alternative employment. A recent study of land acquisition by local experts in China found that 'the present land acquisition system was created during the planned economy era, and (thus cannot meet the demands of the current market economy)' (ADB 2006d). The report went on to identify three major problems: first, the right to acquire land has been exercised on a wide scale and in ways that often disregard genuine public interest; second, inappropriate methodologies and other problems have resulted in low levels of compensation to those who lose assets as a result of land acquisition; and, finally, resettlement policies have failed to guarantee farmers and other affected people the necessary long-term livelihood assistance. As a consequence, the experts argue, flawed land acquisition policies and resettlement practices have not only proved inefficient but have also exposed farmers whose land has been expropriated to the risk of deepened and prolonged impoverishment and contributed to 'unrest'.

In many respects the Chinese Government has accepted these frank criticisms and has acknowledged the urgency of the problems that land acquisition and resettlement pose to the country as a whole and for the development of a 'Socialist Market Economy'. A process of reform since the 1990s, which included the redrafting of a new property law beginning in 1993, saw domestic and international scholars appeal for reform of land laws and the country's expropriation system. A number of important measures have been adopted to improve land acquisition and compensation for both rural and urban populations in a way that seeks to promote protection from impoverishment risks and ensure that affected populations have the necessary assets and resources to build *sustainable* alternative livelihoods or *in situ* livelihoods where land acquisition was only partial. The following section will briefly review the policy framework, laws and regulations on land acquisition in China in order to provide background to a more general discussion about the context within which development-induced 'displacement' occurs in China.

China's present land acquisition system is based on the Land Administration Law and on its implementation regulations, as well as the Decision of the State Council on Deepening the Reform of Strict Land Administration issued in October 2004.[4] Article 10 of the Constitution of the PRC states that land in the cities is owned by the state, while land in rural and suburban areas is owned by collectives, except for those portions which belong to the state in accordance with the law. Collectives also own house sites and private plots of cropland and hilly land. The state may, in the 'public interest', lawfully expropriate land by paying compensation to collectives. Article 2 of the Land Administration Law enshrines the socialist public ownership of land, namely, ownership by the whole people and collective ownership by the working people. State-owned land includes land owned by the state and land originally owned by peasant collectives but subsequently expropriated by the state.

The Act contains principles for what is termed 'compensation resettlement' which specify that land expropriation should be compensated for on the basis of its original purpose of use and compensation payments should be for land, resettlement subsidies, and attachments and young crops on the expropriated land.[5] The Act further sets compensation standards at six to ten times the average annual output value of the expropriated land and should not exceed fifteen times its average annual output value for the three years preceding such expropriation. There are additional and detailed standards for other lost assets and there is flexibility to allow local provincial bodies to set standards for non-cultivable land.

In acknowledgement that these standards for compensation may not accurately reflect the productive or replacement value of acquired land, the Decision of the State Council in December 2004 (Decision

No. 28) on land acquisition reform stated that land acquisition compensation measures should be improved if they are deemed insufficient to help farmers and others who have lost land to maintain their original living standards (the central government, however, retains some authority in setting increased levels of resettlement subsidy and compensation). In line with minimum standards contained in ADB and World Bank Involuntary Resettlement Policies, the Chinese Land Administration Act contains an overall requirement for resettlement at levels sufficient to enable the farmers needing resettlement to 'restore their original living standards'. In acknowledgement that embezzlement has been a continuing problem in resettlement payments, Decision No. 28 contained measures to combat criminal corruption. Compensation payments are made in the form of cash paid directly to those who lose their land and other assets and to local government to support economic development. Decision No. 28 states that: a. within the planned area of a city, the local people's government should include those farmers made landless as a result of acquisition in the urban and town employment system and established social security system; and b. outside the planned area, when collectively-owned land is taken, the local people's government should reserve necessary cultivated land for the farmers or provide corresponding jobs to them within its administrative area. Those landless farmers for whom local provision does not meet basic productive and living conditions should be resettled in different areas; Decision 28 does not, however, specify where such areas might be. There are additional provisions to make available forms of resettlement assistance which could include payments through agricultural production, employment, share holding and dividend distribution, and resettlement through relocation in other places. The Act contains clear procedures for land acquisition and for the formulation of resettlement packages including population, land-use, ownership, value and productivity surveys (with additional verification), consultation, appeals and approval processes. Decision No. 28 allows also for public hearings and dispute resolution mechanisms.

Within the scope of the Act and the 2004 Decision, a number of operational initiatives have been taken to 'improve' land acquisition and the outcomes of land and asset loss and resettlement for affected populations. These include proposals for the 'enhanced inspections' of land acquisition programmes, research into the 'root causes of impoverishment following asset loss and resettlement', initiatives at the local government level to provide additional assistance with the aim of improving the livelihoods of affected populations, new methods for asset valuation and for calculating compensation payments, and attempts to integrate resettlement provisions into the evolving Chinese social security system (specifically in the Zhe Jiang Province); elsewhere emphasis has been placed on enhanced pension payments for affected populations.

Draft Land Laws

In March 2007, Wang Zhaoguo, the Vice-Chairman of the Standing Committee of the National People's Congress (NPC) explained the new Draft Property Law of The People's Republic of China before the Fifth Session of the Tenth National People's Congress in Beijing (see *Xinhuanet*, 8 March 2007[6]). The full implications of the draft law, which is extensive, running to five sections, with 247 articles under nineteen chapters, are not yet known but have considerable relevant implications for any future land acquisition particularly with respect to property relations and in defining what constitutes the property of the state, the collectives and individuals and the rights attached to ownership (usufruct and 'security rights') and also what constitutes 'fair compensation' following acquisition. The extent of public consultation in the drafting of the law was frequently described in government-circles as unprecedented in the history of legislation (-making) in China. According to Wang, the principle aim of the draft law would be to permit continued economic development whilst evolving a new 'Chinese-style socialist property system' in which public ownership remains dominant but new systems of ownership, including private ownership, develop alongside in a manner that 'strengthens both State and collective-ownership' and where non-public ownership contributes to economic development to help 'regulate the socialist market economy' and 'stimulate vigour in creating wealth'. While economic development justifications are strong in Wang's case for reform, he also describes the need to 'safeguard the immediate interests of the people' in pursuit of 'social harmony' and how property law is a 'prop' giving shape to the Chinese socialist legal system at this stage of its development.

The new law appears to be built on a number of interrelated principles:

- equal protection to the property of the state, the collective and the individual in accordance with the provisions of the Constitution (as such the Constitution stipulates, 'Citizens' lawful private property is inviolable …. The State, in accordance with law, protects the rights of citizens to private property and to its inheritance';
- strengthening the protection of state-owned property against the loss of such property (which appears to extend to increasing the opportunity for state ownership);

- giving a full and accurate expression to the basic policies of the Party in the rural areas; and
- safeguarding the interests of the large numbers of farmers.

In relation to compensation for acquired land, the draft law describes land acquisition as a 'general concern of society'. Wang explains that China has insufficient cultivable land to feed its people and the state is committed to retaining or protecting 120 million hectares of land as 'capital farmland': a task he describes as 'Herculean'. To this end the draft law would seek to ensure that any future land acquisition (the translated term is 'expropriation') is conducted within the limits of the law; it also sets out the principles for compensation. In terms of collective-owned land the law stipulates that:

> fees shall be paid as compensation for the land expropriated, subsidies for resettlement, compensations for the fixtures and young crops on land, and the premiums for social security of the farmers whose land is expropriated shall be allocated in full, in order to guarantee their normal lives and safeguard their lawful rights and interests.

The basic principle therefore is that compensation for acquired land must be sufficient to guarantee that living standards will not decline (which is in line with previous laws and international standards) but in addition that livelihoods must be ensured for 'a long time to come'. Wang also confirms that the new law acknowledges that in practice compensation is frequently not paid to farmers who lose their land and other assets and in future where embezzlement transpires penalties (presumably fines) will be incurred.

Despite the strengthened legal framework, a greater openness in discussing the flaws in new laws and their implementation, and quite far reaching initiatives at the Provincial and local government levels, there remains considerable concern in China about the impact on particularly vulnerable individuals who find themselves in the way of fast-tracked development. The main criticisms are as follows.

Public Interest

The Chinese Constitution and Land Administration Act of the PRC states: 'The State may in the public interest take over land for its use in accordance with the law' and 'all units and individuals that need land for construction purposes shall, in accordance with law, apply for use of state-owned land ... [which] includes land owned by the State and land originally owned by peasant collectives but acquisitioned by the State' (Article 43, Land Administration Act). However, there has been consistent concern both within and outside of China that what constitutes 'public interest' is insufficiently defined, opening the way for a broad application of the law.

The broadness of this definition has led to the over use of the right to acquire land. In effect land acquisition rights have been extended to any land that is used for economic construction without distinction between land for public good and land for construction and commercial gain. In most countries land for commercial development is acquired on a willing-seller-willing-buyer basis and on agreed market values. 'Public interest' is typically defined as public facilities and public welfare undertakings that take the state as their investment entity, do not aim to make a profit, but serve the general public good of society and have benefits shared by society. Such infrastructure might include military installations, road used for transport, energy, water conservancy, municipal and other public facilities and other public places invested in by the state such as governmental office facilities and cultural, education, health, technical and other public buildings. The advent of public–private partnerships in transport and other schemes across the world makes such clear cut definitions more problematic.

The important RETA 6091 PRC draft Country Study went so far as to argue that in China:

> According to survey data held by the Ministry of Land and Resources (MLR), land acquisition went beyond the scope of 'public interests' in sixteen provinces surveyed, between 2000 and 2001. Collective land acquisitioned for the use of urban operations such as industry, business and real estate accounted for 21.9 per cent of total area of land acquisitioned, second only to the proportion of land acquisitioned for infrastructure development, such as transportation, energy and water conservancy, which was 52.1 per cent.

> Public interest is equivalent to national development in the law; moreover, public interest is not defined, and therefore, the rights of land acquisition are abused to some extent. In fact, the purpose of land acquisition is no longer confined within the public interest and extends to the interest of companies and individuals. Any company or individual can apply to the government to conduct land acquisition for their use.

Compensation and Livelihood Restoration

A number of government reports and Provincial research projects have shown that compensation levels and forms of compensation under the preferred valuation methods do not and will not guarantee the current living standards of farmers and urban residents whose land and assets are acquired for development purposes. The main problem would appear to be low levels of compensation which are a major cause of social conflict over land acquisition. Research conducted for the RETA 6091 report found that 'the current compensation standards for acquisitioned land, whatever the lower or upper limits, are insufficient to maintain the original living standards of farmers affected by land acquisition'. It further reported that:

> if the average annual output value of the cultivated land in the eastern region of China is RMB 800 per mu, the total compensation for land and resettlement subsidies will be no more than RMB 8000 to RMB 12,800. Even if it is 30 times that stipulated in the Law, the total sum will just be a little more than RMB 20,000, a level that equals 1–2 years' income of a regular civil servant.

And in reality, particularly in the poorer regions of China, the lower limits of compensation are paid while multiples of the kind advanced above are only paid in wealthier urban locations. Payments therefore tend only to cover short-term subsistence needs and do not allow for training or social security provisions.

In line with practice elsewhere in the world, the resettlement package following land acquisition involves mainly: cash compensation, employment or employment skills and training, provision of alternative farmland (through land readjustment), land reallocation, alternative housing, and social security provisions including pension contributions. At present, cash compensation is the main method for compensating for losses and as a one-off payment.[7] Other compensation options such as social security support are only applied on a very small scale and have only recently been introduced. Studies of practice internationally suggest that a combination of compensation methods tailored to the needs of individuals and communities offers the best resettlement outcomes.

The challenges of livelihood rebuilding through government actions should not be underestimated. It is extremely difficult to construct a compensation-based resettlement package that carries people through the 'shock' of land acquisition, displacement, asset loss, cultural upheaval and the potential resettlement to a new location in a manner that guarantees livelihood re-establishment. Each of the methods outlined above contain their own challenges. Cash compensation, while simple to administer and often preferred by affected populations, may work better in more developed economies and suit younger people rather than those in late middle age who have few transferable skills. Farmers who lose their land also lose the basis of their subsistence and will struggle to compete for employment on the open market; they have no inheritance to pass on to their children and find their social status and position in society is much diminished as their role as farmer is no longer valued. Though infrequently used, the provision of alternative employment for resettlers in industries located on acquired land is an attractive addition to other compensation methods. A study has found that in Shanghai between 2000 and 2001, 13.7 per cent of the work force comprised those affected by land acquisition. Such opportunities are timely and offer for a period of relatively secure income. However, as the Socialist Market Economy evolves and other reforms are introduced, competition for jobs is increasing, companies recently established in the new zones are as prone to global market forces as any companies in the world, and resettlers find themselves in an extremely vulnerable position in the increasingly competitive urban labour market since they are typically less educated and have no other skills that are marketable. Outside the major industrial zones, there are limited opportunities in town-run or village-run enterprises to secure employment, but research by one of the authors of this book in resettlement locations has shown that employment remains generally precarious and uncertain with too many resettlers pursuing too few opportunities.

Asset Valuation

Considerable grievances occur when officials wrongly estimate the value of people's assets and living standards. The methodologies for doing so are inconsistent, unclear and prone to being changed without clear explanation. As previously explained, Article 43 states that all units and individuals that need land for construction purposes shall, in accordance with law, apply for use of state-owned land. Consequently, therefore, only the government can act as the legal authority to convert agricultural land for construction purposes. However, as China applies a system of land acquisition compensation paid according to the original purposes of land, but not at the market price, the low cost of land acquisition enables the government to obtain a greater proportion of returns from land acquisition and through selling land use rights for commercial activities. In the eyes of farmers, particularly those that have lost their assets, this situation produces an inequitable economic relationship between the original holder of land use rights and the state. There is no system in place to adequately monitor the legality of land acquisition requests. The review system for land acquisition requests is weak as are the slowly developing appeals procedures. This has led to a profound sense of powerlessness on the part of farmers who do not have the means to influence policy-making in the domain of land acquisition.

India: The Normative Framework for Land Acquisition and Resettlement

In India until 2004, the main instrument governing the acquisition of land and the provision of compensation to those affected was the Land Acquisition Act of 1894 (LAA), amended in 1984; importantly, and in common with other countries' legal systems, the Act was enabling legislation for land acquisition though not for resettlement. The original LAA was supplemented between the 1950s and the mid-1980s by a series of legislation related to sectoral developments in the Indian economy. These included the National Highways Act of 1956 and the Coal Bearing Areas (Acquisition and Development) Act of 1957. Other significant legislation relating to land acquisition adopted at that time included the Mines and Minerals (Regulation and Development) Act of 1957 amended in 1986; the Mineral Concession Rule of 1960; the Indian Railways Act of 1890; and the Indian Electricity Act of 1910. A number of further government, as opposed to individual state-level, laws were introduced, which included compulsory acquisition provisions such as the Ancient Monuments and Archaeological Sites and Remains Act, 1958; Atomic Energy Act, 1962; Damodar Valley Corporation Act, 1948; Defence and Internal Security of India Act, 1971; Petroleum and Minerals Pipelines (Acquisition of Right of User in Land) Act, 1962; Requisitioning and Acquisition of Immovable Property Act, 1952; and Re-settlement of Displaced Persons (Land Acquisition) Act, 1956. The basic principles of the LAA are incorporated into these special laws, with a few exceptions. In addition to these Indian Government laws, several state governments have promulgated their own legislation including Orissa, Maharashtra, Madhya Pradesh and Karnataka.

Under the LAA, compensation for land and houses was paid at the market value (determined by examination of land and structures) on the date of the preliminary notification that acquisition was to take place. An additional 15 per cent of the determined market value was paid as *solatium*, in recognition of the compulsory nature of acquisition.

Interest in cases of delayed compensation was paid at a rate of 5 per cent per year from the date of dispossession. The award was determined by a Land Acquisition Officer but could be appealed in a civil court. The 1984 amendments to the LAA addressed the level of compensation and delays in payment. The rate of *solatium* was increased from 15 per cent to 30 per cent and a time limit of one year was introduced for completing all formalities between preliminary notification and the declaration of notification. The compensation award had to be determined within two years of the issuing of the declaration of notification. Interest was set at a rate of 12 per cent per year from the date of preliminary notification to the date of dispossession. These changes applied to cases before the Civil Courts even for awards made before the enactment of the amendments.

Even after the 1984 amendment, however, a number of significant limitations to the Act remained. These reduced the effectiveness of the Act to guarantee levels of protection and compensation for displaced and resettled populations and thus failed to protect against impoverishment and contributed to the creation of a landless internally displaced population in India. A major limitation was that the Act had no provision for dealing specifically with resettlement and rehabilitation, including restoration of income. There was no provision of compensation for deprivation of Common Property Resources (CPR) especially loss of customary rights to land and forests, which form an integral part of tribal livelihoods in particular; nor did the Act allow for compensation (except for houses) for landless labourers, artisans and those sharing the use of land who have no legal rights to it. In addition, the method of valuation set the market price of land through sales statistics (leading to undervaluation as buyers deliberately undervalue for sales statistics as a method of reducing registration fees) at the date of notification but ignored any subsequent increase in land value. Therefore the actual market value of land, which would have enabled the owner to buy similar replacement land, was not provided for by the framework of the LAA which lead to a large number of court cases resulting in further delays.

The National Highways Act (NHA) introduced in 1956 provided for the maintenance, management and construction of national highways. This Act mandates the acquisition of land through a 'competent authority' i.e. any individual or authority authorised by the central government. The Act identifies the steps required for the purchase of land, including: notice of central government intention to acquire land; power to enter for survey; hearing of objections; the declaration of acquisition; power to take possession; power to enter into the land;

determination of compensation; and deposit and payment of compensation. The NHA retains the principles of compensation from the LAA but stipulates that the processes from issuing of notice of intent to the declaration of acquisition must be completed within a year, thus addressing a key weakness in the LAA under which this process can take up to three years. This is important because lengthy delays in the acquisition, removal and relocation process introduce significant additional risks for affected populations which are difficult to ameliorate through interventions. The NHA covers only legal titleholders and provides for compensation based on market value of the land; additional compensation for trees, crops, houses or other immovable property; and damage due to severing of land, residence and/or place of business. There is no right of appeal to a civil court under this Act – complaints are heard by an independent arbitrator, usually the District Collector.

There are a number of limitations to the NHA in that it does not include entitlements for non-titleholders and does not specify compensation for loss of income due to the acquisition of commercial establishment and agricultural land, nor does it provide Economic Rehabilitation Grants to vulnerable categories. The NHA differs significantly from the LAA in a number of areas. The NHA is for the exclusive use of central government and applies only to land required for national highway construction or maintenance, whereas the LAA only covers land acquisition and may be used by central, state governments, municipalities and, under certain circumstances, private companies. The procedure and timetable for the acquisition of land is different under each act: under the LAA, the acquiring agency (the District Collector) can enter the land only after the award is made stating the amount of compensation payable, whilst the acquiring agency (any person or organisation appointed by central government) can enter the land before this stage under the NHA, making the whole process more expedient. In addition, the hearing of objections under the NHA is reduced to twenty-one days from thirty days under the LAA. Compensation is provided for differently under the two acts: the LAA calculates compensation on market value plus 30 per cent *solatium* and 12 per cent interest (also compensates for damage and a shifting allowance is included), whereas the NHA calculates compensation based on market value and compensation for damage and a shifting allowance. However, no *solatium* or additional interest is payable. The NHA makes no provision for the emergency acquisition of land which can be acquired in fifteen days before compensation is agreed under the LAA.

Land for coal mining has been historically acquired under the provisions of a separate Coal Bearing Areas (Acquisition and Development) Act of 1957. The Act identifies that in the economic interest of India, the State requires greater control over the coal mining industry and its development. The Act provides for acquisition by the State of land containing or likely to contain coal deposits or of rights in or over such land. Under the Act, the State can prospect for coal in any land. If the land is found to have coal deposits, the government can issue notification of intent to acquire the land. The compulsory acquisition of land and compensation is provided for under the Act. The other significant legislation pertaining to coal mining in respect of compulsory land acquisition is the Mines and Minerals (Regulation and Development) Act of 1957, amended in 1986. This Act provides for regulation of prospecting, for granting of leases and for mining operations under the control of the central government. The Mineral Concession Rule of 1960 is also relevant in the context of the granting and renewal of prospecting licences and leases in respect of land belonging to private individuals.

The LAA 1894, the NHA 1956 and the Coal Bearing Areas Act 1957 are the principle pieces of legislation for the expropriation of and compensation for land, houses and other immovable assets acquired by the state for any project defined as being for 'public purpose' and have been used to acquire land and relocate millions of people in India since 1950. However, the introduction of the Government of India's National Policy on Resettlement and Rehabilitation (NPRR) in 2004 meant that recognition would in future be given to the need to support the restoration of livelihoods of those affected by displacement. The NPRR, therefore, marks a major policy shift and sets out minimum standards for rehabilitating affected people including assistance over and above the compensation required by the LAA whilst broadly outlining an approach and institutional framework to achieve these objectives. Kälin (2005d) commended the NPRR for its attempts to implement the Guiding Principles on Internal Displacement and in particular its emphasis on 'providing relief and rehabilitation for the rural poor, including small and marginal farmers and women who have been displaced'. It also aims to encourage, he commented in an address to the ADB in 2005, 'an open dialogue between the displaced and those in charge of administering the development project'.

The NPRR seeks to address resettlement and rehabilitation in a manner not covered by the LAA and ensure that displacement does not result in the state- or development-induced impoverishment that has been a well documented feature of previous infrastructure investment in India since the 1950s. It is seen as pivotal in the development of a systematic approach to addressing resettlement as India rapidly industrialises and urbanises and ever larger projects increase significantly the scale of land acquisition. Strengths of the policy include: provisions to help improve planning, implementation and monitoring at central and state level of involuntary resettlement in development projects; provisions relating to consultation with affected people and disclosure of relevant information at various stages of planning; recognition that affected people without legal rights also need to be assisted (although no specific detail); the treatment of major sons and daughters as separate families (and therefore, eligible for economic rehabilitation); provisions allowing for purchase of privately owned land through open market transactions for the resettlement of project affected people; and provisions clarifying that the cost of resettlement needs to be included in the project cost.

Indian and International Standards

There remain limitations to the scope of the policy, however, and a number of key differences between the NPRR and the ADB's Policy on Involuntary Resettlement which is, along with the World Bank policies, generally regarded as the global standard on involuntary resettlement. The provisions of the NPRR apply only to those projects where 500 or more families have been displaced in so called 'flat areas' and 250 or more families in so called 'hilly areas' as defined by the Constitution. No basis is set for calculating the number of families affected by any one project, nor is a framework identified for projects involving fewer families than these thresholds, whilst the ADB Policy applies to all projects involving compulsory acquisition of land.

The provisions of the NPRR apply only to those who have been resident in the project area for at least three years prior to the date of notification. People who purchased property less than three years before the date of notification are not entitled to receive any additional assistance over and above compensation. This provision may be particularly problematic in urban areas where land and housing is bought and sold frequently and where considerable future land acquisition and resettlement will take place under circumstances which are arguably far more challenging than in rural areas. A further difficulty is that there are no specific provisions for those without legal rights to affected land who constitute a significant portion of the Indian population. Once again this will be a major issue in many development projects, especially those in urban areas. The Policy does not apply to parks and protected areas as the provisions are triggered only in situations involving land acquisition using the principle of 'eminent domain' of the state whereas the ADB's resettlement policy addresses restrictions of access to legally designated parks and protected areas.

Rehabilitation grants and benefits indicated by the Policy are the minimum expected: state governments and project proponents are free to adopt higher compensation packages and in practice some do. However, compensation and rehabilitation provision appear to be inadequate in certain areas, such as the livelihood restoration packages for some categories of landowners, particularly those with significant land holdings, who do not receive sufficient compensation and other assistance to enable them to restore their livelihoods to previous levels. The Policy also fails to make adequate provision relating to 'linear' resettlement where Rs.10,000 is paid to each affected landowner without regard to the area lost or the severity of impact on the respective landowner. Furthermore, whilst the policy recognises that cash compensation alone may not be sufficient for economic rehabilitation, most of the specific mitigation measures proposed are based on cash compensation. There is no reference to the need to provide land based resettlement or allow for the purchase of privately owned land to resettle affected people. However, the area of agricultural land proposed for each affected family is relatively low (maximum one hectare of irrigated land and two hectares of rain-fed land), which may make it difficult for those who lose significantly larger areas of land to be able to restore their standards of living.

In situations involving significant loss of land belonging to indigenous peoples, there is a significant gap between the NPRR and the requirements of the ADB. The NPRR contains provisions for indigenous peoples, including higher cash compensation, but does not feature a special mandate to provide replacement agricultural land, a key pre-requisite for the successful resettlement of indigenous people according to the ADB. The ADB's policy related to resettlement of tribal people, on the other hand, requires special efforts to promote land-based resettlement.

There are a number of other aspects to the NPRR which may require further consideration or clarification in the Implementation Guidelines including: provision for the preparation, review and approval of resettlement plans before anyone is adversely affected; the provision and maintenance of physical infrastructure at resettlement sites; consideration of the house plot size to be provided, which is currently extremely small (62m² for urban areas and 124m² in rural areas); linkage of resettlement implementation with construction activities; clarification of institutional arrangements for resettlement implementation; and scope for donor assistance to establish resettlement capacity at various levels. In addition, the NPRR fails to address some significant issues that are pertinent in urban as opposed to rural resettlement, for example, the need to: relocate affected commercial properties to appropriate locations; compensate for losses of income during transition; provide alternative housing options to the affected people; and compensate affected people, if necessary, for increase in travel distance after relocation.

The key point of divergence between the Indian Government and donor approaches to resettlement issues is a government focus on compensation versus donor concerns for sustainable restoration of incomes of affected people or in the case of the very poor, improvement of incomes. The Indian Government is using a legal framework driven by a concern to compensate for lost assets while donors, as development institutions, approach resettlement as a development matter and strive to reinstate or improve the income base of affected people though this is not an explicit requirement of ADB or World Bank policies. Also, the NPRR only deals with issues related to economic rehabilitation and does not address the provisions in the LAA, which continues to be the basis for calculating and paying compensation for affected assets.

The LAA 1984 is the principle legislation for the compulsory acquisition of land for any public purpose at state level, as well as at national level. It is used at the state level with state amendments introduced appropriate to local requirements. A number of states have introduced additional laws on resettlement and rehabilitation. These were principally aimed at water resource projects, although certain provisions were made to extend the packages to other projects requiring compulsory acquisition of land. Maharashtra took the lead among Indian states as early as the mid-1970s in accepting the responsibility to rehabilitate displaced persons and declared a number of policy intentions, including: affected persons will preferably be allotted alternative land for cultivation rather than cash compensation; an alternative residential plot will be provided for affected persons; settlements (*goathans*) are to be established with civic facilities; employment is to be provided on a priority basis to one member of each affected family; and all expenditure incurred for these rehabilitation measures should be met from the project budget. Similar provisions were made by Madhya Pradesh, Karnataka and Orissa. The state of Gujarat also passed several Government Orders (the best-known package was that covering the Narmada Dam project). However,

Gujarat does not have a state policy on rehabilitation as such. Andhra Pradesh, Tamil Nadu and Rajasthan have also passed several Government Orders on resettlement and rehabilitation, most of them in connection with externally funded aid projects.

Some of the positive elements outlined in the states' policies, which extend the resettlement and rehabilitation provisions beyond those in the LAA, include: increased participation by those affected in the mapping and designing of the new villages and resettlement sites; involvement in the identification of the infrastructure required; and development of common resources. The states' policies, in particular Orissa, include provision for civic amenities such as schools, wells, village ponds, community centres, dispensaries, connecting roads and electrification at the sponsored resettlement sites as well as the provision of timely and transparent information about the resettlement and rehabilitation package with clear guidance to the benefits and amenities.

However, there are still many limitations in state policies; principally perhaps, in line with the provisions of the LAA, such policies use the market value and not the replacement value as the basis for compensation for compulsorily acquired land; market values have consistently proven to undervalue people's assets. Also, all liabilities (mortgage, debt or other encumbrances) on the land held by those affected at the time of acquisition are deemed to be transferred to the land allotted to them at the rehabilitation site, even if this does not have the same value as their previous land which introduces obvious inequities.

Summary

Broadly, the issues that might inform any humanitarian-led discussions on development-created displacement and its human rights dimensions would include the known involuntary resettlement (by which is meant not only physical relocation due to loss of assets, but also livelihood and other quality of life losses incurred as a result of a given development intervention) in public sector projects and the implementation of that resettlement (how relocation was managed, the valuation of asset loss, consultation with the affected people, compensation plus development assistance to restore or improve livelihoods). And any consideration would have to take in to account twenty-first century development demands, rapid urbanisation, rising living standards and demands for clean power, clean water, mobility and environmental protection. Accompanying these demands and their delivery is the shadow of land acquisition and resettlement risks, most importantly large scale landlessness and increasing risks for indigenous and situationally powerless rural people whose livelihoods are dependent on natural resources and – more visibly to those who benefit from such investments – the multiple risks faced by the unprotected urban poor.

Any policy led discussions addressing potential future responses to development-created forced displacement situations where human rights violations may occur would need to consider the existing policy frameworks and question whether together they constitute a valid protective framework to handle the growing scale and complexity of state sanctioned displacement, landlessness and resettlement. Consideration will also have to be given to the powers of recourse for people who are displaced or otherwise affected by development projects where financing for expropriation may be either through the private sector (loans raised on capital markets or through local revenue raising measures) or through loans agreed between international financing institutions (mainly the development banks) and ministries of state where sovereign courts and the laws with which they deal (often colonial in heritage and little changed) offer the individual very little protection against the state exercising eminent domain powers. The ombudsman or oversight role of the development banks in project preparation, public consultation and implementation or recourse, when things go wrong and humanitarian issues may arise, is weak. The situation for those displaced is more precarious still where investments are private and land is acquired on a willing-buyer-willing-seller basis or through the transfer of eminent domain powers from the state to the private sector. These issues are returned to in the concluding chapter.

Notes

1. The authors are grateful to Dr Ruwani Jayewardene for her advice on this section.
2. Examples of problems that arise in failure to apply World Bank resettlement policies can be seen in the documents produced by the Inspection Panel of the World Bank.
3. According to China's laws and regulations, 'land acquisition' refers to the turning of collective ownership of land into state ownership, excluding demolishing and reconstruction in cities 'involuntary resettlement' is referred to by the phrase 'land loss farmers'.
4. Information on Chinese laws is available through Washburn University School of Law: http://www.washlaw.edu/forint/asia/china.html. Accessed 28 June 2009.

5. (i) Compensation for land: this means compensation for losses of investment in and proceeds from land caused by the state's land acquisition against the 'land owners'. 'Land owners' are the object of compensation.

(ii) Resettlement subsidies: this means compensation for land loss to farmers who are disadvantaged because of the state's acquisition of farmers' collective land where those farmers rely on land for their main productive means and income source.

(iii) Compensation for young crops: this means a lump-sum payment for losses of crops grown on the acquired land such as paddy, wheat, corn, potato or vegetables as a result of land acquisition.

(iv) Compensation for attachments on the acquisitioned land: this means fees for relocation and restoration of various buildings and structures on the acquisitioned land, such as houses, wells, roads, pipelines or aqueducts, as well as compensation or felling charges for forest on the acquisitioned land.

(v) Other compensation: this means compensation other than the compensation for land, resettlement subsidies, compensation for attachments on the acquisitioned land and compensation for young crops, namely, compensation paid for losses on other aspects caused by land acquisition against the affected units and farmers, such as water conservancy facilities restoration charges, charges for loss of working time, relocation charges or infrastructure restoration charges.

6. The translation of this address was provided by *Xinhuanet* editor Liu Fang.

7. According to the 2002 survey conducted by the MLR in sixteen provinces (cities, districts) from 2000 to 2001, 60–80 per cent of the resettlement of affected farmers is based on this method. The proportion in Tianjin, Zhejiang, Shanxi, Guangdong, Hebei is over 90 per cent. The proportion in Shijiazhuang, Harbin, Hefei, Lanzhou and Nanning is as high as 100 per cent.

CHAPTER SIX

Environment and Climate Change

While there is no conclusive agreement on the current and eventual impacts of climate change, there would appear to be consensus among scientists and politicians alike that human activity has led to a rise in average global temperatures with the potential to affect the lives of a significant proportion of the world's population. Concerns about the human impacts of climate change have coalesced around the likelihood of mass displacement and related migration occurring in those areas most severely affected by rising sea levels, adverse climatic events and more gradual environmental degradation. The IPCC has been noticeably cautious in its estimation of human impacts including displacement; however, development NGOs and the media are inclined to produce projections predicting displacement on a scale that dwarfs flight from conflict and even voluntary international migration. Christian Aid (2007) went so far as to predict 'a wave' of one billion displaced people by 2050. At the time of writing this chapter, two senior figures in the EU warned that Europe should prepare for a 'flood of climate change migrants' generated by a number of factors triggered by anthropogenic climate change (Traynor 2008). Senior British politicians Paddy Ashdown and George Robertson (*The Times* 2008) forecast in a British newspaper that 'climate change may yet become a contributing factor to population displacement and societal conflicts around the world'.

As discussed in Chapter Two, the current debate about so called 'climate change refugees' resonates with the broader political debate about global migration, and in particular south to north movements which, while largely understood as a result of global economic processes, are generating policy responses that reflect security concerns of Western nations. Writing a decade ago, Kibreab (1997) suggested that politicians in developed countries were using the term 'environmental refugee' to 'depoliticise causes of displacement' in the sense that the environment was seen almost as a 'sphere outside of politics'. In many respects, however, today's debate about the environment and displacement has been repoliticised, overlapping as it does with the agenda of some European states to manage and contain global population movements through, for example, the restriction of access to asylum in Western states. It is yet to be seen whether the recent warnings from EU advisors about climate change-related displacement and new global movements of people will be used by those seeking to accelerate moves towards more regionalised approaches to forced migration management including for example the harmonisation of European asylum systems. Alternatively, humanitarian agencies argue that the 'reality' of environmental migrants or refugees demands the immediate *widening* of the scope of international instruments of assistance and protection to include their protection needs. At the same time there is a tendency among some ecological scientists to use Western fears of climate change-induced displacement and subsequent migration as a wedge to drive home more forceful environmental policies aimed at curbing carbon emissions. Ferris (2007) identified a further strand in the debate which she calls the 'security scare factor' encapsulated in a recent report by a group of former US Generals which linked climate change to terror and extremism and called related displacement one element of 'a threat multiplier for instability' (CNA 2007). There is also the less frequently heard voices of developing nations who, if refugee movements of the past are a guide to the future, will bear the brunt of any displacement but may also see opportunities in bidding for 'emergency' funding from donor nations to cope with the expected challenges in the knowledge that such funding is at present more readily secured than development funding.

The debate on climate change and human displacement is evidently highly politicised and tends to be further confused by the misleading use of legal terms to support a particular argument or to advance a particular agenda (Ferris 2007). The term 'environmental refugee' as we have stated previously is problematic, being legally meaningless (Black 2001, Kolmannskog 2008) and falsely implying a mono-causal linkage between processes of environmental change, displacement and migration to the exclusion of a range of other political, economic, socio-cultural and psychological reasons that constrain and enable behaviour in given circumstances. It will always be the case that a complex set of factors drives human movement (Kolmannskog 2008). Furthermore, confusing the legal status of affected individuals with Convention refugees, as the label 'environmental refugee' deliberately does, potentially places protection for the latter at risk (Ferris 2007; see also McDowell and Morrell 2007).

Clarity is lost in the debate where warnings about rising global temperature are taken at face-value assuming there is no potential for mitigation or human adaptation to the effects of climate change. Since

May 2006, the Climate Change Adaptation in Africa initiative has, for example, identified a range of adaptation measures to enable African countries to cope with climate change, including enhanced preparedness for flooding and disease, water conservation to lessen vulnerability to drought, and new agricultural production techniques to generate secure food supplies in changing agro-ecological conditions. Opportunities such as these are frequently left out of the public debate despite strong evidence that a range of impacts could be incorporated into existing development assistance and disaster risk reduction strategies (van Aalst 2006). Other socio-demographic policies are also often ignored, such as voluntary and anticipatory population resettlement or socio-economic development policies that attempt to diversify opportunities and spread the risk for populations vulnerable to the effects of climate change. Finally, the current debate has tended also to ignore the lessons of history. Changing environmental conditions have always had a role to play influencing patterns of human mobility and settlement. In many cases, migration is temporary or cyclical and is often a solution to environmental (and other) problems rather than an unwelcome consequence. Furthermore, where environmental change contributes to displacement, the extent and permanency of displacement is with few exceptions mediated by socio-political structures.

Having raised these cautions about the environment and displacement debate, this chapter will investigate existing literature in considering the forecast scope and extent of human impacts of climate change. Questions include: what are the mechanisms or the triggers that transform a warmer climate into displacement and later migration? What will be the extent of this phenomenon in the areas most likely to be affected and what will characterise human movement? Is the changing climate the only or even the primary cause of displacement in these areas or should other factors be taken into account? Having considered these questions, the chapter explores the potential for mitigation of and adaptation to the impacts of climate change and argues that tackling underlying political instability and economic underdevelopment will be crucial in minimising displacement and avoiding negative outcomes.

Environment and Migration

As we argue in Chapter Two, it is problematic to make a direct causal link between environmental change and *forced* migration or displacement even, as we shall see, in instances such as earthquakes where the causality cannot be assumed. Physical change has to be understood as one element of a complex interaction of different factors generating migration or displacement (Black 2001, Castles 2002). Environmental change can be plotted on a continuum from typically slow-onset, such as desertification, through flooding and droughts to instant-impact natural disasters. Along this continuum, affected individuals are faced with varying degrees of choice in responding to crises and changed circumstances from a reluctant ostensibly voluntary decision made in response to a failing crop yield for example, to immediate involuntary displacement in the event of homes destroyed by hurricanes or earthquakes. Similarly, environmental events involve different durations of displacement, from a permanent loss of land and home to return after only a few weeks to formerly flooded homes. Some academics conceptualise these factors as reflecting either 'routinised migration' or 'distress migration' (Suhrke 1997). Decision-making in such contexts is always constrained by social structural and political factors.

Types of Environmental Change and Migration

Various typologies have been developed to capture new flows of 'environmental refugees' or 'environmental migrants' but rather than adding to available typologies, we focus on historical evidence linking displacement and migration to specific environmental processes that have been widely researched: desertification, drought and floods, and natural disasters. These events and processes cover a range of impacts from slow-onset to immediacy, incorporate a range of migration responses and durations of displacement and involve interactions with existing social and political structures.

Desertification, according the United Nations Convention to Combat Desertification, is described as land degradation in arid, semi-arid and dry sub-humid areas resulting from mainly climatic variations and human activities and is an example of a slow-onset disaster as described in Chapter Two. A number of factors may contribute to desertification, including the over-exploitation of the natural resource base, short-term and harmful production methods, unsustainable population density, poverty and underdevelopment (Schwartz and Notini 1994). Studies suggest that the unsustainable exploitation of land results in localised degradation, triggering displacement from land that is no longer able to sustain populations and placing similarly destructive pressures on neighbouring land (UNU 2007). However, there is also substantial research which paints a more complicated picture and questions assumptions that land degradation and specifically desertification under such conditions is inevitable. Research by the International Institute for Environment and Development (Mazzucato et al. 2001) analysing data on soil fertility in Burkina Faso casts doubt on the dominant account of degradation that depicts African farmers as careless miners of soil nutrients who are perpetually vulnerable to displacement as a result of degradation. It argues that farmers are well aware of land degradation processes and how to halt them and have extensive social networks that sustain their livelihoods. In Burkina Faso, and elsewhere, contrary to expectation farmers are able to increase output through local agricultural systems that arrest desertification and reduce the likelihood of involuntary displacement and migration (see also Mortimore 1989, Tucker et al. 1991).

Elsewhere, however, Schwartz and Notini (1995) reviewed research from Central America and Africa and found a statistical correlation between emigration and aridity. In response Black argues that because slow-onset environmental change takes place over an extended period of time, often across generations, it is difficult to assert a causal certainty from a statistical correlation. Across any timescale numerous economic, social and political changes and varying capacities for adaptation will undoubtedly influence people's decision to leave an area in response to changes they observe and anticipate. It is noteworthy that a recent report (UNU 2007) drawing on state of the art knowledge on desertification made a number of recommendations to combat the problem, yet did not address displacement as a significant outcome; in fact the only mention of displacement in the report is to be found in the Foreword, which comments that the number of people *at risk* of displacement by desertification may 'exceed 50 million over the next ten years'. Although the report does not substantiate or even expand on this claim, press coverage of its release was nevertheless dominated by this figure.

It is generally the case that rural to urban as well as rural to rural migration occurring in situations of environmental stress takes place alongside other significant dynamics, including changing production structures, demand for labour in cities or political upheaval, and in the presence of cultural drivers of migration, including nomadic lifestyles and long-distance trade. Sally Findley (1994), conducting research in the drought-prone Senegal River Valley in Mali in the 1980s, observed a counter-intuitive effect where the failure of crops and the local economy deprived many potential migrants of the necessary income to set migration in motion. It is difficult, therefore, to accurately pinpoint situations where populations have become displaced exclusively as a result of the effects of localised drought. Of course this is not to deny that desertification may interact with other significant changes to increase the likelihood of displacement and migration in any given context.

The flooding of land increases migratory pressures and generates displacement where physical protection against flooding is insufficient and where social protection is unable to provide adequate assistance, promote resilience, underpin responsive livelihoods and permit return. Some of the most severe examples of floods in recent times have been seen in Mozambique and Bangladesh. Bangladesh in particular has extremely high population density in areas prone to flooding and over 80 per cent of the country's population survives on less than two US dollars a day (Government of Bangladesh 2005). Flooding in such areas has frequently led to a chain of events that has forced people from their homes, some moving internally and others moving to neighbouring India. Despite this, even where flooding has caused prolonged displacement and the permanent migration of populations it is described by some academics 'as both a positive and negative resource' (Haque and Zaman 1993), able to create opportunity as well as crisis. It has been shown that knowledge and experience of dealing with extreme weather events has led to locally developed methods to respond to risk and this may include migration most markedly in those situations where other migratory pressures exist and in particular where ineffective local institutional response, inequitable land ownership patterns and ethnic division are significant factors causing people to move (Lee 2001).

Extreme and instant environmental change caused by natural disasters such as cyclones, tsunamis, earthquakes or hurricanes would also appear to provide clear-cut causal links to displacement. Since the 2004 Asian tsunami – which was the world's most devastating natural disaster in recent memory – there have been a series of destructive natural disasters causing damage on an unprecedented scale. These have included earthquakes in Kashmir in 2005, China in 2008 and Haiti in 2010, while Cyclone Nargis caused widespread devastation in Burma in 2008, and Hurricane Katrina in New Orleans in 2005. It was evident from media coverage including startling statistics of their human impacts that these events generated physical displacement due to the collapse of the physical infrastructure and further environmental destruction. With the exception of the Szechuan earthquake in 2008, however, where the town of Bechuan was largely abandoned with many of its residents permanently relocated, according to Chinese government reports, the majority of those displaced in these recent emergencies remained close to the area of the disaster and along with humanitarian aid workers, state institutions and military personnel were engaged in clearing and rebuilding affected areas in preparation for their return. In the overwhelming majority of cases, those displaced by natural disasters wish to return and are able to do so. While those displaced by disasters face many of the same initial challenges as other displaced persons and have many of the same needs, ensuring their return in most cases requires a humanitarian and operational response rather than a political, diplomatic or military one. Furthermore, as with the more incremental environmental changes discussed previously, the role of the state is crucial in keeping displacement to a minimum and as short-lived as possible. Castles (2002) gives a clear illustration of the effects a strong and efficient state can have in comparison to unstable, failing or corrupt states. It is often cited that in Japan, the Kobe earthquake initially displaced 300,000 with fewer than 50,000 people remaining displaced three months after the event, whereas by contrast following the Mount Pinatubo eruption in the Philippines a majority of the 100,000 people displaced remained living in camps or were described as squatting several years later.

It is clear therefore that underdevelopment and state incompetence or neglect play a critical role in prolonging displacement in the event of floods, drought, desertification and famine. There are, as Black (2001) points out, areas of the world prone to flooding and drought or even earthquakes and hurricanes that do not experience mass displacement. More specifically, there are low-lying cities prone to flooding or cities on fault lines prone to earthquakes where the number of inhabitants continues to rise. Institutional planning and responses to these events can allow local populations to adapt to the impacts of environmental change by transforming local production structures and infrastructure. In areas of the world that are underdeveloped or lacking funds to put into place these safeguards, international institutions and developed nations have a role to play in working with governments and local communities to share knowledge and in combination with traditional coping strategies develop new frameworks to manage the unavoidable effects of environmental change of all kinds.

The current challenge is to understand how climate change will create conditions where environmental factors, interacting as they will with other changes, more directly impact on societies and their ability to adapt and cope with those changes. If populations have historically dealt with incremental environmental change or regular high-impact natural disasters using some of the strategies explored above, how does man-made change impact on these environmental processes and affect this dynamic? In Chapter 7 we consider briefly the growing body of literature suggesting that accelerated or erratic environmental change and resource scarcity caused by climate change may, as Ashdown and Robertson would argue, exacerbate existing conflict and generate new ones (Homer-Dixon 1991, Homer-Dixon and Percival 1996, Gleditsch et al. 2007).

Climate Change, Displacement and Development

The previous section provided a discussion of the historical and conceptual links between the environment and displacement and questioned the assertion that environmental change alone can increase migratory pressure and generate displacement. This section builds on that analysis by exploring the effect that anthropogenic climate change may have and is already having on these relationships and dynamics. As discussed in the introduction to this chapter, there is significant scientific agreement, set out in the Fourth Assessment Report of the IPCC, that human activity is responsible for raising the earth's average temperature. The report is also notable for containing a number of new claims about the effects of climate change most likely to lead to displacement, such as predicting with high confidence an increase in droughts and floods. Taking into account the findings of Chapter Two with respect to the terminology used in relation to climate change and displacement and the established relationship between migration and the environment identified in the previous section, the aim of this section is to address what we know about climate change, how it is likely to impact upon displacement and whether the potential for increased pace and intensity of environmental change can really be said to represent a shift in the relative significance of the factors that generate displacement.

What Do We Know?

The 'hockey stick' graph, illustrating temperature fluctuation against CO2 emissions that have been observed over the last twenty years (Gleditsch et al. 2007) has become an iconic representation of global warming. Scientists of the IPCC argue that the earth is warming and almost all national governments and regional and international institutions are in agreement. There is almost as strong a consensus that human activity is responsible for the accelerated increase in global temperatures, specifically the emission of greenhouse gases (IPCC 2007). The primary greenhouse gas emitted is carbon dioxide formed in the process of burning fossil fuels, which traps heat in the earth's atmosphere preventing its escape beyond that point (van Aalst 2006). Since the industrial revolution in the mid-eighteenth century the concentration of carbon dioxide in the atmosphere has increased by one third to what is likely to be the highest level in the last twenty million years (IPCC 2001). Evidence from studies incorporated into the Fourth Assessment Report leads the IPCC to be 'highly confident' that this is the result of human activity, with 89 per cent of 29,000 observable data series monitored by recent studies changing in the direction expected in response to warming (IPCC 2007).

The rising average temperature has a knock-on effect on a number of environmental processes and patterns. It is argued that a warmer climate in the polar regions is accelerating the rate at which polar ice caps, as well as glacier regions around the planet, are melting; however, many found the IPCC report's claim that the Himalayan Glaciers would disappear by 2030 to be misleading. The impact of environmental changes are most likely to be observed through disruption to local ecosystems and habitats but also, more significantly, in rising sea levels. Although low-elevation land vulnerable to rising seas only accounts for 2.2 per cent of dry land, 10.2 per cent of the world's population inhabit that land (Piguet 2008) and population density in these areas is increasing rapidly. According to the Stern Report commissioned by the UK Government in 2006, a 4ºC rise in average temperatures would each year result in flooded lands affecting 170–300 million people. The IPCC also predicts with a high level of certainty that the rising temperature will have a significant impact on hydrological systems. This could manifest itself in a number of forms that vary across different regions. Average river run-off and, therefore, water availability in high latitude and tropical regions is likely to increase by up to 30 per cent; dry, mid-latitude areas are likely to experience at least as large a decrease in water availability (IPCC 2007). The Stern Report calculates that if average temperatures rise by 4ºC, southern Africa and the Mediterranean could suffer a fall in water availability of up to 50 per cent. The corollary of all this is that areas prone to flooding are likely to receive more rain and areas prone to drought are likely to receive less. The evidence is less certain on the impact of climate change on food production. In some areas, a moderate rise in temperatures could increase crop productivity and crop varieties with others seeing a fall in productivity, depending on crop type (IPCC 2007). However, in the case of more significant temperature increases, productivity and absolute production potential is likely to decrease severely, increasing the risk of hunger. The IPCC makes these assertions with only medium confidence.

Projections such as these have generated alarming and some alarmist scenarios though scientists will acknowledge that predictions are ambiguous in terms of severity of impact as this is dependent upon by how many degrees temperatures actually increase, which is itself dependent on human activity, and further attempts at mitigation of impact are additionally dependent on conditions in specific locations. However, some impacts of climate change are already observable, notably enlarging glacial lakes, changes in polar ecosystems (IPCC 2007) and more frequent and intense natural disasters (EM-DAT/IFRC 2007). Furthermore, as carbon emissions are unlikely to stabilise in the near future, it is probable that temperatures will continue to rise (van Aalst 2006). The IPCC makes clear that a temperature rise of less than 1–3°C above 1990 levels would initially generate both costs and benefits in different locations and sectors, yet goes on to say that temperature rises of above 2–3°C would see any net benefits reduced, costs increased and the capacity to adapt diminished in all countries and sectors. Irrespective of which scenario is ultimately played out, it is unequivocal that the impacts of climate change will be unequally distributed. Impacts will differ between and within regions. Within this diversity, however, it is likely to be those least responsible for emissions that bear the brunt of their forecast negative effects – specifically the world's poor. According the IPCC (2007), Africa and Asia are the most vulnerable continents, though Latin America and small island states will also be significantly affected. It is not just geography or ecology that determines this: these are also the regions least able to adapt to or mange the impacts of climate change. And within these it will be the poorest, the 'hyper-vulnerable', that are most likely to be at risk. The impact of climate change at a macro regional and micro personal level will depend largely on governments' ability to manage change, available resources, planning and adaptation policies.

Mechanisms of 'Climate Displacement'

The science, as presented by the UNIPCC, provides evidence that the planet is warming but is uncertain about the magnitude of the impact of rising temperatures. The range of many of the predictions is testament to this ambiguity. One step further removed from this are even more uncertain predictions about specific human impacts, in particular the issue of human displacement and migration as a result of these changes which are, as we have already pointed out, fundamentally shaped and influenced by social and political structures, economics and personal decision-making. There is a paucity of credible evidence on the actual impact of predicted climate change on displacement and further research in this area is urgently required on the many questions that remain unanswered (Ferris 2007, Kolmannskog 2008). There are a number of complex ways in which the potential for environmental change identified above may interact with other factors to generate displacement. Below, we focus on three of the most significant generative mechanisms that could directly cause displacement, examining what we know about how climate change is likely to affect current trends and forms of displacement generated in this way. We would caution once again that it remains difficult to sustain a direct causal link between environmental phenomena and displacement, even accounting for the exacerbating impacts of climate change.

1. Increased frequency and intensity of sudden onset natural disasters.
A number of recent reports have noted an observable correlation between rising global temperatures and an increase in the frequency and intensity of natural disasters, particularly certain types of disaster (Helmer and Hilhorst 2006, Ferris 2007, Kolmannskog 2008). Data from the Emergency Events Database (EM-DAT), the most comprehensive database monitoring global natural disasters, charts a significant rise in the frequency of hydro-meteorological events since the 1980s. As Ferris (2007) argues, some of this increase can be attributed to better data collection and monitoring, though this cannot account for the greater severity of these disasters, reflected in increasing human and financial costs. Van Aalst (2006) proposes a number of potential causal links between this qualitative change in the nature of hydro-meteorological disasters and the earth's rising temperature. The increased prevalence of flooding can be linked partially to increased precipitation in tropical areas linked in turn to climate change. Areas most likely to be affected are the mega-delta regions of Africa and Asia (IPCC 2007). Van Aalst (2006) is also careful to point out that other factors affect the extent and impact of flooding and cannot be put down exclusively to warming temperatures. In some areas of Europe prone to river flooding, winter flooding has actually decreased and summer flooding remained relatively unchanged over a the past one hundred years (Mudalsee et al. 2003). A further difficulty of isolating a link between climate change and flooding is that existing models for monitoring rainfall provide information on too large a scale to make specific claims. The resolution of these models would need to improve ten-fold to make claims about specific areas of flooding, something that is not possible with existing technology (van Aalst 2006). The set of environmental circumstances that generate cyclones, however, is more complex than floods and,

therefore, the link with climate change is more subtle (ibid.). Essentially, there is no model accurate enough to unequivocally determine the impact of climate change on these or any other forms of high-impact natural disasters. Despite this, the frequency and intensity of cyclones – a term which incorporates typhoons and hurricanes – has been increasing since 1970 in the North Atlantic (IPCC 2007) with the number of category 4 and 5 cyclones doubling (Webster et al. 2005). It has been suggested that the increased energy in the atmosphere and the rising temperature of the oceans can generate cyclone activity that is more intense and prolonged with rising sea levels also compounding the after effects (van Aalst 2006).

As discussed in the previous section, natural disasters do cause mass human displacement. To what extent do the potential impacts of climate change on the frequency and intensity of disasters fundamentally alter the extent and permanency of this displacement and methods of prevention and protection? While it is likely that cyclones will become more intense and floods more severe, technological and managerial advances are also being made to combat the financial and human consequences of these events. Most experts appear to conclude that the impact of climate change on disasters is unlikely to result in or contribute to the supposed apocalypse of waves of 'climate refugees'; nor is it considered that the disaster displacement dynamic is likely to change. Piguet (2008) reminds us that in instances of disaster displacement, most affected persons tend only to be displaced close to their homes and furthermore have a 'high propensity to return' once rebuilding is complete or to contribute to the rebuilding process (see also Castles 2002, Kolmannskog 2008). An increase in the number of displaced disaster victims is unlikely to transform into long-term displacement or long-distance, cross-border migration. In terms of planning to combat the effects of disasters and providing protection for the unavoidable displacement that will take place most experts argue that climate change represents only one other factor to take into account rather than representing a fundamental change or threat. For van Aalst (2006) anticipating and planning for the greater intensity of disasters can and should be incorporated into existing disaster risk reduction (DRR) strategies. Benefiting largely from the graphically illustrative nature of the suffering these disasters cause, those displaced in such circumstances are comparatively well protected and assisted. Though there are always operational and political barriers to relief work following disasters, an extensive operational framework for the protection and assistance of disaster victims already exists to act on van Aalst's recommendation.

2. Accelerated slow-onset environmental change.

Climate change is also likely to cause more gradual change in local environments affecting people's capacity to make a living from the land and potentially diminishing already scarce resources. Specific examples of this include longer periods of drought, the degradation of once fertile land (or 'desertification') and reductions in food productivity by quantity or quality. While evidence for the impacts of climate change on the latter is mixed and uncertain there is evidence to suggest that warming temperatures have already contributed to increased drought and desertification. In dry regions of Africa and Asia the frequency and intensity of droughts has increased over the last twenty years (van Aalst 2006), while a new finding of the Fourth Assessment Report is that a future increase in droughts can be predicted with high confidence, with stark consequences for the availability of freshwater. Piguet (2008) adds that this environmental impact is compounded by demographics and development: rising population and rising income is increasing the demand for water at the same time that climate change may be reducing supply. The IPCC (2007) calculates that 'water stress' from this combination will affect 75–250 million people in Africa by 2020 and potentially up to one billion in Asia by 2050. Drought is also linked to desertification, though the phenomenon does have other causes. Despite the questioning of the concept of desertification discussed earlier in this chapter academics continue to use the term and describe the potential risks it poses to humanity, such as depriving many of the inhabiting population of their traditional livelihoods, putting millions at risk of displacement (UNU 2007). A direct link between climate change and desertification, as opposed to other human activities such as exploitation, mismanagement and damaging farming practices, is as we have already discussed more difficult to substantiate. Once again, for both drought and desertification it is likely to be the hyper-vulnerable, those exposed to multiple stresses and with a livelihood linked to subsistence agriculture, that are most at risk (Kolmannskog 2008). But it is argued that both drought and desertification illustrate the potential for climate change to severely restrict the supply of productive resources in already resource-poor areas. The IPCC acknowledges that it is on less confident ground making specific assertions about food availability and productivity as noted above, although it does predict that anything more than a moderate rise in temperature (2º–3ºC) is likely to result in escalating net losses for crop productivity.

While scientific links between climate change and these progressive changes in the environment can be made with reasonable confidence, it is more problematic to suggest that this will generate mass displacement.

As with natural disasters, this is a more difficult calculation as we need to take into account the interaction of actual and potential environmental change with the capacity for human agency in the face of these risks. Firstly, the slow-onset nature of these impacts means that flight from the land is also likely to be incremental (Piguet 2008). Conceptually, it is difficult to sustain such movement of people as displacement: one would need to examine why some people moved earlier and others later. Those moving first may have the resources to do so and are therefore risking less in making that active decision. Others are more likely to move as a last resort, a response to the failure to reform a subsistence livelihood in changing circumstances. Therefore, while many of these individuals will have been forced to migrate or, recalling Cernea's (2003) definition, be displaced due to economic dislocation, it will be difficult to identify the particular element of force in each case (Kolmannskog 2008). Furthermore, while it is not clear that migration from areas affected by progressive environmental change can be considered displacement, nor is it unequivocal that the environment is primarily responsible for the people leaving the areas (ibid.). A number of other factors are also likely to have played their part as shown by a study of migration within drought-affected Burkina Faso that suggests only 5 per cent could be accounted for by environmental factors (Henry et al. 2003). Even where the common reasons for leaving these areas, as mentioned, are a loss of livelihood, scarcity of other resources and in the worst cases famine, environmental change may trigger famine but it is rarely responsible for it. Rather it is poor management, inequitable distribution and corrupt or undemocratic government that is culpable for the hunger of the population and therefore the ensuing displacement. Armatya Sen's (1981) respected insight is worth further repetition here, that famine has never taken place in a democracy. Even in instances where displacement from areas of drought or desertification can be detected in most cases it will more accurate to consider it (lack of) development displacement or politically generated.

3. Rising sea levels.

The causal link between anthropogenic climate change and rising sea levels is a phenomenon distinct from the other environmental impacts we have discussed in that it is ostensibly irreversible and does not represent an extension or exacerbation of existing environmental risks or hazards that are already experienced on a regular or seasonal basis. What it does have in common with other impacts of climate change is that there is evidence that rising seas are already affecting some areas with small island states, river delta islands and low-lying coastal regions being most at risk. Ferris (2007) cites research findings observing that 80km² of the Sundarban islands in India have disappeared since the 1970s displacing six hundred families. Island states in the Pacific Ocean, such as Tuvalu, are at risk of inundation, not only displacing inhabitants but making them technically stateless. Other low-lying areas are likely to be at risk in the future. Worst case scenarios see the west Antarctic and Greenland ice sheets breaking off and the east Antarctic sheet becoming less stable, raising sea levels by more than 15 metres (ibid., Gleditsch et al. 2007) and putting huge metropolitan areas such as London and Tokyo at risk (HM Treasury 2006). More moderate projections, such as the IPCC's A1B scenario based on maintaining current levels of economic growth and moderate use of fossil fuels, would see a rise of less than one metre by 2300 (Piguet 2008). Whichever scenario becomes reality, over 600 million people, a number that is increasing, live in coastal areas less than ten metres above sea level and may be impacted in some way by climate change.

Where the scientific evidence of the human impact on sea levels remains certain, there must once again be questions as to whether this phenomenon can be considered the exclusive cause of displacement. In certain cases, such as the small island states, there will undoubtedly be displacement as the population will have no 'choice to remain'; resettlement agreements with regional neighbours will most likely follow but there will be a clear chain of causal links from climate change to displacement in these instances. In coastal areas of large land masses, the links are less clear. A report for the NRC (Kolmannskog 2008) argues that, similarly to drought and desertification, the gradual nature of migration from the affected areas clouds the distinction of the migration as forced. Furthermore, there remains an opportunity for governments of the areas at risk to plan for the impending rise of sea levels – either through state-sponsored resettlement programmes (Piguet 2008) or demographic engineering projects encouraging and incentivising early voluntary migration (see Castles 2002 for an analysis of the Transmigrasi programme in Indonesia). There is also the prospect of technological and engineering solutions to rising sea levels emulating cities in the developed world that inhabit reclaimed land. In sum, despite the potential numbers at risk in coastal areas and the 'absolute displacement' faced by inhabitants of small islands, the impact of rising seas does not, in reality, square with the apocalyptic scenarios of one billion climate refugees headlined in the 2007 Christian Aid report. It is unlikely that all those at risk would all at once become wandering migrants (Piguet 2008). Migration is more likely to be gradual, regional and 'contained'.

The climate change–displacement relationship is a complex one. At times, the science is ambiguous and where the science is more certain it is not clear that the impacts would actually generate displacement. Where it can be substantiated that displacement would be generated it is not without the influence and interaction of variables additional to the change in environmental conditions caused by anthropogenic climate change. In fact, in many instances, effective planning, technological development and political stability could prevent displacement. Where this is not the case, however, it will be the hyper-vulnerable that are least able to migrate on the one hand and, on the other, for whom displacement will be most prolonged and devastating due to a lack of resources or social networks that render them immobile. In protection terms, NGOs, the international community and environmentalists might better serve their mandates with concern about those that *do not* migrate or are displaced close to their homes – most likely the vast majority. These issues are dealt with further below.

Mitigation, Adaptation and Vulnerability

Thus far, this chapter has analysed the potential for climate change to cause displacement without fully considering the capacity for human agency to rise to the challenge of arresting the rising temperature or developing strategies for coping with the effects. The scenarios contained in the IPCC, Stern Report and other authoritative studies tend only to consider human activity that will augment the effects of climate change, though these reports do acknowledge that some mitigation and adaptation measures are currently available and can be developed in order to limit the negative impacts of warming temperatures. In addition experts from scientific and conflict studies backgrounds tend to agree that vulnerability is crucial to assessing the impacts of climate change and is determined by the success of global mitigation efforts and the effectiveness of local adaptation strategies. The success of mitigation efforts will depend upon international co-operation, political will and levels of investment in carbon neutral technologies. This section briefly assesses some of the options for mitigation and adaptation, their potential efficacy, the likelihood of their implementation and the impact on the vulnerability to displacement of affected populations.

The fourth IPCC report concluded that many of the impacts of warming temperatures can be 'avoided, reduced or delayed by mitigation', with the potential to stabilise the concentration of greenhouse gases. The Kyoto Treaty provides a framework for action on mitigation by setting binding targets for most industrialised European countries and providing knowledge for other states on how to reduce emissions. A raft of measures, including carbon trading, taxes and incentives, and integrated carbon emission reduction strategies at a national level aim to meet these objectives. Under articles 5, 7 and 8 of the Protocol signatory states are committed to reporting on their performance. Meeting these targets requires not only a reduction in emissions but also economic restructuring. In 2008 the EU also developed a framework for making Europe the first economy for the low-carbon age through the harnessing of green energy sources such as wind, solar and nuclear power. Furthermore, although yet to ratify the Kyoto Protocol, the United States has developed its own targets for reducing carbon emissions. Performance in meeting these targets has been mixed across the industrialised world. The difficult balance that national governments are trying to achieve is to meet environmental commitments without significantly affecting domestic economic growth. Furthermore, while developing countries have historically only contributed fractionally to warming temperatures in absolute terms and per head, the rapid industrialisation and population growth in countries like China and India means that an increased contributions to emissions is unavoidable. The international community faces a similar difficult balance at the global level in attempting to encourage developing countries to factor environmental concerns into their development strategies without unduly restricting their development capability – China, India and others rightfully believe in their 'right to develop'. Mitigation efforts will in future rely on technological development and the public and political will to implement emission reducing strategies. Many argue that for this to happen, particularly in the developed world, a fundamental shift in attitudes and lifestyles is required, something very difficult for governments to advocate or legislate for.

Even if mitigation efforts are successful the range of impact will be low particularly as emission levels show no sign of stabilising in the short term. Adaptation needs to take place primarily at a local and regional level, although technology transfer, knowledge sharing and collaboration will also be important and should be a priority (Gleditsch et al. 2007). There are specific practical policies that can be put into place in order to, as a DfID report into Bangladesh puts it, 'avoid the unmanageable and manage the unavoidable'. The impact of flooding can be prevented or minimised by improved irrigation or land reclamation; the same can be said of the impact of rising sea levels in low-lying coastal regions. Where such things are not possible, such as small island states or areas where these techniques would further degrade the surrounding environment, other solutions must be found. Government-sponsored resettlement programmes, similar in scale to those put into place in response to large development projects, are likely to be a common response. In the case of small island states, these agreements will have to be reached through negotiation with other states in the region. There is a wealth of research and experience to draw upon in designing these programmes as discussed in Chapter Five.

In the case of increasingly frequent and intense natural disasters, adaptation can take a number of forms. Extensive thinking and strategic organisation already goes into DRR and van Aalst (2006) suggests that measures to combat the increased risk from natural disasters caused by climate change can be incorporated into existing DRR strategies. The Hyogo Framework for Action (HFA) adopted by the World Conference on Disaster Reduction in 2005 identifies several ways in which states and communities vulnerable to the effects of natural disasters can strategically reduce risks through prevention rather than only engaging after the event. Investment in technologies that improve early warning systems will be important. For example, the effects of the 2004 Asian tsunami could have been significantly reduced were vulnerable populations given more warning (Kälin 2005a). Of course, millions would still have been displaced and a significant number would have lost their lives, but many deaths may have been avoidable. In addition, the impact of natural disasters is often exacerbated by buildings constructed in a manner unsuitable for areas at risk from earthquakes or hurricanes for example. It is true to say that earthquakes rarely kill people, buildings do; similarly, flooding following hurricanes is more likely to cause death and displacement than the event itself. Building regulations, particularly in developing countries, need to be improved and adhered to (Kälin 2005a). The HFA attempts to incorporate these and other measures to reduce underlying risk factors and improve preparedness. While there has been visible progress at a number of levels, there remains delay between the adoption of policies and the translation into specific operational measures and a need to develop more strategic partnerships between different levels of government and across borders. The latter is illustrated by the separate institutional and operational frameworks of the disasters relief, international development and climate change communities (Helmer and Hilhorst 2006).

As noted in Chapter Three, the risk of death or displacement from a natural disaster in the developing world is considerably higher than in the developed world. This leads on to a key factor influencing the success of adaptation: the role of the developed world in sharing knowledge and technology with poorer states vulnerable to natural disasters. The developed world needs to do more of this if it is to fulfil its responsibility for being most culpable for climate change yet least vulnerable. Many of the most vulnerable states are not only politically unstable but also do not have the economic capacity to embark on expensive adaptation schemes. With this in mind it is, however, crucial that the international community consults with and empowers local communities to deal with the effects of climate change from within. This is particularly the case with respect to desertification and drought, where local knowledge and traditional coping strategies need to be harnessed to increased financial resources and improved technology. Finally, the success of adaptation strategies involving technology transfer and increased international aid will depend upon political stability and governing institutions in the areas at risk. Corruption, autocracy and political repression are all likely to undermine adaptation efforts. According to Castles (2003) it is imperative, therefore, that the international community does more to tackle the underlying causes of civil conflict that he sees as embedded in unequal social and economic relations between the global North and South. In addition to this, however, others would argue that domestic governments, civil society groups and the general population in developing countries should also take responsibility for their own response to the effects of climate change, grasping the individual and collective human agency. Information provision is key to empowering public participation in following this course, norms of which have evolved in human rights law and been adopted in international environmental law.[1] Whether or not the global North, the UN and other international institutions are able to further develop these conditions and tackle the underlying causes of conflict and repression is dealt with briefly in the final section of this chapter and in more depth in Chapter Seven.

Taking the mitigation and adaptation responses together, it is clear that vulnerability to the effects of climate change depends on the success of technological development and international diplomacy at the macro level and local ingenuity, co-operation and democratisation at the micro level. The IPCC (2007) suggests that an internationally collaborative portfolio of mitigation and adaptation strategies can limit the impact of climate change on migration and displacement; equally, combining holistic strategies with local knowledge and giving the power and capacity to communities at risk will enhance the effectiveness of global strategies.

Notes

1. Notably Principle 10 of the 1992 Rio Declaration on Environment and Development, and the 1998 Convention on Access to Information, Public Participation in Decision-making and Access to Justice in Environmental Matters.

CHAPTER SEVEN

Unstable Peace

This chapter is concerned with the political, development and humanitarian challenges displacement poses in situations of mainly localised, but occasionally generalised instability and hostility that would not be defined as armed conflict under international humanitarian law. Whilst, as we have previously discussed, there is no consensus on what constitutes armed conflict, the authors follow a recent ICRC (2008) position on 'international armed conflict' as existing whenever there is resort to armed force between two or more states; and 'non-international armed conflict' existing in protracted armed confrontations occurring between governmental armed forces and the forces of one or more armed groups, or between such groups arising on the territory of a State'.[1] Essentially the chapter is concerned with two very broad categories of displacement where there is direct involvement of the state. The first could be described as violence-induced, that is displacement occurring in violent situations that do not reach the threshold of armed conflict. The second is displacement occurring as a result of government fiat or private sector activities, which commonly are described as forced evictions. The chapter is further concerned with events resulting in violence, displacement, vulnerability and human insecurity where the state is not involved directly but may be said to be neglectful of its protection obligations towards those displaced.

Particular attention will be paid to politically-motivated displacement including election and post-election violence, pastoralist dispute-related violence, livelihoods vulnerability and economic-induced displacement, forced resettlement and relocation, and forced evictions. It is also an aim of this chapter to explore local-level context-specific displacement; specifically the structural factors causing displacement and multiple sequential displacement, and locate this causation in the context of political, economic and social inequality, poverty, economic stagnation, state repression, government neglect and environmental degradation. Finally, the chapter will also discuss the links between climate change and ensuing resource scarcity on these episodes of violence and in areas of instability.

The displacement and migration of populations in countries that would not be described as being in a state of armed conflict is on the rise (Guterres 2008) and is regarded as presenting threats to international security and national development, as well as causing human rights violations. The displacement of populations is frequently included as a key determinant in various indices measuring state fragility or breakdown. In recent years, political violence and forced evictions in Zimbabwe, Kenya, Mexico and Burma have received extensive media coverage and while not triggering international intervention have been the source of debate as to how far international obligations, including R2P, could or should be invoked to intervene in such situations. Displacement of this kind is most frequently associated with political processes (elections, and the deliberate repression of populations for political gain), imposed economic shocks (unchecked inflation, collapse of health and social services, dramatically reduced employment opportunities), land seizures and resettlement programmes by state and non-state interests, combined with rapid social change (including internal migration).

Political-type displacement is often justified by states as both legal and warranted in pursuit of national development (growth, environmental conservation and land preservation, reducing population pressure on land) but such justifications are frequently unsupported. In practice rights are widely violated and justice unavailable thus nullifying any development benefits that may arise. In other cases actors engaged in the displacement of populations for reasons ostensibly of national interest act outside of the law with or without state collusion. There are additional circumstances, including in the aftermath of natural disasters, where displacement is prolonged for political reasons, where violence may be used to achieve such ends and where return is denied.

As already stated, the authors would include in the category of political displacement, displacement that cannot be attributed directly to actions by the state but for which the state has a responsibility to prevent and to provide protection and justice but fails to do so. The draft Convention for the Prevention of Internal Displacement and the Protection of and Assistance to IDPs in Africa presented to the Africa Union in 2006 refers explicitly to such displacement by neglect as 'displacement induced by a lack of development'. This might include the failure to act in circumstances that Moser and Rodgers (2005) call the 'change–violence' nexus and would cover wide ranging displacement events arguably taking the form of trafficking (trade in sex, drugs and illegal movements) and escape from gang-related territorial violence linked to lack of economic opportunity and the collapse of livelihoods (this would include so called social violence 'mob attacks' and the deliberate displacement of foreigners in South Africa in early 2008). In this much broader understanding, the situations resulting in displacement may well be exacerbated by a number of the environmental factors described in Chapter Six. These might include increasing inequality in access to natural resources, particularly land, at its sharpest in those countries where climate change, the loss of water and reduced access to common property resources and secure cultivable land are already intensifying such resource competition. The likelihood is that in those areas of severe economic decline where displacement is a deliberate act to preserve advantage, power becomes severely imbalanced and recourse to violence is common. This is discussed further below in relation to the current situation in parts of Cambodia.

A Typology of Violence-related Non-conflict Displacement

Any attempt to build a typology of 'non-conflict displacement' raises a series of difficulties and anomalies. All of the 'types' of displacement we discuss in this chapter are likely to take place in, or lead to, conflict that may reach the international humanitarian law threshold of armed conflict and are triggered by and lead to violence that in any common sense understanding would be regarded as 'conflict'. Furthermore, as suggested above, it may not be useful to separate out displacement occurring in conflict situations but which is not directly attributable to that conflict. Arguably one could include in any typology displacement that arises as a result of insurgency or counter-insurgency-type activities taking place in situations where internal armed conflict has not been internationally recognised, yet such insurgency-related displacement (as witnessed in for example, Iraq, Turkey, Yemen and Palestinian land over the past two decades) has not been included. This chapter therefore is concerned to address displacement occurring in those circumstances where there are less serious forms of violence such as internal disturbances and tensions, riots or acts of banditry that have not (yet) reached a certain threshold of confrontation. It is recognised that in many crisis situations governments are eager to downplay the gravity of the crisis or the number of the affected populations and their circumstances, as they are aware that such outcomes are frequently a direct result of a number of actions they have sanctioned.

Politically Motivated Displacement/Forced Evictions

It was a feature of twentieth century history that both forced displacement and forced evictions were frequently used by the state and non-state groups in society for overtly political purposes. This has included the displacement of political opponents or the internal deportation of ethnic minorities and others for political gain. It is a practice that continues in the twenty-first century.

Post-election violence in Kenya in 2007, for example, created the displacement of over 500,000 people, mostly Kikuyu living in the Rift Valley, into camps and dispersed among host communities. The reasons for the violence were complex but should be understood in relation to the ethnicisation of Kenyan politics, and the politicisation of land issues. At the time of writing, the number of people internally displaced was fluctuating as people returned to ancestral homelands, relocated from one camp to another or left their host families. The UN anticipated that 150,000 people would remain in camps throughout 2008. The displacement resulted in the disruption of livelihoods over broad sectors of Kenyan society, including among farmers displaced from Rift Valley and Western provinces. Small and medium-sized entrepreneurs were particularly affected in urban, peri-urban and slum areas where businesses were looted or destroyed and an estimated 400,000 professionals (including civil servants in the Central province) and formal labourers and up to one million informal workers reportedly lost their jobs.

In Zimbabwe also, as we have previously discussed in this volume, there were significant 'political evictions' linked again to election processes and land issues. In 2005 it is estimated that more than half a million people were made homeless by Operation Murambatsvina when the government embarked on a nation-wide campaign to destroy supposedly illegal structures in towns and cities. The UN estimates that a total of 700,000 were directly affected, that is losing either their home or their business, or both, and many more were indirectly affected. Further forced evictions came in late 2006 and early 2007, in Operation Chikorakoza Chapera (Operation End Illegal Gold Panning) when thousands of mine workers were made homeless after their houses were destroyed by government forces. In the case of both Operations, the motivation for the destruction of homes is generally believed to have been political.

Operation Murambatsvina began shortly after the 2005 elections, in which most of the urban areas voted for the opposition Movement for Democratic Change (MDC). The evictions were seen as a straightforward punishment of the urban population and an attempt to drive people out of the cities to prevent food riots that could have evolved into political demonstrations. The rural areas in Zimbabwe are generally under the control of the ruling party, ZANU-PF (something that was partly seen to have changed in the last elections on 29 March 2008), and the political strategy may have been to drive people from the urban areas into the rural areas thus weakening the support base for the opposition. Evictions, albeit at a lower level, and crackdowns on vendors continued after Operation Murambatsvina and resulted in additional displacement. For example, there were reports on 20 April 2006 that police in Masvingo forcibly moved around two hundred households from a squatter camp and set shacks alight. The impacts on those displaced, according to international and national human rights groups, as a result of the evictions included disrupted access to antiretroviral drugs for those HIV positive and a general deterioration in health standards and access to healthcare, an increase in poverty, school non-attendance, chronic overcrowding and psychological stresses with fears of an increase in domestic violence. At the time of writing, thousands of people remained displaced in Zimbabwe as a result of violence following the elections in March 2008 despite moves towards power-sharing arrangement in the second half of the year.

What could be termed displacement occurring as a result of politically-motivated violence has occurred in other parts of Africa in recent years. For example, thousands of Abidjan residents were displaced by attacks on their houses following the September 2002 coup attempt led by disaffected soldiers. The ensuing fighting left the country divided with the rebels of the Movement Patriotique pour la Côte d'Ivoire (MPCI) in control of much of the centre and the predominantly Muslim north of the country, and government forces holding the largely Christian south. The government of Cote d'Ivoire had openly accused neighbouring states of supporting the rebels, Burkina Faso in particular. This accusation allegedly gave security forces and civilian supporters of the government a green light to systematically attack and burn down Abidjan shantytowns housing west African migrants, refugees and Ivorians accused of supporting the rebels.

In the two weeks following the attempted coup, UNHCR reported that in Abidjan more than six thousand Ivorians, migrants and refugees were made homeless by the demolition policy. Residents often received little or no notice of the demolitions and lost all their possessions as bulldozers razed their homes. Although the government assured that this was not an operation against foreigners, as many Ivorians were also concerned, the main targets of the demolition appeared to be migrants whom the government accused of supporting the rebellion. Thousands of migrants in Cote d'Ivoire, especially Burkinabes, reportedly returned to their home countries to escape reprisals.

In Abidjan, the most immediate need of the victims of the demolitions was shelter and in the days after the uprising, human rights groups reported that an estimated two thousand people were sheltering at night in churches, private courtyards and buildings under construction. The displaced sought shelter at UNHCR and IOM centres normally used for processing refugees, although their capacity was limited. Subsequently, the Government also housed a small percentage of the displaced in social centres, while others found shelter with families, friends and relatives, or at churches and mosques.

In the Middle East, political evictions in pursuit of ethnic politics have been widespread. From the 1960s, activities by the state in Kurdish areas of Iraq rendered many thousands of Kurds stateless and such actions were coupled with a strategy of populating Kurdish areas in the north of Iraq with Arab communities by offering state incentives, providing, it is alleged, a 'safe Arab belt' in the north. The question of Kurdish statelessness remains unresolved despite state promises to resolve the issue in 2007. The situation in Syria has similarities, though is far less draconian than forced displacement of Kurdish and Shi'ia communities in Iraq in the 1980s and through the 1990s.

Ethnicity or Caste-motivated Forced Evictions

In India forced evictions take place on a daily basis in various parts of the country. Among those frequently targeted are Dalits (or so-called 'untouchables', known in Indian legal terms as scheduled castes). In a typical scenario, Dalit villages are attacked and looted by neighbouring upper-caste villagers, forcing them to settle for months in temporary homes on government property. The perpetrators largely enjoy impunity and little is done to help the displaced Dalits return home or to prosecute those responsible for the attacks. The Indian Government has also been known to forcibly evict those who have fled conflict and are living as IDPs. In a recent example, IDPs who had fled the Maoist conflict in Chhattisgarh State and were living in forest settlements in neighbouring Andhra Pradesh State reportedly had their shelters destroyed by forest department officials and faced forced eviction.

Resettlement and Forced Displacement under the Guise of Development

As we have explained elsewhere in this volume, most state-sanctioned resettlement is carried out legally with the intention of providing a solution for those resettled in the name of overriding public benefit. Too frequently, however, international standards for resettlement and relocation are not reached, protective frameworks are weak and policies poor. Involuntary resettlement creates deepened impoverishment, contributes to new conflicts and increases vulnerability to further displacement and human rights violations if the resettled do not enjoy legal title to land and do not receive legal protection or economic assistance. Forced evictions with recourse to violence in pursuit of ostensible development objectives in particular are cited as creating a distinct group of persons requiring protection under international human rights law. The human costs of forced evictions can be substantial and can involve negative impacts on the lives and livelihood of those affected with humanitarian consequences and needs that are frequently unaddressed.

The situation in the Chittagong Hill Tracts in Bangladesh is often cited as an example of politically motivated displacement justified in the cause of national development. The cause of displacement of the Buddhist Jumma or thirteen groups of indigenous people living in the Chittagong Hill Tracts in Bangladesh is related to the politics of nation-building and ensuing conflicts between the minority and majority population. Since Bangladesh gained independence in 1971, armed conflict between the tribal population and the government as well as a government-sponsored transmigration programme of Bengali Muslim settlers from the plains have forced large numbers of Jumma to flee their homes. Violence and tension continues in the Chittagong Hill Tracts over army attempts to settle Bengali families on land occupied by Jumma families.

We have already mentioned that transmigration programmes were also undertaken in Indonesia with the aim of transferring populations from the poor and overcrowded areas of the central islands (Java, Lombok, Bali and Madura) to less densely populated areas of the outer islands (Borneo, New Guinea and Sumatra). Initiated by the Dutch, this policy was implemented on a large scale under President Suharto's regime with financial support by the World Bank. From 1976 to 1986, the World Bank lent 500 million dollars to fund the project. Some seven million people were relocated during this period, half of them on their own initiative. One of the main objectives of the programme, it is widely thought, was geopolitical, primarily the control of indigenous peoples of the outer islands through forced integration. In many cases, the programme violated property rights of the indigenous peoples and forest dwellers.

The relocation of large groups, often from Java to under-populated areas, led to growing ethnic imbalance and land disputes. These deepening tensions broke out into conflicts when the political vacuum created by Suharto's fall triggered new local political aspirations and power struggles. In the wake of the financial crisis that hit Indonesia in 1998 and the fall of the Suharto regime the same year, religious and ethnic violence started to spread throughout the country. Against a backdrop of economic recession, widespread political discontent fuelled separatist aspirations. The resulting unrest saw more than 1.4 million people displaced between 1999 and 2002.

It has also been widely recorded that the military junta in Burma/Myanmar has carried out urban evictions and forcibly relocated at least half a million people in the 1980s and 1990s from around Rangoon and other cities to new satellite towns. Those displaced were, it is alleged, offered little compensation and were ordered to pay for their plots of land at the new locations. Since 2005, at least 10,000 local people have been uprooted due to construction of the new capital in Naypidaw.

Displacement of populations in urban areas in many developing countries has taken place with a development justification (mostly urban upgrading) but accompanied by discernible political objectives. Between 2003 and 2007, for example, hundreds of thousands of people were reportedly forcibly evicted from their informal settlements in Abuja, Nigeria within the framework of the 1979 Abuja Master Plan. The implementation by the administration of the Federal Capital Territory of this urban development plan was conducted according to human rights groups without adequate consultation with the affected communities, without adequate notice of the date of the eviction and without a careful strategy for compensation or adequate alternative housing. Violence against residents and business owners appeared in some instances to have been perpetrated by security forces. Demolitions systematically targeted those people that the administration considered to be 'non-indigenes' or 'settlers', people who had moved to Abuja in the past thirty years, after the establishment of the federal capital.

Violence-induced Displacement

A further category of displacement that occurs outside of internationally recognised conflict is related to the use of forced resettlement by states, either as official policy or through covert action, to depopulate an area by relocating people against their will.

This process has been seen in Burma, where the junta has targeted civilians in conflict areas using a tactic known as the Four Cuts policy whereby the state military clear large areas of villages following a scorched-earth strategy, forcing people to move to government-controlled relocation sites, usually with little or no warning. The Four

Cuts has been official policy since the early 1970s, but the present military junta, human rights reports would suggest, has made its implementation much more systematic than previously. In the mid-1990s, the SPDC launched programmes to forcibly move or eliminate all rural villages in areas outside its control; the numbers of displaced increased dramatically as a result. The purpose of the policy is believed to be to separate insurgents from their civilian base which is perceived to be providing support to the insurgency. The insurgents and civilians are from ethnic minority groups who have been fighting the Burman-dominated central government for more than forty years.

There are reports that in Nigeria's oil producing region, the Niger Delta, armed militia groups have used increasingly violent means to gain greater control of oil wealth and criminal rackets, clashing with the Nigerian army, kidnapping numerous foreign oil workers and destroying oil installations, drastically reducing the country's oil input. Violence between local militia groups and security forces, as well as inter-militia fighting and widespread destruction of property, has frequently forced people to flee their homes. Many civilians are, for example, regularly caught in crossfire in fighting between security forces and the Movement for the Emancipation of the Niger Delta (MEND), most recently in September 2008 when up to twenty thousand people were reported to have been displaced from the affected communities.

Violence-induced Displacement (Pastoralist)

A subdivision of violence-induced displacement could be identified in pastoralist societies where much displacement has taken place against the backdrop of land disputes that would not necessarily be included in a typology of non-conflict displacement. Particular attention in the media has been paid to pastoral conflict in the East Africa drylands where intra-clan conflicts (sections of one community or clan or one sub-county/division fighting with one another), inter-district conflicts (Karamajong against other tribes or communities living in the districts neighbouring the Cluster, possibly within the same country) and cross-border conflicts between tribes are all causing displacement. Clearly these are forms of violence linked to a complex of socio-cultural, economic, political and environmental factors that have led to intensification of resource competition in the region and a rise in displacement.

The Karamoja region of Uganda is cited here as an example of pastoralist violence-induced displacement that is inseparable from livelihood vulnerability. The Karamoja region continues to suffer from violence, mainly related to cattle-rustling by semi-nomadic pastoralist

Karamojong warriors. Traditionally, clans fought each other with spears, sticks, bows and arrows, but in the post-colonial period these traditional weapons have been replaced with more lethal small arms. The violence in Karamoja is rooted in a history of colonial and post-colonial neglect, shrinking access to pasture and grazing land for cattle, and successive years of drought. Commercialisation of cattle-rustling has further fuelled incentives to carry out raids. The result is a cycle of violence in which victims of the raids, particularly rival Karamojong clans, acquire weapons to protect themselves and retaliate against attacking clans.

Karamoja has the worst humanitarian and development indicators in Uganda, including the lowest primary school enrolment, highest maternal and infant mortality and the lowest life expectancy in all of Uganda. The continuing inadequacy of government services, such as social, medical and judicial institutions, has contributed to an overall breakdown in the rule of law and the flight of women and children in search of food and employment. Such movements have increased vulnerabilities and contributed to a protection crisis. People who flee from Karamoja to Kampala in search of livelihood opportunities, including children, are regularly rounded up by the government and returned to Karamoja.

A heavy-handed government disarmament campaign has disrupted traditional movement patterns and has caused displacement within Karamoja. However, there are no accurate estimates of the number of people displaced, and it is difficult to distinguish the forced displacement from the ordinary movement patterns of the semi-nomadic Karamojong. Nevertheless, a representative of the international humanitarian community in Uganda has estimated that about 30 per cent of all displacement in Karamoja is related to the ongoing disarmament campaign.

Resource conflict between pastoral groups and conflict between farmers and herders are common causes of displacement in pastoral areas of Ethiopia, Kenya and Somalia.

Livelihoods Vulnerability and Economic Displacement

The linkages between livelihoods vulnerability, displacement and an ongoing vulnerability to future displacement are discussed in greater detail below in relation to Cambodia. However, there are numerous examples from elsewhere that aid our understanding of the complex processes involved.

Limited economic opportunities in parts of South Africa have led to 'locals' using force and violence to displace 'outsiders'. In mid-2008, at least thirty thousand foreigners living in South Africa, including many thousands of Zimbabweans, were displaced from their homes and forced to seek refuge in police stations, churches and community centres, and later government-run 'refugee camps'. More than three weeks of so called 'xenophobic violence' left at least eighty people dead and tens of thousands homeless in a situation that was described as a humanitarian crisis. Many foreigners decided to return to their home countries to seek safety with some three thousand people reported to be returning to Mozambique every day at the height of the violence. Loren Landau at the University of the Witwatersrand confirmed that some of the Zimbabweans displaced in what was called 'mob social violence' had been previously displaced within Zimbabwe as a result of Operation Murambatsvina and unsuccessfully sought refugee status in South Africa (personal correspondence).

As stated above, displacement has been closely linked to oil production in the Niger Delta region. While the region has been volatile for many years, with impoverished local communities accusing successive governments as well as oil companies of depriving them of their fair share of revenues, tensions have escalated dramatically since early 2006. The violence in the Niger Delta is due significantly to poverty and unequal access to resources. Despite its oil wealth (Nigeria is Africa's leading oil producer, and the seventh largest in the world), it is reported that at least two thirds of Nigerians live on less than one dollar per day. The cause of the conflict rests on the allocation of oil revenue and on the sense of relative deprivation that this induces among the huge pools of destitute and frustrated youth. Many analysts believe that this sense of deprivation is used by politicians, particularly those linked to the former military regime, to create social divisions and violence that can quickly spread and take on a momentum of its own. The region's extensive pollution, due in large part to gas flaring, the process of burning off surplus gases from oil wells, has affected many people's health and limited the access of many more to their traditional livelihoods.

Northern Niger has been affected by fighting since February 2007 when an insurgent Tuareg group, the Niger Movement for Justice (MJN), announced it was launching an armed campaign against the government. The stated aim of the insurgency is to win more economic and political autonomy for people in the uranium- and petrol-rich region from the central government in the capital Niamey, 1,200 km to the south. Although displacement is not directly a consequence of economic conditions in the area, livelihoods vulnerability and an unequal share of resources are at the centre of the conflict that has resurfaced since early 2007. An estimated eleven thousand people have been displaced by the conflict so far.

Environmental Roots of Instability and Displacement

Throughout the above typology it is evident that subtle and less subtle processes of environmental change, linked in many cases to climate change, are exacerbating resource competition and intersecting with other social pressures to increase instability and in turn create the conditions that may lead to displacement. It is in this domain of unstable peace that attention has turned to the potential future impact of climate change and the potential for increased displacement discussed in the previous chapter. The growing debate about climate change-related instability is in part a product of the securitisation of the climate change discourse but is also rooted in the reality that instability overlaps with vulnerability to climate change as can be seen in many of the countries listed above. Figure 7.1 illustrates the fact that the majority of the regions most at risk of the environmental impacts of climate change are areas of recent or current conflict or political instability (Kolmannskog 2008).

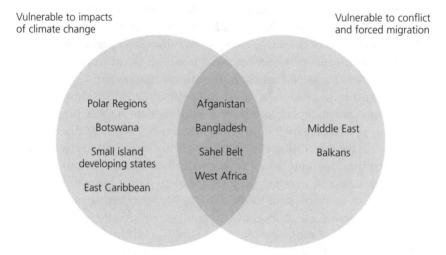

Figure 7.1. Correlation of Risks Related to Impacts of Climate Change, Conflict and Forced Migration

While the environment–security dynamic has emerged recently as a key issue for international politics, academics have been debating links between environmental change, resource scarcity and instability for several decades. Following a combination of the scenarios outlined by Gleditsch et al. (2007) and Kolmannskog (2008), two pathways can be identified from environmental change or climate change to conflict, one directly and the other using migration as the transmitter:

Scenario 1 – environmental/climate change ➔ conflict from region A ➔ migration

Scenario 2 – environmental/climate change ➔ migration from region A ➔ conflict in region B

Slow-onset environmental stresses, such as drought and desertification, as discussed in the previous chapter, have the potential to limit already scarce resources and livelihood opportunities. Grievance models of conflict suggest that those affected by this kind of progressive change may resort to violence as they see their own personal circumstances decline (Gleditsch et al. 2007). This chain of events can be particularly prevalent in areas where large sections of the population are reliant upon the kind of subsistence agriculture most at risk from environmental stresses of this nature. Those inclined to view this as a framework for understanding conflicts in Darfur and elsewhere are likely to point to a study of conflicts between 1980 and 1992 by Hauge and Ellingsen (1998). This study found a positive correlation between civil conflict and a number of types of slow-onset environmental change – many of which are likely to be intensified by climate change. However, academics have been quick to point out the magnitude of the effect of environmental change on conflict identified was small, increasing the probability of conflict by only 1 per cent (Castles 2002). Although the effects of climate change have the potential to increase this probability, more recent studies have failed to replicate the results of Hauge and Ellingson (Gleditsch et al. 2007). A survey by Black (2001) of eleven conflicts, many of which generated mass internal displacement, found that few can count environmental conditions (particularly not resource scarcity as a consequence of slow-onset disasters) as primary drivers of conflict. Black insists that other factors, such as poverty, governance and political instability, carried far greater weight: something actually confirmed by the Hauge and Ellingson study (Castles 2002). Other factors, such as existing ethnic division or inequitable resource distribution, are also likely to determine the propensity for conflict in areas of progressive environmental change. According to a working paper for the International Peace Academy instability is more likely where income and resource inequality already exists along ethnic lines (Gleditsch et al. 2007). In these instances, it cannot be said that environmental change is, nor predicted that climate change will be, the sole cause of conflict that then generates displacement (Goldstone 2001). In fact, there are examples of some good emerging out of often tragic events. In the case of the devastating effects of the tsunami on

Aceh, the response to the human suffering is believed to have been instrumental in starting a process of cooperation between competing factions in the region and ultimately contributed to a peace agreement (Ferris 2007). Moreover, when environmental stress has threatened violence between states rather than within, there are numerous instances of cooperation between states over water rights and access (Castles 2002).

In instances of natural disasters there is the possibility that an inadequate government response that fails to provide satisfactory assistance and protection for the affected population can heighten existing political unrest if not directly cause it. A paper by the NRC (2008) argues that the indifferent response from centralised authorities to the devastating typhoon that hit what was then East Pakistan in 1970 strengthened the separatist movement that ultimately created Bangladesh. Castles (2002) also highlights misuse of international aid by the Somoza regime following the earthquake in Nicaragua in 1972. The German Advisory Council on Global Change (2007) has argued that the world will see an increase in 'sudden disaster conflict' as many of the areas most at risk, such as Central America, are politically unstable. When natural disasters strike areas that are not currently experiencing heightening ethnic, nationalist or religious tensions, the propensity for violence is lower. Where violence does break out it is likely to be unorganised, localised and purely with the aim of securing suitable assistance. The events that followed Hurricane Katrina's devastation of New Orleans show that some violence, if not conflict, can be generated by inadequate responses, particularly if the provision of assistance is perceived to be inequitable. The NRC report (2008) argues that this shows that even developed countries can 'have their weaknesses and injustices revealed by climate change'. The effects of these events certainly have the capacity to exacerbate existing social and political tension or result in spontaneous violence or lawlessness.

The evidence for the first scenario of climate change generating new outbreaks of conflict that would reach the threshold set in international humanitarian law in region A appears limited and, consequently, it is equally unlikely that migration or displacement would be generated as a result. The types of environmental stress climate change may cause are more likely to lead to migration in the first instance rather than conflict. There is, therefore, a stronger case for a link between climate change and conflict that sees migration as a consequence of environmental stress in region A generating conflict in region B. This is particularly likely when people move into areas that are already politically unstable (Kolmannskog 2008). Newcomers arriving spontaneously to areas of underdevelopment that cannot provide suitable camps will exacerbate existing competition for resources, often developing urban slums in cases of rural to urban migration (Castles 2002) or degrading land and food stocks by using hunting and agricultural methods unsuitable to their new location.[2] Two US think tanks published a report suggesting that, in security terms, this phenomenon is the most worrying aspect of climate change (CSIS/CNAS 2007). Gleditsch et al. (2007) analyse thoroughly the accuracy of these claims, providing a number of reasons why 'ecomigrants' may contribute to conflict in receiving areas. One example cited is the movement of Bengalis to the northern Chittagong Hills where local tribes have clashed with state authorities and to the Assam region of India which has developed social frictions between religious groups. Gleditsch et al. go on to argue that in instances of climate change exacerbating existing conflict, the resulting flow of displaced people can have particular implications for security. Displaced persons from some conflicts are known to maintain local and transnational ties with military factions at home. Where displacement forces people into neighbouring countries, cross-border attacks can be frequent, which further jeopardise the security of the region and increase the risk of displacement. Despite acknowledging these links between climate change, migration and conflict, Gleditsch and his colleagues argue that displacement from the impacts of climate change does not in itself lead to conflict in receiving areas. Most of the people at risk of displacement from the effects of climate change are unlikely to contribute to organised violence or have a political agenda beyond receiving suitable protection and assistance.

As discussed above, the effects of climate change are most likely to cause either short-term displacement with a high propensity for return or progressive migration over a long period of time; whether this is internal displacement or cross-border movement, states can either provide temporary assistance with the help of the international community for the former or develop strategies and capacity for incorporation of newcomers for the latter. Where these are not put in place, the probability of conflict is higher, though it is still inaccurate to say that this conflict will have been caused by climate change: the environmental impact is merely one of many factors that determine a state's capacity to prevent either displacement or conflict. Political stability, democratic institutions, economic capacity and social characteristics of host and arriving populations will all play a role in the outbreak or prevention of conflict. We have covered a number of examples above where the effects of climate change have contributed to migration, displacement or conflict in region A or region B. In these cases, one or more of the crucial factors listed in the table has been absent. There are also a number of cases counterfactual to those used by environmentalists and others as proof of the link between climate change and conflict. What these examples instead show is that theories of mono-causality for either displacement or conflict in areas affected by climate change are inaccurate and reductionist. Firstly, assertions that civil and border wars are increasingly fought over scarce resources does not square with the dynamics of a number of recent conflicts. Black (2001) points to conflict in Rwanda, Sierra Leone and Liberia as well as unrest in Central Asian states that stems not from resource scarcity but from the desire of factions within these nations to control potentially rich and abundant natural resources. Furthermore, examples can be cited where resource scarcity, famine or drought has not led to conflict but only temporary displacement. The famine in Ethiopia in the 1980s failed to generate organised internal or cross-border violence, while the 2001 flooding in Mozambique generated large-scale but only temporary displacement (ibid.).

The conflicts in Sudan and Somalia are often considered as paradigmatic cases of the climate change and conflict link. Events in Darfur are often held up as a vivid example of a conflict directly linked to resource scarcity, where drought has reduced crop-yields and challenged traditional livelihood strategies leading to migration and conflict over remaining meagre resources. Yet this can be challenged on two fronts. Firstly, as Black (2001) reminds us, oil is also a significantly rich resource in Sudan and influencing factor in the conflict in Darfur. Secondly, the conflict is much more complex and dynamic than a simple resource-based conflict incorporating cross-border and internal political relations and tribal, ethnic and religious division. In some respects, it is the conflict that is exacerbating environmental degradation rather than the other way round (see Bromwich 2007). In Somalia, a conflict over control and access to resources is being played out through antecedent complex socio-political structures of clan, class and religion. The origin of this struggle lies not in environmental change or resource scarcity, though Somalia has experienced both, but in the inability or incapacity of government or government-like institutions to provide equitable distribution of resources along a number of dividing lines in Somali society (de Waal 2007). Ultimately, the effects of climate change need to be understood and incorporated into accounts of some current conflicts and assessment of the risk of future conflict, but only as an additional variable not as the overriding or decisive factor.

Post-conflict Displacement: Vulnerability to Further Displacement – Evidence from Cambodia

Drawing on evidence from Cambodia there are indications of increasing incidence and severity of forms of each of the displacement types discussed above intersecting with detrimental cumulative impacts on livelihoods and aspects of human security particularly for the rural poor. It is possible to observe situations where displacement takes place in the context of a 'perfect storm' of land and resource loss and intensified resource competition due to illegal or barely legal activities of the state, state officials acting independently or private companies; (unmanaged) economic shocks; and accelerating environmental degradation leading to deepened impoverishment, political marginalisation and stress reactions including migration. Displacement may occur as a result of one of these 'shocks' confronting households or communities, or may occur as a result of a number of shocks intersecting with differing degrees of intensity at different times. The journey on which people find themselves is one in which displacement, land loss, migration and impoverishment become embedded and reinforcing in the sense that the net effect is to compound the vulnerability of the rural poor to repeated or sequential displacement.

Such a pattern is not unique to Cambodia and can be found in other countries, particularly those that have emerged out of international or internal armed conflict and where humanitarian responses and post-conflict development interventions have failed to break the displacement–poverty–return to conflict cycle. However, what might be new is that the cycle is also a feature of relatively stable and even prosperous societies that have not experienced serious internal conflict, but rather have enjoyed longer periods of relative stability, relatively good governance, transfers of international aid and expanding economies. This would suggest that displacement, migration and impoverishment are not abnormal or exceptional but are in some circumstances structural outcomes of current development and growth models combined with a political (and arguably broader social) tolerance of displacement. If this is the case then it raises questions for policy makers about where and how there can or should be interventions to break the cycle and to restore rural livelihood security. One issue policy makers will have to tackle is the role of migration in this displacement–vulnerability cycle.

In Cambodia, Pilgrim and McDowell[3] identified a number of structural processes that contribute to this rural insecurity and which are both contributing causes and consequences of increased displacement and vulnerability to displacement. They include the *disruption to land rights* and the impact such disruption has on the household's developmental cycle including impacts on traditional processes of land acquisition and transfer through inheritance, or the expansion of farms by purchase or bush clearance as principal means for the acquisition of resources. This has additional impacts on the management of the means of livelihood by individuals in the group or of the group as a whole. Second, they point to *land shortage as a result of population increase* in which there are simply too many people living off and subdividing insufficient land. Without non-agricultural sources of income the majority of households are in poverty because their land holdings are insufficient to support subsistence. Population growth has, moreover, given rise both to a general land shortage and to a growing differential in sizes of land holding within rural communities; this is a differential which tends to become greater because of the ability of wealthier farmers to acquire land, often land which poor members of the community are obliged to sell in times of crisis (notably of health crisis) because of indebtedness.

Third, Pilgrim and McDowell argue that the *economic costs of displacement and migration,* both hidden and obvious, are significant in compounding the negative impacts of displacement and thus increasing the vulnerability to displacement at some point in the future. These costs commonly mean that households are obliged to sell food crops to pay for other food and essential expenditure on health, clothes and education, resulting in food deficits for periods of the year. Fourth, they argue that there is a need to consider the cumulative impacts of the *social and health costs of displacement and migration.* For example Biddulph (2000) records that 44.7 per cent of rural people migrating have lost their land due to illness and 67 per cent of the families taking out loans due to family health problems have become landless. The incidence of sickness linked to land loss in 1998 and 1999 included 170,000 people suffering from HIV/AIDS (NCHADS 1999). Four other major diseases led to widespread land loss: malaria, dengue fever, TB and typhoid. Yagura (2005) found that 38.1 per cent of the people in Svay and Trapeang Ang sold their land to pay for medical expenses, as the major cause of landlessness. Finally, as research has demonstrated, a lack of access to or failure in the effectiveness of legal process is a major factor in land losses among rural households and communities in conflict with private or government agencies seeking to acquire land. Cambodia is suffering from a more or less continuous process of illicit land acquisition by powerfully placed individuals and corporations displacing rural communities and subsistence farming.

As a result of these structural processes in Cambodia and the failure of development intervention or humanitarian programmes to address them, Pilgrim and McDowell contend that there is a growing vulnerability to multiple and compounded displacement and migration – of which there are two recognisable variants. First is the repeated experience of migration as a household, changing location several times, seeking land, homes, employment, sustainable livelihoods in the context of oppression and dislocation brought about by the action of military forces, government agencies and municipal developers, speculators and expropriating companies or internally through the impact of local population pressure, land shortage and indebtedness. Second, the migration of individual members of the household, most often young adults continuing to provide remittances to the parental household while seeking a basis of stability and sustainability for their own long-term livelihoods and family development.

At the same time, migration is increasingly a systematic and institutionalised strategy employed by rural households and communities to achieve sustainable livelihoods and to escape from poverty. Clearly migration brings benefits to the rural poor and these have been recognised as: enhancing income and smoothing fluctuations; contributing to commercialisation, the flow of new goods between migrant areas; and development of social capital. Migration is also seen to impact on household structures and gendered norms, influencing who makes decisions about migration and the use of remittances, as well as which people become migrants. It has also been identified, however, that rural production may suffer as a consequence of out-migration by the most productive community members. Migration may also increase inequality and is itself a very unequal process. This returns us to Moser and Rodgers' (2005) caution that displacement and migration have the potential to increase the instability that leads to further displacement.

In terms of policy implications, a number of Western governments, the World Bank and parts of the UN are promoting the benefits of migration for development and poverty alleviation. There are discussions taking place in the UNHCR considering how labour migration could be part of the solution to forced migration crises for people who otherwise would have gone on to seek asylum. However, a close examination of the causes and consequences of displacement and migration in fragile and unstable contexts would suggest that policy makers need to take into account the possibility that migration may increase inequality and instability. They need to be aware of the way migration is embedded in social relations, the disadvantages this may have for some members of households and the community, and the opportunities this creates for supportive policies.

Political and Humanitarian Responses to Non-conflict Displacement

We discussed the governance and management of non-conflict displacement in Chapter Four, but it is worth noting in relation to this particularly problematic 'grey zone' of political displacement that governance is most open to scrutiny and criticism. It is a widely held view that the international community and in particular the UN was unable or seemingly unwilling to mobilise political support to address the protection and humanitarian needs of people displaced within the borders of their own countries as a result of actions by the state and non-state actors where that displacement (or neglect of the displaced) was a deliberate political act including deliberate neglect. Observers of events in Zimbabwe in 2005, after the publication of the powerful Tibaijuka and Egeland UN-commissioned human rights report on the situation following Operation Murambatsvina and the 2008 elections, were shocked at the apparent inaction. Failure to criticise the government or to ensure the implementation of UN recommendations were considered serious failings on the part of the UN and the international community as a whole.

There remains an impression that over the issue of Zimbabwe the international community has been passive and devoid of ideas. However, this is misleading. Since 2005 there has been a raft of measures constituting quite forceful, though ultimately unsuccessful, advocacy proposed by international bodies and individual governments to force change in Zimbabwe on the economy including: on structural reform (World Bank, IMF), monetary policy (IMF), governance (World Bank) and relations with the international financial community (IMF); on land reform and agriculture in general (Commonwealth, UN's Tibaijuka report, IMF, United Nations Development Programme, EU); on the humanitarian situation including food security (African Commission on Human and People's Rights, World Food Programme, EU); on the restoration of political stability including human rights legislation and the rule of law (African Commission on Human and Peoples' Rights, joint UE-ACHPR); and on political intimidation and violence (Commonwealth, EU, ACHPR). Official voices from outside the country at least have been loud and the recommendations have been specific in relation to Operation Murambatsvina and its aftermath including calls by the UN for full humanitarian access to those displaced and evicted, for international monitoring of the situation, and further calls to suspend or repeal a number of laws and constitutional provisions which contravene international human rights standards such as the Public Order and Security Act and amendments to the Constitution.

However, with limited support from Southern African Development Community states and the African Union, such calls have gone largely unheeded and within the UN it is understood that there is a need to rethink the limits of humanitarian and political action in such situations and the general responsibilities of all parts of the UN system. A key practical and operational issue is the challenge related to non-conflict displaced populations and the need to develop humanitarian response mechanisms to address the shortcoming. There is an emerging viewpoint among some officials that 'displacement' crises of the type we are addressing in this chapter are fundamentally more political than other crises and as such present far greater challenges to the international system. This has led some to the view that a rights-based vulnerability approach to protection (rather than one that focuses on displacement as the event and the category of person in need) would be more pragmatic and workable given current constraints. The main issue emerging from this would be how to enhance protection in complex environments which include multiple causes of displacement, lack of options to flee, repeated cycles of secondary or tertiary displacements and multiple causes of vulnerabilities amongst all segments of an affected population. This would have the added advantage of extending the protection and assistance to all affected populations and not just those who have moved and are reachable but also those who remain behind or are affected by the movement of others. The relevance of this is clear in the case of Zimbabwe where evictions and related displacement became an international humanitarian issue with an unknown number of those displaced crossing into South Africa and subsequently becoming displaced once more and seen as 'people of concern' by those UN agencies assisting the South African Provincial authorities in their relief and protection activities.

It is in these complex, ambiguous areas of displacement occurring between political actions, disasters and development, where state policies may be the source of forcible displacement and where national authorities are unwilling to protect or assist, that the international humanitarian community is restricted by overriding political considerations. But the restriction on action, as we have suggested throughout this volume, emerges also from within the system, from within the frameworks on displacement (the labelling and definitions, the divisions of responsibility) that determine responses and to a large extent determine how agencies and their donors perceive the problems they are required to address.

Notes

1. The armed confrontation, the ICRC proposes, must reach *a minimum level of intensity* and the parties involved in the conflict must show *a minimum of organisation.* The ICRC also cautions that a situation can evolve, and indeed does evolve, from one type of armed conflict to another, depending on the facts prevailing at any given time and the evolution is by no means predictable.
2. See an account of this phenomenon in the Ivory Coast on the Intercontinental Cry blog: http://intercontinentalcry.org/west-africa-from-desertification-to-migration-to-conflict/.
3. The analysis included in this section was undertaken by Professor John Pilgrim and Christopher McDowell in preparation for upcoming research in Cambodia.

CHAPTER EIGHT

Conclusion – Displacement Challenges for the Twenty-first Century

This volume has examined the human, economic and political outcomes of non-conflict displacement occurring as a result of natural disasters, as part of the development process, and in situations of peace, hostility and instability that do not reach the threshold of armed conflict as recognised in international humanitarian law. It has reviewed national and international institutional, legal and policy responses to displacement and considered current reforms. It is in many respects through the observed outcomes – the effects – of non-conflict displacement, mediated increasingly through media coverage, that the causes of displacement are sought and culpability or responsibility is assigned. It has previously been discussed that this process of identifying outcomes and ascribing responsibility has in part shaped the rethinking taking place within the international humanitarian community to identify weaknesses in humanitarian responses and propose system-change options for addressing identified protection and material assistance needs. Conceptually, examination of effects and outcomes of displacement is leading also to a reconsideration of the different categories, causes and complicating factors of displacement including a renewed focus on the common causation rooted in vulnerability to displacement, including importantly land insecurity, political marginalisation, economic development processes and poverty. It is a finding of this study that the distinctions between displacement taking place in traditionally understood conflict and so called non-conflict situations, and also within that non-conflict domain, are increasingly difficult to sustain conceptually or operationally. At the most obvious level it is a feature of contemporary displacement that causes are interrelated, displacement is not an isolated unexpected outcome of events and decisions, and that vulnerability to multiple and sequential displacement is a growing phenomenon that is insufficiently understood.

In the most part, the outcomes of non-conflict displacement are assessed through the knowledge and understanding we have of internal displacement and cross-border refugee movements, repatriation, return and reintegration resulting from conflict, particularly in those conflicts where the state is weak or has collapsed and where displacement and migration are seen as destabilising and threatening to neighbouring and distant states. More than twenty years ago Lance Clark writing in the 1988 World Refugee Survey suggested the term 'internal refugees' for all those displaced within the borders of their own countries and since then conflict-created humanitarian outcomes as witnessed in refugee situations have provided the baseline against which other forms of displacement outcomes and dynamics in non-conflict contexts are measured and have in turn shaped our understanding of displacement more generally. This can be seen in the small amount of contemporary literature that seeks to compare the similarities and dissimilarities in displacement outcomes underpinned by a concern to identify commonalities and in turn to identify opportunities for assistance, protection and intervention based on past practice (see for example Cernea and McDowell's 2000 World Bank study comparing the circumstances of development displacees with refugees).

One weakness in the current refugee discourse-driven approach to the challenge of human insecurity and vulnerability has been somewhat of a preoccupation with displacement as the only, or at least the principal indicator of humanitarian need and the trigger for action. Clearly, movements of people are the most visible manifestation of insecurity and a sign that people's options are severely limited and individuals and groups of people are prepared to take risks to protect their futures. However there is an increasing awareness that neither the act of displacement itself nor the distance people move can be used as a proxy to measure need. Indeed there is evidence, particularly from natural disaster situations that the most critical need may be with those who are unable to leave or who choose not to. For many of those who remain behind it is not a voluntary decision to do so and to assume choice would be misguided. Situations of immobility present their own dangers and protection needs. Those populations may be the most difficult to access, are beyond the news cameras and are in a humanitarian and protection blindspot. Similarly, it is a finding of this study that traditional definitions of displacement and the labelling that follows are exclusive in the sense that 'displacement' takes many forms and there is a need to reconsider an over-reliance on assumptions of movement.

Whilst small, the body of comparative literature on displacement is growing as academics, practitioners and policy makers seek to disentangle the conceptual and observed differences and similarities between displacement outcomes. Ferris (2008) has identified three 'overarching similarities' between those displaced by natural disasters and those by conflicts. First, Ferris identifies similarities in the human experience of disasters and conflict including loss of family members, separation and trauma. This involves shared protection needs, a similar gendering of displacement where women are more likely to be immediate and ongoing victims of both situations. There is also a class dimension where the poor are disproportionately affected and least able to recover. Both sets of displaced people, Ferris argues, will likely face difficulties in securing return or resettlement in another location. Second, she finds that people displaced by disasters and conflict will most likely become IDPs as governments, in both the developing and industrialised world, put in place measures designed to contain displacement and 'make it more difficult for people fleeing violence to seek safety' beyond their national border. And third, Ferris argues that the displacement occurs in the world's poorest countries revealing the close relationship between poverty and conflict and between poverty and vulnerability to the worst consequences of natural disasters, and poorer states' inability to respond to displacees' needs.

Ferris draws out a range of additional similarities between these two emergency situations. She argues that conflicts, like natural disasters, have harmful environmental consequences beyond the immediate event. These could include the impact displaced people have on the environment through the construction of camps and the concentration of displaced people in fragile environments with the effect of degrading and depleting the natural resource base. She sees further similarities in the politics of response to these two types of emergency, quoting research which shows that the level and duration of commitment to support is overridingly determined, at least in the US, by domestic and foreign policy considerations rather than on the basis of need.

The differences between the two situations Ferris notes are of degree rather than substance. In terms of solutions open to people displaced by natural disasters or conflicts, for the former to return home may not be an option where impacts are at their most severe. In conflict situations there is typically advanced warning of the upcoming risk of displacement and therefore some opportunity to anticipate or prepare. Evidence presented by the Calcutta Research Group (Ferris 2007) on the duration of displacement would suggest that in most cases victims of natural disasters are able to return home sooner than other categories of displaced people. Data gathered from four South Asian countries suggested that 80 per cent of those displaced by natural disasters had been displaced for one year or less, while 57 per cent of those displaced by armed conflict and 66 per cent of those displaced by development project construction and land acquisition had been displaced for more than five years. In terms of international assistance, with very important exceptions including Burma in May 2008, governments are normally more prepared to accept international governmental, military as well as nongovernmental assistance to aid in natural disaster operations than they are to accept assistance in conflict situations.

The following section draws together some of the findings of this study as they relate to two common sets of outcomes, namely the risk of impoverishment and human rights violations, that would seem to define the experience of displacement in non-conflict situations for the majority of those involved.

Looking broadly across the literature on the different domains of displacement – be they as a result of development projects or disasters, or for environmental and conservation projects – some of the most telling analysis has been on the impoverishing and marginalising effects of rapid externally imposed change resulting not necessarily in physical relocation but in the creation of new impoverishment and livelihood risks that extend beyond the immediately affected population, are intergenerational and which affect all populations irrespective of movement. Cernea, echoing Deng's earlier use of the term 'dispossession', would shift the focus of our attention away from uprooting and instead towards impoverishment and a deeper examination of the historical and structural causes and consequences of human insecurity and vulnerability. Both conceptually and operationally this is already the underpinning rationale to the IFRC framework which has consistently shied away from what it perceives to be unhelpful distinctions between categories of human need based on a physical condition and pragmatic labels such as civilian/combatant, displaced/non-displaced, or IDP/refugee in favour of responses based on humanitarian principles of impartiality, neutrality and universality. There are enormous challenges to the preservation of the humanitarian space in current conflict and intervention situations, and impracticalities in terms of the capacity and political will of governments to take responsibility and action for generalised human insecurity.

Shared Outcomes of Displacement

Impoverishment and Marginalisation

The work of Cernea and McDowell (2000) comparing the situations of development affected populations with refugees displaced by conflict supports one of Ferris's key findings, namely that impoverishment –

indeed new forms of impoverishment and dispossession – would appear to be common in all displacement whatever the immediate cause. This volume has suggested that for displacement to avoid being the catalyst for embedded impoverishment and human rights violations, it may benefit from being understood in wider development frameworks that promote the building of secure sustainable livelihoods. Evidence finds, and McDowell (2002) has argued this elsewhere, that the displacement and resettling of populations is frequently a particular and dramatic example of enforced, exogenous rapid social change, and suggests there are combinations of factors and processes that, in certain cases, are common whether the initial displacement was caused by conflict, planned development or natural disasters. As Ferris and others have suggested there may be particularly close parallels between the experiences of disaster-affected and development-affected populations in circumstances where the populations are poor and relatively marginalised, where displacement is arbitrary and where international standards in protection and resettlement assistance are not achieved.

Indeed, key to this failure to provide 'durable solutions' to displaced populations is the failure to properly manage the complex challenge of relocation and livelihood reestablishment for populations who are unable to return home. In common with many disaster, environment and climate change-affected populations, and for people displaced by many types of development projects, the possibility of return will increasingly be removed as houses, land and familiar environments are irrevocably degraded, lost beneath rising waters, dismantled or built over. For affected populations who are involuntarily relocated, the sense of belonging is for many shattered as attachments to land and place are severed. Academic researchers including Scudder (1996, 2005) and Colson (1999) with a focus on the gendered aspects of uprooting have recognised that involuntary relocation and loss of original 'home' are stressful in unique ways, and that stress has wide implications over a number of generations.

We have shown in Chapter Five that the expectation that whole communities can be transplanted to a new location, and that permanent and sustainable lives, livelihoods and cultural communities can be rebuilt in a short space of time with limited resources, is the misplaced basis for economic and development decision making by states that result in construction works that knowingly displace settled populations. It is an assumption that also underpins post-disaster planning and may also shape resettlement programmes for people displaced by rising sea levels and other climate change-related events within countries and possibly across borders. Populations relocated by disasters or uprooted by government actions are not alone in the world in having to farm inferior or marginal lands, and nor are they alone in living in sub-standard housing with few government services, and without international recognition of their plight. However, displaced and relocated communities are a particular case because they are compelled or forcibly displaced and relocated in a situation in which past securities have been removed, and vulnerability suddenly in the case of disasters, and usually more gradually in the case of development projects, is externally but legally imposed and often sanctioned or at least acquiesced to by the majority population – though often on the basis of partial information.

Certainly there are differences between displacement domains: the experience of being uprooted in a city to make way for a new road is different in important ways to the experience of being displaced and resettled by a dam in a remote mountainous area or made homeless through a volcano eruption. The commitment of governments, private corporations and other agencies to resettlement varies from country to country, and project to project, and as shown in Chapter Five the legal and protective frameworks in which displacement and resettlement occur also vary widely and are differently applied.

Research across displacement/relocation domains has benefited from Cernea's identification of the key risks that cause asset loss and impoverishment through involuntary displacement. Cernea does not suggest that resettlement processes play out in isolation from the wider historical, political, economic, social or cultural context. Rather, in proposing that there are distinct and identifiable processes in involuntary resettlement that account for the onset and unfolding of impoverishment, a number of studies have sought to explore the involuntary resettlement dynamic in terms of its own logic, but also in the broader context. The ADB (see Chapter Five) has commissioned a number of studies to further understand impoverishment risks and to develop new procedures to both anticipate and ameliorate such risks in the resettlement planning process.

McDowell (2002, and see Moser and Rodgers 2005) has proposed an analysis of resettlement-created impoverishment that combines both Cernea's impoverishment risk analysis and more recent rural development theories and methods derived from the sustainable livelihoods body of work which seeks to analyse and understand rural development processes but with a consistent focus on impoverishment as a common outcome of displacement, poor households, and the decisions people take about how to achieve successful sustainable livelihoods and what support they need to do so. The approach would benefit future planning when seeking to understand the impacts of disasters and forced displacement on the livelihoods and human rights of affected populations, and the process of post-disaster livelihood reconstruction. The challenge of re-establishing livelihoods is a complex one in particular because in the process of uprooting and relocation, institutional arrangements are fundamentally altered, relocated populations confront increased insecurities and new dynamics influence people's abilities to compete for and control resources. Displacement research, following natural disasters or conflict, or as a result of development projects, has documented well the impacts of forced uprooting on institutional and livelihood processes particularly in relation to improving what Albala-Bertrand (2000) terms 'emergency' (short-term relief) and 'restitution' (long-term social and physical reconstruction) compensatory responses through risk and livelihood analysis.

Cernea's (Cernea and McDowell 2000) Impoverishment Risks and Reconstruction model highlights the intrinsic risks or sub-processes that cause impoverishment through forced relocation, as well as the ways to counteract – eliminate or mitigate – such risks. According to Cernea, the key impoverishment sub-processes and components for reconstruction of involuntary resettlers' livelihoods, are: landlessness, joblessness, homelessness, marginalisation, food insecurity, increased morbidity, loss of access to common property resources, and community disarticulation.

Community disarticulation is arguably the most complex part of the displacement and reconstruction process. The term is used to refer to the tearing apart of social structures, interpersonal ties, and the enveloping social fabric as a result of forced resettlement. Cernea and McDowell have described the main elements of community disarticulation as the scattering of kinship groups and informal networks of mutual help. The unravelling of spatially and culturally based patterns of self-organisation, social interaction and reciprocity represents loss of valuable social capital that compounds the loss of both natural and man-made capital (Cernea and McDowell 2000). While these components of impoverishment were identified in relation to involuntary resettlement induced by planned development processes, evidence suggests that the same risks – though in different combinations, and with different intensities – are critical in other domains of forced displacement.

Part of the future challenge will be to explore existing and alternative routes to sustainable livelihoods for displaced people in contrasting agro-ecological and political settings with a focus on the issue of land. A broad aim of any approach would be to ask: what is a sustainable livelihood in a given setting, and why is it that some displaced households achieve adequate livelihoods when others fail? These questions are important for understanding the situation of displaced populations and their ongoing assistance and protection needs. Resettlement planning for displaced people will essentially involve accounting for changes to the basic material and social, tangible and intangible assets that people have in their possession, and tracking the impact of these changes – more specifically losses – on their livelihood and survival strategies. In terms of disaster response, resettlement policy and operational strategies, through such an approach it may be possible to identify where investments to promote livelihoods should be focused in light of the risks people confront, the assets they lose and the trade-offs they are obliged to make in pursuing survival and livelihood strategies. Central also will be the identification of the key conditions for improvement in sustainable livelihoods, and an analysis of which institutions (exogenous, endogenous, formal and informal) mediate people's access to and control over the resources necessary to pursue those strategies in the resettlement phase. Pilgrim and McDowell's work in Cambodia (see Chapter Seven) suggests that livelihood insecurities as a result of resettlement (be it relatively minor partial asset losses and social disruption) or relocation to a new place compound impoverishment and reduce livelihood options.

The authors of this volume would therefore suggest that far greater attention needs to be paid to the as yet poorly understood impacts of rapid change brought about by forced displacement and involuntary resettlement on people's livelihoods throughout the displacement–resettlement cycle. Our paucity of knowledge challenges researchers to map the 'variables of impoverishment' (Cernea 2000) and understand the ways in which those variables are interlinked, and influence one another in ways that lead to livelihood reconstruction or further impoverishment, or both in all displacement situations. Such analysis based on dynamic processes, livelihood systems and vulnerability would reach beyond the narrowly economistic to examine, for example, hypothesised linkages between the experience of resettlement with weakening social cohesion, or inequality and increased morbidity and mortality. Further, it is proposed that livelihoods-based displacement and resettlement research should focus not on poor households as a given category, but rather on the sub-processes of displacement- and resettlement-created impoverishment, to explain why households become poor, why they stay poor in post-disaster and resettlement situations, and why the risks associated with involuntary resettlement and disaster-related displacement demand targeted responses from governments, financing institutions and community organisations with the achievement of sustainable livelihoods as the key objective. Key to this analysis is the political context within which displacement and resettlement takes place, the robustness of domestic laws, the engagement of those displaced and civil society in decision making and external scrutiny to ensure international standards are adhered to where international funding is secured.

Displacement's Human Rights Challenges

As we have shown in this volume, the deliberate and arbitrary displacement of populations is responsible for a range of serious human rights violations. In addition, there are several significant violations that may occur as a consequence of displacement whether from environmental change, natural disasters or in situations of political instability. While, as we have previously described, the Guiding Principles provide a framework for protection in accordance with fundamental humanitarian principles, the failure to abide by these principles may increase the risk of human rights violations. In all displacement situations it tends to be the poorest, marginal populations, those who are distanced from the centre of power and whose livelihoods are dependent on an insecure resource base, who are most at risk of these violations, generated not only by unequal exposure to risks of displacement but also by limited capacity to adapt to their displacement. The volume has highlighted a series of human rights violations and impoverishment risks associated with displacement and the barriers that prevent states, humanitarian agencies and international institutions from eliminating or minimising these risks.

In complex displacement emergencies it is always difficult to safeguard people's basic rights of access to food, water, housing and shelter and considerable work has been undertaken through the humanitarian reform process, building in part on The Sphere Process, to identify these gaps and weaknesses and to address them. The actions of the Burmese junta following the 2008 Cyclone Nargis which included the deliberate blocking or delaying of international aid and foreign aid experts coming to assist in the relief operation reminded the international community that universal guarantees of access to essential assistance are far from assured. There were additional reminders from Zimbabwe following the 2008 election that governments will deliberately violate people's rights both through eviction and displacement of who they characterise as political opponents and in the failure to subsequently provide basic assistance in the face of proven need for short-term political gain.

Once humanitarian agencies have negotiated physical barriers a further set of problems arise in terms of ensuring equitable distribution of aid provision. Discrimination disproportionately affecting displaced populations can be a major human rights risk in the aftermath of natural disasters, particularly where there are existing ethnic, national or religious divisions. There can also be discrimination along other lines, notably between types of displaced person. Although the effect of natural disasters can be to de-politicise the issue of international aid, they can also lead to the diversion of resources away from conflict displaced persons to those affected by disasters. In the aftermath of the Asian tsunami, particularly in Aceh and Sri Lanka, Kälin detected a tendency to neglect the needs of conflict IDPs in favour of providing immediate assistance to disaster victims. While it must be acknowledged that in this extreme case, decisions about the distribution of limited resources would have been extremely challenging, with some groups inevitably losing out, such discrimination violates the humanitarian principles noted above and has the capacity to contribute to further tension, violence and localised conflict.

Discrimination can also be a factor that affects the make-up and conditions within camps that are set up to provide protection for the displaced. These issues are common across all types of displacement, though in situations of natural disaster, those who are displaced may wish to return to their homes to protect property as soon as possible rather than languish in camps. It is a balancing act for authorities to make sure that return only takes place in safe circumstances without contravening people's freedom of movement. Where this balance is not found, it can often be the case that certain groups, contrary to Guiding Principle 4, are excluded from official and spontaneous shelters and camps on the grounds of ethnicity or by local people concerned about the influence of unknown newcomers to the area. Within the camps, discrimination is also a problem, although a larger set of human rights risks exist in what are often unsanitary, overpopulated and militarised settlements. Camps can often come to resemble a microcosm of conditions that put people at risk of violence and displacement in the first place. Resources are scarce and controlled, often necessarily in the first instance, by military organisations. There is a high potential for violence, heightened risk of sexual exploitation and discrimination in the case of a politicised military presence. Children in camps are also vulnerable to recruitment by fighting forces.

Women and children face further specific and heightened human rights risks in all situations of displacement. As noted with respect to camps, women face heightened vulnerability to sexual violence throughout the displacement process, though the conditions of displacement from natural disaster are unlikely to exacerbate this further, unless in an area of conflict. As noted above, however, the impacts of natural disasters can destroy existing livelihoods. If this occurs in an area of conflict where male members of households are likely to be involved in organised violence, single-parent households are less likely to be able to adapt to these conditions and access other livelihood opportunities. In these situations, where livelihoods are completely destroyed, women and children are exposed to greater risks of trafficking and military recruitment. Vulnerability is increased for people who lose everything and have little to risk when there appears to be no other option than to take what traffickers are offering. The risk of family separation is heightened in these circumstances, contravening Guiding Principle 17. Authorities should work to avoid family separation and, where this is unavoidable, make efforts to ensure family reunion once the effects of the natural disaster have passed. In addition, authorities are required, where possible, to provide continued education for children. Obviously, the disruption caused by disasters and displacement makes it difficult to organise education and particularly unlikely that it can be organised to coincide with each child's current level or abilities. Despite this, given the high propensity to return in the case of displacement by natural disasters it may be easier to organise educational facilities and activities on a temporary basis, unlike other situations where return is either unlikely or uncertain. Furthermore, it is argued that providing some form of educational activity is not only useful in and of itself but also reduces the vulnerability of displaced children to recruitment by fighting forces.

The loss of personal documentation (birth or marriage certificates, passports, identity cards for example) during natural disasters or subsequent displacement is a significant problem that can lead to numerous human rights risks. For slow-onset forms of environmental change, loss of documentation is perhaps less likely given that the gradual nature of movement generated in these instances would allow for some planning of movement. However, in instances of natural disasters documents are more likely to be lost. According to Kälin (2005) 70 per cent of people lost documentation in areas affected by the 2004 Asian tsunami. This creates immediate problems for those displaced in terms of accessing services and aid as well as receiving full entitlements for families. Without documentation the potential for corruption is heightened, but it can also affect people's right to free movement within countries and across borders. It is operationally and logistically difficult to re-issue documentation, particularly in cases of mass displacement requiring an immediate response. Kälin (2005) cites good practice from Sri Lanka following the tsunami, where power to re-issue documents was devolved to regional agencies and local administrative officials. In instances of displacement by natural disasters – and many other forms of displacement – while the loss of documents may not inhibit freedom of movement given the high propensity to return, it is still likely to be an issue on return. Loss of vital documents related to land and property, particularly where official local records are also lost, can create additional problems with respect to property restitution. Furthermore, in some areas vulnerable to natural disasters and the effects of climate change there may be no formal titles to land in existence, leading to significant human rights and impoverishment risks. This has the potential to make temporary loss of livelihood more permanent if people are unable to formally stake their claim for their own land. In addition those displaced by natural disasters will be keen to return to protect their property yet limited freedom of movement, potentially exacerbated by lost documentation, renders some people immobile and their property and belongings vulnerable to looting.

The final considerations with respect to human rights risks are consultation and participation. As the Guiding Principles emphasise throughout, it is crucial for organising authorities to involve displaced people in decisions about their lives: where they are moved to, how camps are organised, when and how they are returned and how property disputes are resolved. The risk of human rights violations can be reduced through this sort of consultation, particularly with women in respect of camp management and resource distribution as they tend to be most knowledgeable about families' and communities' needs. There are obstacles to achieving sufficient consultation and participation, however, notably the often necessary need to centralise operations and decision-making in the immediate aftermath of natural disasters and mass displacement. As noted throughout this chapter, many of the areas vulnerable to the risks of climate change are politically unstable and undemocratic, often lacking in lines of communication and consultation between the state and citizens. The failure of central authorities to relinquish power and resources to local officials and communities can heighten the sense of helplessness among those displaced impacting negatively on morale, mental health and people's optimism for the future.

Addressing the Challenges

As we show in this volume the best available current data suggests that fifteen million people annually are 'involuntarily resettled' as a result of development projects in the developing world. In India where it is estimated that more than sixty million people were displaced by development interventions between 1947 and 2000 – of which forty million were affected by water resource development – at least twenty million hectares of land were expropriated for development between 1951 and 1993 including seven million hectares of forests and six million hectares of common property resources. Some twenty-five million people lost both their land and houses, and fifteen million people lost common property (land and houses). It is assessed that about 70 per cent were further impoverished after resettlement. Meanwhile in China, between 1950 and 2005, over 70 million people were displaced, and currently it is estimated that 3.3 million farmers are being affected by land loss as a result of action taken by the state; the figures for urban displacement are unknown. According to Chinese official statistics from 2001 to 2010 approximately 26.5 million farmers will require resettling. This does not include the recent updates for the Three Gorges dam of a projected additional four million people who will be relocated due to potential environment risks.

In Chapter Six we show how the increasing focus on climate change will result in ever increasing measures for forestland protection, prevention of land degradation and return of land to forest or conversely the conversion of inhabited forestland for bio-fuel production. The primary threats from these measures will be to indigenous populations and the most marginalised social groups who have been pushed by poverty towards marginal lands.

Elsewhere we have argued that the line between public and private development is increasingly blurred as governments are faced with limited public funds to meet the demands of infrastructure development. The establishment of SEZs in India, for example, has led to continuing conflict as people protest against public-private land acquisition.

Land acquisition and displacement are a growing cause of social unrest in many developing countries. The Oxford University China scholar, Professor Frank Pieke, recently described 'land acquisition as the most import source of discontent and exploitation in rural China at the moment' (personal correspondence).[1] Increasing social unrest or the fear of unrest has prompted the Government of India in the past few years to approve for the first time a Resettlement and Rehabilitation Policy, focusing on both public and private sector investments. The adoption of the policy is a clear indication of the importance of this issue to one of the world's major economies.

Elsewhere in this Conclusion we have shown that particularly vulnerable in the development and displacement process are tribal and indigenous populations and those urban dwellers unable to prove ownership of the lands they occupy or depend upon for subsistence. These populations have been historically at greater risk of summary eviction in the development process.

In policy terms, the growing and immediate challenge of managing the development process while protecting the rights of citizens in situations of displacement and land acquisition is a complex matter involving policy making at many different levels and in all areas of governance. At the heart of this are a number of land-related issues:

- a lack of available unoccupied public land for development purposes;
- increased forced acquisition involving the use of violence – of both private lands and public lands occupied by the landless;
- the non-availability of alternative replacement land to ensure those who lose their lands to development are able to regain sustainable livelihoods;
- increasing private sector investments with minimal regulatory oversight by the state;
- and finally, a rise in public private investments with state involvement in expropriation but where investments are profit-oriented rather than in the public interest.

The Guiding Principles on Internal Displacement provide one critical mechanism to address some of these complex issues at an international level, and in recent years ties have been strengthened between the Representative of the Secretary-General on the Rights of IDPs and the multilateral development banks which are engaged in lending money for infrastructure projects that seek to confront these challenges. Indeed, the World Bank through its work on post-conflict reconstruction and its position as a standing invitee on the Inter-Agency Standing Committee has integrated the Guiding Principles into aspects of its work, though this does not extend to its recently revised policies on involuntary resettlement. Addressing the ADB in December 2005, Walter Kälin underscored the relevance of the Guiding Principles to development-created displacement specifically highlighting their usefulness in identifying displacement that could be considered 'arbitrary' and thus in violation of human rights standards, and more generally their contribution towards identifying those rights that are at risk in any involuntary resettlement process. He described as 'rare' the circumstances under which the sorts of development projects funded by the ADB and other banks are likely to be considered arbitrary and not in the public interest. Kälin reminded his audience that Principle 6 of the Guiding Principles ensures that development cannot be used as an argument to disguise discrimination or any other human rights violations by stressing that development-related resettlement is permissible only when the requirements of necessity (in public interest) and proportionality are met. In very practical terms this means looking again at the size of projects and their impacts, genuinely considering viable alternatives, taking into account all opportunities to minimise displacement and, where unavoidable, making special provisions for vulnerable populations, with all affected persons being fully consulted and their fully informed consent given. Kälin's aim was to build momentum behind joint efforts on the part of the UN; development, financial and humanitarian institutions; governments; national human rights institutions; civil society; and affected communities, aimed at ensuring the Guiding Principles were applied to development-induced resettlement programmes. Kälin's comments to some degree anticipated Guterres's call in 2008 for a global compact on all forms of displacement and the upholding of displacees' human rights (Guterres 2008).

While the structures and consensus necessary to secure a global compact of this kind are some way away, there have been policy developments in other areas that offer modest improvements in the protection of people who lose their land and other assets in the development process. States, in adopting national and regional resettlement policies and laws (for example Vietnam, China, India, Sri Lanka, Lao PDR), and acknowledging past damage (as the Chinese have recently done in paying reparations to the twenty-three million people displaced by dams in that country since 1949), could be giving out signals that they are accepting their responsibilities and acknowledge that development and economic progress cannot be achieved by disenfranchising and leaving behind populations who by happenstance live in the path of a particular version of 'progress'.

Within the main lenders, most notably the World Bank and the ADB, there have been over the past decade strong pressures from some staff and also from NGOs on the outside to strengthen their safeguard policies to ensure that development funded in part or whole by ADB or World Bank loans did not have the perverse counter development impacts of increased impoverishment, marginalisation of indigenous population and women, and accelerated damage to the environment. Consequently, throughout the 1990s there was encouraging dialogue between the International Financing Institutions and lender governments on new legislative frameworks within which land acquisition and involuntary resettlement would be conducted. There was encouragement also that the Banks' oversight role was being strengthened.[2]

However, in recent years the Development Banks would appear to have stepped back somewhat from this commitment and initial momentum towards improving legislative frameworks is in danger of being lost. Despite operational improvements in calculating and making reparations for assets lost as a result of land acquisition, the record remains poor and impoverishment remains by far the most likely outcome for the majority displaced from their lands and communities as a result of development investments. This volume has discussed a number of new uncertainties in the coming decades that may present greater challenges for policy makers, civil society, academic researchers and the affected populations, for example:

- the fast evolving *shift towards commercial development* for example in highways and energy development, in the construction of dams for power generation (for example the Nam Theun 2 hydro power project in Laos), and in the potential development of the Mekong river for serving the energy needs of the region;
- with *conflict-related internal displacement* on the increase, as we have already described, it is more commonly the case that development-forced displacement is inter-meshing with conflict population displacement – with clear protection implications;
- similarly, *disaster-related displacement* is on the rise and again there is a dangerous intersection of types of displacement that raise complex response and protection challenges (Bangladesh, particularly, faces enormous challenges in finding sufficient land for re-establishing displacees from disaster and development projects);
- *climate change*, it is predicted, will add considerably to this complex humanitarian, development and political situation;
- finally, the rise of new investors, such as China in Africa and the Mekong Region, raises potential social risks that have not been documented.

It is clear that development displacees in unstable and undemocratic countries and where development is often little more than a thin disguise for politically motivated actions, such as those described in Chapter Seven, are particularly susceptible to human rights violations and multiple displacements. Future policy directions need to focus on developing far stronger national and international legal instruments to avoid and minimise resettlement and include sufficient protection measures particularly for untitled and vulnerable indigenous people. This is particularly important in areas of rapid urbanisation where large slum populations need support.

Policies will in addition need to address the growing risks inherent in the extractive industries and large-scale private sector investments. Very little is known in the public domain about how the private sector actually handles their investments that involve involuntary resettlement or about what kind of laws and regulatory frameworks bind them. Certainly, the resort to national land acquisition laws which are generally weak and lack transparency may result in weakened protection for displaced populations. Acquiring land using nineteenth century domestic laws may be less controversial for the private sector but generally does not provide the necessary protection to those whose lands are being expropriated. There may therefore be an argument for a single international legal instrument that binds all transnational private or public sector investments with recourse available through an independent global court.

It remains the case that voices within UN humanitarian agencies, and specifically the UNHCR, despite calls by the agency's head for a more joined up approach to tackling the issue of displacement whether caused by conflict, disasters, development or environmental change, are sceptical about the value of humanitarian agencies 'taking on' state-mandated land acquisition and development-induced displacement as a protection and response challenge alongside its existing responsibilities. The authors of this volume share that scepticism. There is acknowledgement that the dissimilarities between the displacement occurring in the development process and as a result of conflict are difficult to sustain conceptually and may add to public confusion about the governance of and responsibilities towards the challenge of displacement. There is further the sense that a legal and political process is underway in a number of countries that may result in a genuinely robust protective framework for those who stand to lose land and other assets in the development process. Towards the latter half of 2008, for example, and in response to growing unease and anger at land acquisition for the construction of SEZs in many Indian states, referenda were held giving local populations a voice in these decisions. Beyond their concerns that the sheer numbers of people affected by involuntary resettlement arising out of land acquisition would eclipse the numbers of conflict displacees and perhaps divert people's attention from the growing needs of IDPs and refugees, voices in humanitarian agencies expressed concern that major states in the south, most notably the Chinese and Indian Governments, would continue to strongly oppose UN humanitarian engagement in what are regarded as internal and sovereign economic and social development issues. Land acquisition and involuntary resettlement are politically sensitive and any suspicion of 'interference' may place further unnecessary strain on the relationships between those governments and the UN system.

It is all too easy to be overawed by the present and future scale, complexity and scope of the challenge presented by human displacement. The volume cautions against accepting at face value the more intemperate and alarmist predictions of instability and human insecurity arising out of anticipated environmental change, the impacts of natural disasters and as a result of rapid population growth, industrialisation and urbanisation. While we consider the insufficiencies of the current regimes to avoid, minimise, manage and respond to the needs of people who will be displaced or forced to migrate as a consequence of these changes in the coming decades, the overview leaves room for optimism.

In the preceding section we have argued that important dialogue is taking place between the state and the citizen (often mediated by a professionalising civil society) in fast developing countries to find new ways to modernise economies and manage the environment in a manner that recognises and guarantees the rights of those who in the past have lost out in the 'development' process. In many places it remains a dialogue; policy and legal frameworks are weak and unenforced and it is the least visible in society who remain most vulnerable in the face of this protection deficit. However, forms of global resistance and demands for democratic participation in development decision making are taking root. And in the private sector, voluntary initiatives such as the Equator Principles are beginning to institutionalise a corporate responsibility for practice that matches – and not just in rhetoric or for the back pages of the Annual Report – international standards in social and environmental protection. As governments are slow to adopt and enact national resettlement policies that offer genuine protection, so corporations are only gradually changing their practice and appear unnecessarily fearful of external scrutiny. But there are positive signs of new 'contracts' emerging between the state, the developer and the citizen to avoid past injustices.

For this reason we have argued that population displacement and involuntary resettlement occurring as a consequence of legal land acquisition for development purposes, for the mean time at least, should not be at the forefront of UN or other related activities to promote the critically important UN Guiding Principles. We say this in large part out of an interest to buttress support for the Guiding Principles, particularly within those states where the political will to implement the protections they include needs to be won and cannot be taken for granted. The volume reflects concern that the issue of legally sanctioned involuntary resettlement may threaten the cooperation required to undertake the processes necessary for states to fulfil their responsibilities to displaced persons in those situations where human rights abuses and humanitarian needs are most acute.

Throughout the volume the authors argue for greater accuracy and precision in the use of terms. We do so because despite the wide scale recognition of the Guiding Principles there remains public confusion about who constitutes an internally displaced person and what rights and entitlements they have in international and domestic legislation. Public confusion on any important public policy issue opens the way for political manipulation and inaction. We therefore remain sceptical that attaching the label IDPs to people displaced by land acquisition for the purposes of building a dam or a road – and thus positing equivalence between their vulnerability and protection needs to 'internal refugees' forced from their villages by government troops or insurgency forces – will reduce confusion or build confidence in any new legislation. In fact we believe it may cause the opposite.

Elsewhere the volume supports the view that the other categories of displacement discussed in this volume – politically motivated and unjust displacement, following natural disasters and in some situations of environmental change – there is a strong case for identifying and recognising them in law as a specific category so as to ensure their basic rights. And furthermore that this recognition should be part of the process of adopting new national resettlement laws and policies for people affected by disasters or other environmental reasons and internal conflicts. The progress made recently in drafting such resettlement policies in various Asian countries could prove a useful and instructive parallel process.

While national laws are critical to achieving the protection of those displaced, the Guiding Principles as more than a simple restatement of legal values have a critical role to play in not only shaping the protection activities of the UN and other humanitarian agencies (acting after the event) but in developing binding instruments to prevent the harmful displacement we have described. Evidence presented suggests that the displacement challenges confronting states and international bodies require collective action, similar to that now evolving to tackle climate change, that link states to regional and global bodies underpinned by coherent action involving the UN, development banks, civil society, donor governments and the private sector. The current legal and normative framework is likely to prove insufficient to address all the challenges that lay ahead, and the task is to construct a new framework built around the Guiding Principles that is capable of mobilising international action and rise to the displacement challenges outlined here.

Notes

1. The absence of a land market in China, coupled with the absence of legal provision to limit expropriation for public purpose development, has resulted in farmers losing their land to unscrupulous local governments and private developers who work in tandem investing in golf courses, property development and SEZs to name a few. Protests by farmers increase daily as they find their lands taken away for development.
2. For example, the Mumbai Urban Transportation Project (funded by the World Bank), which displaced some twelve thousand people, failed to plan for commercial opportunities for displaced small businesses and was finally suspended after the Bank's Board approved the Inspection Panel's critical report. The suspension was lifted after the approval of a remedial action plan.

Notes on Authors

Christopher McDowell is a political anthropologist specialising in population displacement, forced migration and involuntary resettlement in the developing world. He has held research and teaching positions at Oxford University's Refugee Studies Programme, Institute of Development Studies at Sussex University, Macquarie University in Sydney, Australia and King's College London. Christopher has undertaken consultancy and advisory work for UN agencies, governments, development banks and NGOs. He is currently a Reader in the Department of International Politics at City University London.

Gareth Morrell is a Research Director in the Qualitative Research Unit at the National Centre for Social Research, London where he manages a number of social policy research projects for government departments. He has previously held a Senior Researcher position at the Information Centre about Asylum and Refugees (ICAR), City University London, where he conducted original research on asylum, refugees and community cohesion in the UK and contributed to journal articles on development and displacement and the EU asylum system.

Bibliography

Adams, M., Sibanda, S. and Turner, S. 1999. 'Land tenure reform and rural livelihood in southern Africa', Natural Resource Perspectives, No.39, February. Overseas Development Institute. London.

*ADB. 1995a. Involuntary Resettlement, Doc. R179–95, 12 September, Manila.

*ADB. 1995b. 'Involuntary Resettlement: Policies and Strategies', Manila.

*ADB. 1998a. 'Handbook on Resettlement: A Guide to Good Practice', Manila.

*ADB. 1998b. 'Summary of the Handbook on Resettlement: A Guide to Good Practice', Manila.

*ADB. 2001. 'Reorganization of the Bank, Doc. R152–01, Revision 1 Final, 18 September', Manila.

*ADB. 2006a. 'Involuntary Resettlement, Operations Manual, Bank Policies (BP)', 25 September, Manila.

*ADB. 2006b. 'Involuntary Resettlement, Operational Manual, Operational Procedures (OP)', 25 September, Manila.

ADB. 2006c. 'Capacity Building for Risk Management, India Country Report, March', Manila.

ADB. 2006d. 'Capacity Building for Risk Management, China Country Report, March', Manila.

ADB. 2007. 'Capacity Building for Resettlement Risk Management', Manila.

*Adelman, H. 2001. 'From Refugees to Forced Migration: The UNHCR and Human Security', International Migration Review 35(1): 7–32.

*Ager, A., W. Ager and L. Long. 1995. 'The Differential Experience of Mozambican Refugee Women, and Men', Journal of Refugee Studies 8(3): 265–287.

*Agnihotri, A. 1996. 'The Orissa Resettlement and Rehabilitation of Project-affected Persons Policy, 1994: An Analysis of its Robustness with Reference to Impoverishment Risk Model', in A.B. Ota and A. Agnihotri (eds), Involuntary Displacement in Dam Projects. New Delhi: Prachi Prakashan, pp. 19–42

Albala-Bertrand, J. 2000. 'What is a 'Complex Humanitarian Emergency'? An Analytical Essay'. Working Paper 420, Queen Mary University, London.

Alberts, R.C. et al. 1996. Land Management and Local Level Registries. Windhoek: Ministry of Lands, Resettlement and Rehabilitation.

Aleskerov, F. et al. 2005. 'A Cluster-based Decision Support System for Estimating Earthquake Damage and Casualties', Disasters 29(3): 255–276.

Ali Badri, S., A. Asgary, A.R. Eftekhari and J. Levy. 2006. 'Post-disaster Resettlement, Development and Change: A Case Study of the 1990 Manjil Earthquake in Iran', *Disasters* 30(4): 451–468.

Alvesson, M. 1995. *Management of Knowledge-intensive Companies*. Berlin: Walter de Gruyter.

Arzu Iseri Say, A., A. Toker, H.L. Akin and G. Altay. 2005. 'A Cluster-based Decision Support System for Estimating Earthquake Damage and Casualties', *Disasters* 29(3): 255–276.

Ashton, J. 2006. 'Climate Security and Diplomacy of Interdependence', UK Foreign and Commonwealth Office, London, April.

Asif, M. 2000. 'Why Displaced Persons Reject Project Resettlement Colonies', *Economic and Political Weekly*, 10 June: 2006–2008.

Banerjee, P., S. Basu, R. Chaudhury and S.K. Das (eds). 2005. *Internal Displacement in South Asia*. New Delhi: Sage.

Bayefsky, A. and J. Fitzpatrick. 2000. *Human Rights and Forced Displacement*. Boston: Martinus Nijhoff Publishers.

Benn, H. 2004. Statement Before the Overseas Development Institute, London, December 15.

*Bhabha, J. 2002. 'International Gatekeepers? The Tension Between Asylum Advocacy and Human Rights', *Harvard Human Rights Journal* 15: 134–154

*Biddulph, R. 2000. 'Making the Poor Visible', Cambodia Land Project, Phnom Penh: Oxfam GB.

*Bird, J., L. Haas and L. Mehta. 2005. 'Rights, Risks and Responsibilities: approach to implementing stakeholder participation', *Scoping Report for the IUCN*. Retrieved 2 March 2007 from http://www.iucn.org/en/news/archive/2005/10/rrr_scoping_report.pdf.

*Biswas, A.K. 1997. *Water Resources: Environmental Planning, Management and Development*. New York: McGraw-Hill Professional.

Black, R. 2001. 'Environmental Refugees: Myth or Reality?', *UNHCR Working Papers*, No. 34, Geneva: UNHCR.

Borjas, G. and J. Crisp. 2005. *Poverty, International Migration and Asylum*. Basingstoke: Palgrave MacMillan.

*Brockington, D. and K. Schmidt-Soltau. 2004. 'The Social and Environmental Impacts of Wilderness and Development', *Oryx: The International Journal of Conservation* 38: 140–142.

Bromwich, B. 2007. 'Environment, Relief and Conflict in Darfur', Paper presented at the Overseas Development Institute, 2 August.

Castles, S. 2002. 'Environmental Change and Forced Migration: Making Sense of the Debate', *UNHCR Working Papers*, No. 70, Geneva: UNHCR.

Castles, S. 2003. 'Towards a Sociology of Forced Migration', *Sociology* 37(1): 13–34.

Centre for International and Environmental Law. 2001. Memo to Mr Ian Johnson. http://www.ciel.org/Ifi/Johnson_Memo_8May01.html.

Centre for Strategic and International Studies (CSIS) and Centre for a New American Security (CNAS) 2007. *The Age of Consequences: The Foreign Policy and National Security Implications of Global Climate Change*. Washington DC: CSIS and CNAS.

*Cernea, M.M. 1990. 'Internal Refugee Flows and Development-induced Population Displacement', *Journal of Refugee Studies* 3(4): 320–339.

*Cernea, M.M. 1994. 'Bridging the Divide: Studying the Refugees and Development Oustees', Washington, D.C.: World Bank, Environment Department.

*Cernea, M.M. 1996. 'Understanding and Preventing Impoverishment from Displacement: Reflections on the State of the Knowledge', in C. McDowell (ed.), *Understanding Impoverishment: The Consequences of Development-induced Displacement*. Oxford: Berghahn Books.

*Cernea, M.M. 1997. 'The Risks and Reconstruction Model for Resettling Displaced Populations', *World Development* 25(10): 1569–1587.

*Cernea, M.M. 1999. 'The Need for Economic Analysis of Resettlement: A Sociologist's View', in M.M. Cernea (ed.), *The Economics of Involuntary Resettlement: Questions and Challenges*. Washington, DC: World Bank.

*Cernea, M.M. 2000. 'Risks, Safeguards, and Reconstruction: A Model for Population Displacement and Resettlements', in M.M. Cernea and C. McDowell (eds). *Risks and Reconstruction: Experiences of Resettlers and Refugees*. Washington, DC: World Bank, pp. 11–55.

Cernea, M.M. 2003. 'For a New Economics of Resettlement: A Sociological Critique of the Compensation Principle', *International Journal of Social Sciences* 55(1): 37–45.

Cernea, M.M. 2005. 'The Ripple Effect in Social Policy and its Political Content', in M.B. Likosky (ed.), *Privatising Development: Transnational Law, Infrastructure and Human Rights*. Boston: Martinus Nijhoff.

Cernea, M.M. 2006. 'Re-examining "Displacement": A Redefinition of Concepts in Development and Conservation Policies', *Social Change* 36(1): 8–35.

Cernea, M.M. and C. McDowell (eds). 2000. *Risks and Reconstruction: Experiences of Resettlers and Refugees*. Washington, DC: World Bank.

Cernea, M.M. and K. Schmidt-Soltau 2006. 'Poverty Risks and National Parks: Policy Issues in Conservation and Resettlement', *World Development* 34(10): 1808–1830.

Cernea, M.M. and H.M. Mathur (eds). 2007. *Can Compensation Prevent Impoverishment?: Reforming Resettlement Through Investments*. Oxford: OUP.

Chambers, R. 1969. *Settlement Schemes in Tropical Africa*. London: Routledge.

Christian Aid. 2007. 'Human Tide: The Real Migration Crisis'. London.

*Clark, D. 2002. 'The World Bank and Human Rights: The Need for Greater Accountability', *Harvard Human Rights Journal* 15: 205–226.

Clark, L. 1988. 'Internal Refugees – The Hidden Half', *World Refugee Survey – 1988 in Review*, American Council for Nationalities Service. Washington, DC

CAN. 2007. 'National Security and the Threat of Climate Change'. Alexandra, VA.

Cohen, R. 2004. 'The Guiding Principles on Internal Displacement: An Innovation in International Standard Setting', *Global Governance* 10: 459–480.

Cohen, R. 2007. 'Response to Hathaway', *Journal of Refugee Studies* 20(3): 370–376.

*Cohen, R. and F. Deng. 1998a. *The Forsaken People: Case Studies of the Internally Displaced*. Washington, DC: The Brookings Institution Press.

Cohen, R. and F. Deng. 1998b. *Masses in Flight: The Global Crisis of Internal Displacement*. Washington, DC: The Brookings Institution Press.

COHRE (Centre on Housing Rights and Evictions). 2006a. 'Global Report'. Geneva.

*COHRE. 2006b. Letter to Sudanese President Bahir, Forced Evictions, Khartoum and Meroe Dam. Geneva.

Colson, E. 1971. *The Social Consequences of Resettlement: The Impact of the Kariba Resettlement on the Gwembe Tonga*. Manchester: Manchester University Press.

Colson, E. 1999. 'Gendering Those Uprooted by "Development"', in D. Indra (ed), *Engendering Forced Migration: Theory and Practice*. Oxford: Berghahn, pp. 23–29.

Colson, E. 2007. 'Displacement', in D. Nugent and J. Vincent (eds) *A Companion to the Anthropology of Politics*. London: Blackwell, pp. 107–120.

Condé, J. and P. Diagne. 1986. 'South–North International Migrations: A Case Study: Malian, Mauritanian and Senegalese Migrants from the Senegal River Valley to France', *Development Centre Papers*, Paris: Organisation for Economic Cooperation and Development.

*Crisp, J. 2001. 'Mind the Gap! UNHCR, Humanitarian Assistance and the Development Process'. Working Paper Number 43, New Issues in Refugee Research. Geneva. Retrieved 3 March 2007 from http://www.jha.ac/articles/u043.htm.

Dai, Q. 1998. *The River Dragon Has Come!: The Three Gorges Dam and the Fate of China's Yangtze River and Its People*. Armonk, NY: M.E. Sharpe. Translated by Ming Yi.

*De Mello, S.V. 1999. 'Briefing before the UN Security Council'. New York: UN Office for the Coordination of Humanitarian Affairs, Inter-office Memorandum, 3 June.

*Deng, F. 1993. *Protecting the Dispossessed: A Challenge for the International Community*. Washington, DC: The Brookings Institution Press.

*Deng, F. 2001. 'The Global Challenge of Internal Displacement', *Journal of Law and Policy* 5: 141–155. Retrieved 3 March 2007 from http://law.wustl.edu/journal/5/p141%20Deng.pdf.

Desbarats, J. 1987. 'Population Redistribution in the Socialist Republic of Vietnam', *Population and Development Review*, 13(1): 43–76.

De Waal, A. 2007. 'Class and Power in a Stateless Somalia'. Retrieved 5 October 2008 from http://hornofafrica.ssrc.org/dewaal/printable.html.

*De Waal, A. and O. Khin. 2008. 'Against Gunboat Philanthropy', *Prospect Magazine*, Issue 147, Opinions.

De Wit, P. and J. Hatcher. 2006. 'Improving International Peace Operation Responses to Housing, Land and Property Issues in Post-conflict Countries', unpublished.

*Downing, T. 2002. 'Avoiding New Poverty: Mining-induced Displacement and Resettlement', *IIED/WBCSD* 58(April). Retrieved 2 March 2007 from http://www.poptel.org.uk/iied/ mmsd/mmsd_pdfs/058_downing.pdf.

*Dwivedi, R. 1997. 'Why Some People Resist and Others Do Not: Local Perceptions and Actions Over Displacement Risks on the Sardar Sarovar', *Working Paper Series 265*. The Hague: Institute of Social Studies.

*Dwivedi, R. 1999. 'Displacement, Risks and Resistance: Local Perceptions and Actions in the Sardar Sarovar', *Development and Change* 30(1): 43–78.

*Dwivedi, R. 2002. 'Models and Methods in Development-induced Displacement', *Development and Change* 33: 709–732.

Feeney, P. 2000. 'Globalization and Accountability: The Corporate Sector in Involuntary Displacement and Resettlement', *Forced Migration Review* 8: 22–24. Oxford: Refugee Studies Centre.

*Feller, E. 2006. 'UNHCR's Role in IDP Protection: Opportunities and Challenges', *Forced Migration Review* December (Special Issue): 11–14. Oxford: Refugee Studies Centre.

FERN. 2007. 'Human Rights Abuses, Land Conflicts, Broken Promises', Media release. Moreton-in-Marsh, UK, 12 January.

Ferris, E. 2007. 'Making Sense of Climate Change, Natural Disasters, and Displacement: A Work in Progress', *Calcutta Research Group Winter Course*, 14 December 2007.

Ferris, E. 2008. 'Natural Disaster and Conflict Induced Displacement: Similarities, Differences and Interconnections'. Address given at the Brookings Institute, Washington, DC, March 27.

Findley, S. 1994. 'Does Drought Increase Migration? A Study of Migration From Rural Mali During the 1983–1985 Drought', *International Migration Review* 28(3): 539–553.

*Fitzpatrick, J. 2001. *Human Rights Protection for Refugees, Asylum-Seekers, and Internally Displaced Persons: A Guide to International Mechanisms and Procedures*. PAIL Institute Publications.

*Geisler, C. 2003a. 'Your Park, My Poverty: Using Impact Assessment to Counter the Displacement Effects of Environmental Greenlining', in S.R. Brechin et al. (eds), *Contested Nature: Promoting International Biodiversity Conservation with Social Justice in the Twenty-first Century*. New York: SUNY Press, pp. 217–229.

*Geisler, C. 2003b. 'A New Kind of Trouble: Evictions in Eden', *International Social Science Journal* 55(1): 69–78.

Geisler, C. and R. De Sousa. 2001. 'From Refuge to Refugee: The African Case', *Public Administration and Development* 21(2): 59–170.

German Advisory Council on Global Change. 2007. *Climate Change as a Security Risk*. London: Earthscan.

Gleditsch, N.P., R. Nordås and I. Salehyan. 2007. 'Climate Change and Conflict: The Migration Link', Coping with Crisis Working Paper Series, International Peace Academy.

Goldstone, J.A. 2001. 'Demography, Environment and Security: An Overview', in M. Weiner and S.S. Russell (eds), *Demography and National Security*. New York and Oxford: Berghahn Books, pp. 38–61.

Government of the People's Republic of Bangladesh. 2005. National Adaptation Programme of Action (NAPA), Final Report. Ministry of Environment and Forests. http://www.preventionweb.net/files/8133_1569ban01.pdf.

Gutteres, A. 2008. 'Millions Uprooted: Saving Refugees and the Displaced', *Foreign Affairs* 87(5).

Hall, R. 2007. 'The Impact of Land Restitution and Land Reform on Livelihoods'. Research Report 32. Programme for Land and Agrarian Studies. University of the Western Cape.

Haque, C.E. and M.Q. Zaman. 1993. 'Human Response to the Riverine Hazards in Bangladesh: A Proposal for Sustainable Floodplain Development', *World Development* 21(1): 93–108.

*Hathaway, J. 1991. 'Reconceiving Refugee Law as Human Rights Protection', *Journal of Refugee Studies* 4(2): 113–131.

Hathaway, J. 2007. 'Forced Migration Studies: Could We Agree Just to "Date"?', *Journal of Refugee Studies* 20(3): 349–369.

Hauge, W. and T. Ellingsen. 1998. 'Beyond Environmental Scarcity: Causal Pathways to Conflict', *Journal of Peace Research* 35(3): 299–317.

Helmer, M. and D. Hilhorst. 2006. 'Natural Disasters and Climate Change', *Disasters* 30(1): 1–4.

Helton, A. and E. Jacobs. 2006. 'What is Forced Migration?', in A. Bayefsky (ed.), *Human Rights and Refugees, Internally Displaced Persons and Migrant Workers*. Boston: Martinus Nijhoff.

Henry, S., P. Boyle and E.F. Lambin. 2003. 'Modelling Inter-provincial Migration in Burkina-Faso: The Role of Socio-demographic and Environmental Factors', *Applied Geography* 23(2–3): 115–136.

HM Treasury. 2006. *The Stern Review on the Economic Impacts of Climate Change*. Cambridge: Cambridge University Press.

Hildyard, N. 2000. 'What Went Wrong', Presentation to Chatham House Conference, July 10, 2000. London.

*Hitchcock, R., T. Scudder, J. Ledger and M. Mentis. 1999. 'Lesotho Highlands Water Project, General Review, Report No. 20', Report Prepared for Lesotho Highland Development Authority.

*Holtzman, S.B. and T. Nezam. 2004. *Living in Limbo: Conflict-induced Displacement in Europe and Central Asia*. Washington DC: World Bank.

Homer-Dixon, T. 1991. 'On the Threshhold: Environmental Changes as Causes of Acute Conflict', *International Security* 16(2): 76–116.

Homer-Dixon, T. 1994. 'Environmental Scarcities and Violent Conflict: Evidence from Cases', *International Security* 19(1): 5–40.

Homer-Dixon, T. and V. Percival. 1996. *Environmental Security and Violent Conflict: Briefing Book*. Toronto: University of Toronto and American Association for the Advancement of Science.

*Hong, Y-H. and B. Needham (eds). 2007. *Analyzing Land Readjustment: Economics, Law and Collective Action.* Cambridge, MA: Lincoln Institute of Land Policy.

*Horowitz, M. and M. Salem-Murdock. 1993. 'Development-induced Food Insecurity in the Middle Senegal Valley', *Geo-Journal* 30(2): 179–184.

Human Rights Watch. 2005. *Clear the Filth: Mass Evictions and Demolitions in Zimbabwe.* September, New York.

*IASC. 2006a. 'Protecting Persons Affected by Natural Disasters: IASC Operational Guidelines on Human Rights and Natural Disasters'. June, New York.

*IASC. 2006b. 'Guidance Note on Using the Cluster Approach to Strengthen Humanitarian Assistance'. 24 November, Geneva.

*Ibanez, A.M., A. Moya and A. Velasquez. 2006. *Toward a Proactive Policy for the Displaced Population.* Executive Summary, Secretariado Nacional de Pastoral Social, Caritas Colombia. February, Bogota.

ICAR. 2004. 'Media Image, Community Impact: Assessing the Impact of Media and Political Images of Refugees and Asylum Seekers on Community Relations in London'. Report Commissioned by the Mayor of London, London: GLA.

ICAR. 2006. 'Reflecting Asylum in London's Communities – Monitoring London's Press Coverage of Refugees and Asylum Seekers'. Report Commissioned by the Mayor of London, London: GLA.

ICAR. 2007. 'Reporting Asylum – The UK Press and the Effectiveness of PCC Guidelines'. Report Commissioned by the National Refugee Integration Forum for the Home Office, London: ICAR.

ICRC. 2006. 'ICRC Position on Internally Displaced Persons'. May, Geneva.

ICRC. 2007. *Internally Displaced People.* Geneva: ICRC.

ICRC. 2008. 'How is the Term "Armed Conflict" Defined in International Humanitarian Law?' Opinion Paper, March, Geneva.

ICRC. 2010. Protocol Additional to the Geneva Conventions of 12 August 1949, and relating to the Protection of Victims of Non-International Armed Conflicts (Protocol II), 8 June 1977. Geneva. http://www.icrc.org/ihl.nsf/7c4d08d9b287a42141256739003e636b/d67c3971bcff1c10c125641e0052b545.

*IDMC. 2007a. *Internal Displacement: Global Overview of Trends and Developments in 2006.* Geneva: IDMC.

*IDMC. 2007b. *Disaster-induced Displacement – Training on the Protection of IDPs.* Retrieved 28 March 2007 from http://www.internal-displacement.org/8025708F004BE3B1/(httpInfoFiles./7CE8640E88EEB381C125711500479885/$file/Protection%20during%20module%20handout%20natural%20disaster.pdf.

*IDMC. 2007c. *Forced Migration/Internal Displacement in Burma, with an Emphasis on Government-controlled Areas.* Geneva: IDMC.

IDMC. 2008. *The Many Faces of Displacement: IDPs in Zimbabwe.* Geneva: IDMC.

IDMC. 2009. *Monitoring disaster displacement in the context of climate change.* Geneva: IDMC.

*Independent Commission on International Humanitarian Issues. 1986. *Seeking Sanctuary: Displaced People within Developing Countries, Refugees: Dynamics of Displacement.* London: Zed Books.

International Federation of Red Cross and Red Crescent Societies. 2007. *World Disasters Report 2006.* Geneva: IFRC.

IOM/RPG. 1992. *Migration and the Environment.* Geneva and Washington, DC: International Organisation for Migration and Refugee Policy Group.

IPCC. 2001. *Climate Change 2001: The Scientific Basis. Contribution of Working Group I to the Third Assessment Report of the Intergovernmental Panel on Climate Change.* Cambridge: Cambridge University Press.

IPCC. 2007. *Working Group II Contribution to the Intergovernmental Panel on Climate Change Fourth Assessment Report.* Cambridge: Cambridge University Press.

*IRIN. 2007. 'Guns Out of Control: The Continuing Threat of Small Arms', Interview with Barbara Frey. Retrieved 24 June 2007 from http://www.irinnews.org/InDepthMain.aspx?InDepthId=8&ReportId=58967.

Jacobson, J. 1988. 'Environmental Refugees: A Yardstick of Habitability', *World Watch Paper* 86. Washington, DC: World Watch Institute.

*Jayal, N.G. 1998. 'Displaced Persons and Discourse of Rights', *Economic and Political Weekly* 33(5): 30–36.

Johnson, R.W. 2007. 'In Time of Famine', *London Review of Books* 29(4): 32–33.

Kaimovotz, D., A. Faune and R. Mendoza. 2003. 'Your Biosphere is My Backyard: The Story of Bosawas in Nicaragua', *Policy Matters* 12: 6–15.

*Kälin, W. 1998. 'The Guiding Principles on Internal Displacement – Introduction', *International Journal of Refugee Law* 10(3): 557–562.

Kälin, W. 2000. 'Guiding Principles on Internal Displacement: Annotation', *Studies in Transnational Legal Policy* 32, The American Society of International Law and The Brookings Institution Project on Internal Displacement. Retrieved 3 March 2007 from http://www.asil.org/pdfs/study_32.pdf.

*Kälin, W. 2005a. *Protection of Internally Displaced Persons in Situations of Natural Disaster,* Brookings Institute. Retrieved 3 March from http://www.brook.edu/fp/projects/idp/20050227_Tsunami.pdf.

*Kälin, W. 2005b. 'The Role of the Guiding Principles on Internal Displacement,' *Forced Migration Review* Supplement: October.

*Kälin, W. 2005c. *UN Expert Voices Concern for Internally Displaced Persons in Georgia,* media release. New York: UN, 27 December.

Kälin, W. 2005d. 'Regional Workshop: Capacity Building for Resettlement Risk Management Keynote Address'. Asian Development Bank Headquarters, December. Manila, Philippines. http: http://www.adb.org/Documents/Events/2005/RETA-6091/w-kalin-speech.pdf.

Kälin, W. 2006. *Cote d'Ivoire Facing Protection Crisis in Terms of Human Rights of Internally Displaced Persons,* media release. New York: UN, 24 April.

*Kälin, W. 2007a. *The Representative of the Secretary-General on the Human Rights of Internally Displaced Persons Concludes his Visit to the Central African Republic,* media release. New York: UN, 2 March.

*Kälin, W. 2007b. *UN Expert on the Human Rights of Internally Displaced Persons Concludes Visit to Azerbaijan*, media release. New York: UN, 6 April.

*Khagram, S. 2004. *Development, Democracy and Dams: Transnational Struggles for Power and Water*. New York: Cornell University Press.

*Khodka, C. 1999. *House Construction After Displacement Under Nepal's Kali Gandaki Hydropower Dam Project*. Photostudy. Beltari, Nepal: KGEMU.

*Kibreab, G. 1997. 'Environmental Causes and Impact of Refugee Movements: A Critique of the Current Debate', *Disasters* 21(1): 20–38.

*Kibreab, G. 2001. *Displaced Communities and the Reconstruction of Livelihoods in Eritrea*, Discussion Paper No. 2001/23, WIDER, United Nations University.

Kolmannskog, V.O. 2008. *Future Floods of Refugees: A Comment on Climate Change, Conflict and Forced Migration*. Oslo: Norwegian Refugee Council.

*Koser, K. 2008. 'Gaps in IDP Protection', *Forced Migration Review* 31: 17.

*Lassailly-Jacob, V. 2000. 'Reconstructing Livelihoods through Land Settlement Schemes: Comparative Reflections on Refugees and Oustees in Africa', in M.M. Cernea and C. McDowell (eds), *Risks and Reconstruction: Experiences of Resettlers and Refugees*. Washington, DC: World Bank, pp. 108–124.

*Leckie, S. 2008. 'Human Rights Implications', *Forced Migration Review* 31: 18–19.

Lee, S.-W. 2001. *Environment Matters: Conflict, Refugee and International Relations*. Seoul and Tokyo: World Human Development Institute Press.

*Leslie, J. 2005. *Deep Water: The Epic Struggle Over Dams, Displaced People, and the Environment*. Farrar: Straus and Giroux.

*Likosky, M. 2003. 'Mitigating Human Rights Risk in International Infrastructure Projects', *Indiana Journal of Global Legal Studies* 10(2): 65–96.

*Likosky, M. 2005. 'Beyond Naming and Shaming: Towards a Human Rights Unit for Infrastructure Projects', in M. Likosky (ed.), *Privatising Development: Transnational Law, Infrastructure Projects and Human Rights*. Boston: Martinus Nijhoff, pp. 3–26.

*Loescher, G. 1996. *Beyond Charity: International Cooperation and the Global Refugee Crisis*. Oxford: Oxford University Press.

*Loescher, G. and J. Milner. 2005. *Protracted Refugee Situations: Domestic and International Security Implications*. London: Routledge.

Maisels, F. et al. 2007. 'Central Africa's Protected Areas and the Purported Displacement of People: A First Critical Review of Existing Data', in H.K. Redford and E. Fearn (eds), *Protected Areas and Human Displacement: A Conservation Perspective*. Wildlife Conservation Society Working Paper No. 29, New York: WCS, pp. 75–89.

Martin, S. 1999. *Handbook for Applying the Guiding Principles in Internal Displacement*. Geneva: UNOCHA/Brookings Institute.

Martin, S. et al. 2006. *The Uprooted: Improving Humanitarian Responses to Forced Migration*. New York: Lexington Books.

Mazzucato, V., D. Niemeijer, L. Stroosnijder and N. Roling. 2001. 'Social Networks and the Dynamics of Soil and Water Conservation in the Sahel', IIED, London, Gatekeeper Series No. 101.

*Mburugu, E. 1993. 'Dislocation of Settled Communities in the Development Process: The Case of Kiambere Hydroelectric Project', in C.C. Cook (ed.), *Involuntary Resettlement in Africa*, World Bank Technical Paper No. 227, Washington, DC: World Bank.

*McCully, P. 1996. *Silenced Rivers: The Ecology and Politics of Large Dams*. London: Zed Books.

McDowell, C. 1996a. *A Tamil Asylum Diaspora: Sri Lankan Migration, Politics and Change in Switzerland*. Oxford: Berghahn Books.

McDowell, C. (ed.). 1996b. *Understanding Impoverishment: The Consequences of Development-induced Displacement*. Oxford: Oxford University/Berghahn Books.

McDowell, C. 2002. 'Involuntary Resettlement, Impoverishment Risks and Sustainable Livelihoods', *Australasian Journal of Disaster and Trauma Studies* 2.

*McDowell, C. 2003. 'Privatising Infrastructure Development: "Development Refugees" and the Resettlement Challenge', in R. Sullivan (ed.), *Human Rights and Business: Dilemmas and Solutions*. London: Greenleaf Publishing, pp. 155–168.

*McDowell, C. 2005. 'An Asylum Diaspora: Tamils in Switzerland', in C.R. Ember, M. Ember and I. Skoggard (eds), *Encyclopaedia of Diasporas Immigrant and Refugee Cultures Around the World, Part Two: Topics – Types of Diasporas.* Yale: Kluwer, pp. 534–543.

*McDowell, C. 2006. 'Displacement, Return and Justice in the Creation of Timor Leste', in N. Van Hear and C. McDowell (eds), *Catching Fire: Containing Complex Displacement in a Volatile World*. Lanham, Maryland: Lexington, pp. 181–212.

*McDowell, C. and M. Eastmond. 2002. 'Transitions, State-building and the "Residual" Refugee Problem: The East Timor and Cambodian Repatriation Experience', *Australian Journal of Human Rights* 8(1): 7–27.

McDowell, C. and G. Morrell. 2007. 'Development and Displacement: Institutionalising Responsibility', *Development* 50(3): 33–38.

*McNamara, D. 2006. 'Conflict and Displacement: Breaking the Cycle – An Address at Harvard University', *Africa Policy Journal* 1: 107–113.

*Mehta, L. and J. Gupte. 2003. 'Whose Needs are Right? Refugees, Oustees and the Challenges of Rights-based Approaches in Forced Migration', *Working Paper T4*, Institute of Development Studies, Sussex. Retrieved 2 March 2007 from http://www.migrationdrc.org/publications/working_papers/WP-T4.pdf.

*Mintzberg, H. and J. Quinn (eds). 1996. *Readings in the Strategy Process*, 3rd edn. New Jersey: Prentice Hall.

Mooney, E. 2005. 'The Concept of Internal Displacement and the Case for Internally Displaced Persons as a Category of Concern', *Refugee Survey Quarterly* 4(3): 9–26.

*Morse, B. and T.R. Berger. 1992. *Sardar Sarovar: Report of the Independent Team*. Ottawa: Resource Futures International Inc.

Mortimore, M. 1989. *Adapting to Drought: Farmers, Famines and Desertification in West Africa*. Cambridge: Cambridge University Press.

Moser, C. and D. Rodgers. 2005. 'Change, Violence and Insecurity in Non-conflict Situations', Working Paper 245, London: Overseas Development Institute.

Mudalsee, M., M. Börngen, G. Teltzlaff and U. Grünewald. 2003. 'No Upwards Trend in the Occurrence of Extreme Floods in Central Europe', *Nature* 425: 166–169.

*Muggah, R. 2000a. 'Through the Developmentalist's Looking Glass: Conflict-induced Displacement and Involuntary Resettlement in Colombia', *Journal of Refugee Studies* 13(2): 133–164.

*Muggah, R. 2000b. 'Conflict-induced Displacement and Involuntary Resettlement in Colombia: Putting Cernea's IRLR Model to the Test', *Disasters* 24(3): 198–216.

Muggah, R. 2003a. 'A Pressing Humanitarian and Development Issue: Reflections on Internal Displacement and Resettlement', *GSC Quarterly* 9. Retrieved 2 March http://www.ssrc.org/programs/gsc/publications/quarterly9/muggahpressing.pdf.

Muggah, R. 2003b. 'A Tale of Two Solitudes: Comparing Conflict and Development-induced Internal Displacement and Involuntary Resettlement', *International Migration* 41(5): 5–31.

*Myers, N. 1993. *Ultimate Security: The Environmental Basis of Political Stability.* New York and London: W.V. Norton.

Myers, N. 1997. 'The Population/Environment Predicament: Even More Urgent than Supposed', *Politics and the Life Sciences*, 16(2): 211–213.

Myers, N. and J. Kent. 1995. *Environmental Exodus: An Emergent Crisis in the Global Arena.* Washington, DC: The Climate Institute.

NCHADS, Ministry of Health, Government of Cambodia. 1999. 'HIV Sentinel Surveillance in Cambodia', Phnom Penh.

*Newman, E. 2003. 'Refugees, International Security, and Human Vulnerability: Introduction and Survey', in E. Newman and J. van Selm (eds), *Refugees and Forced Displacement: International Security, Human Vulnerability, and the State.* Tokyo: UNU Press.

*Oliver-Smith, A. 1991. 'Involuntary Resettlement, Resistance and Political Empowerment', *Journal of Refugee Studies* 4(2): 32–149.

Overseas Development Institute. 1999. *Land Tenure Reform and Rural Livelihoods in Southern Africa.* Retrieved 23 April 2007 www.odi.org.uk/nrp/39.html.

*Parasuraman, S. 1993. 'Impact of Displacement by Development Projects on Women in India', *Working Paper Series Number 159.* The Hague: Institute of Social Studies.

*Parasuraman, S. 1999. *The Development Dilemma; Displacement in India.* Delhi: MacMillan Press and The Hague: Institute of Social Studies.

Piguet, E. 2008. 'Climate Change and Forced Migration', New Issues in Refugee Research No. 153, Geneva: UNHCR.

Pottier, J. 1993. 'Migration as a Hunger-coping Strategy: Paying Attention to Gender and Historical Change', in H. Marcussen (ed.), *Institutional Issues in Natural Resource Management.* Denmark: Roskilde University.

Redford, K.H. and E. Fearn. 2007. *Protected Areas and Human Displacement: A Conservation Perspective,* Wildlife Conservation Society Working Paper No. 29, New York: WCS.

Richmond, A. 1994. *Global Apartheid.* Oxford: Oxford University Press.

Robertson, G. and P. Ashdown. 2008. 'We must beef up the UN and the EU'. June 12, *The Times* (London).

Robinson, C. 2003. 'Risks and Rights: The Causes, Consequences, and Challenges of Development-induced Displacement', *Occasional Paper,* The Brookings Institution-SAIS Project on Internal Displacement.

*Robinson, J. (ed.). 2002. *Development and Displacement.* Oxford University Press.

*Rofi, A., S. Doocy and C. Robinson. 2006. 'Tsunami Mortality and Displacement in Aceh Province, Indonesia', *Disasters* 30(3): 340–350.

*Roy, A. 1999. 'The Greater Common Good', *Frontline* 16(11), 4 June.

*Salama, P., P. Spiegel and R. Brennan. 2001. 'No Less Vulnerable: The Internally Displaced in Humanitarian Emergencies', *The Lancet* 35(9266): 1430–1431.

Sanders, T.G. 1990–1991. 'Northeast Brazilian Environmental Refugees: Where They Go. Parts I and II', *Field Staff Report, Number 21.* Washington DC: Universities Field Staff International.

Schmidt-Soltau, K. 2003. 'Conservation-related Resettlement in Central Africa: Environmental and Social Risks', *Development and Change* 34: 525–551.

Schmidt-Soltau, K. 2007. 'Is Forced Displacement Acceptable in Conservation Projects?', *id12 Research Highlight.* Retrieved 25 July 2007. http://www.id21.org/zinter/id21zinter.exe?a=0&i=insights57art2&u=46aa2cba.

Schwartz, M.L. and J. Notini. 1995. *Desertification and Migration: Mexico and the United States,* Research Paper for the U.S. Commission on Immigration Reform.

Scudder, T. 1973. 'The Human Ecology of Big Projects: River Basin Development and Resettlement', *Annual Review of Anthropology* 2: 45–55.

Scudder, T. 1996. 'Development-induced Impoverishment, Resistance and River-Basin Development', in C. McDowell (ed.), *Understanding Impoverishment: The Consequences of Development-induced Displacement.* Providence and Oxford: Berghahn Books, pp. 49–76.

Scudder, T. 2005. *The Future of Large Dams: Dealing with Social, Environmental, Institutional and Political Costs.* London: Earthscan.

Sen, A. 1981. *Poverty and Famines: An Essay on Entitlement and Deprivation.* Oxford: Clarendon Press.

Singh Juss, S. 2006. *International Migration and Global Justice.* Aldershot: Ashgate.

South, A. 2007. *Burma: The Changing Nature of Displacement Crises. RSC Working Paper Series,* No. 39. Oxford: Refugee Studies Centre.

*Spink, P. 2004. 'A Closing Window? Are Afghanistan's IDPs Being Forgotten?', *Forced Migration Review,* Issue 21: 34–36.

*Stanley, J. (n.d.). 'Development-induced Displacement and Resettlement – A Literature Review'. Retrieved 2 March 2007 http://www.reliefweb.int/library/RSC_Oxford/data/FMO%20Research%20Guides%5Cdidr.pdf.

*Stavropoulou, M. 1998. 'Displacement and Human Rights: Reflections on UN Practice', *Human Rights Quarterly* 20(3): 515–554.

Steil, S. and D. Yuefang. 2002. 'Policies and Practice in Three Gorges Resettlement: A Field Account', *Forced Migration Review* 12: 10–13.

Stein, M. 1998. 'The Three Gorges: The Unexamined Toll of Development-induced Displacement', *Forced Migration Review* 1: 7–9.

*Suhrke, A. 1994. 'Environmental Degradation and Population Flows', *Journal of International Affairs* 47(2): 473–496.

Suhrke, A. 1997. 'Environmental Degradation, Migration, and the Potential for Violent Conflict', in N.P. Gleditsch (ed.), *Conflict and the Environment.* NATO ASI Series, Dordrecht: Kluwer Academic Publishers.

*Thukral, E. 1992. *Big Dams, Displaced Peoples: Rivers of Sorrow, Rivers of Joy.* Delhi: Sage Publications.

*Thukral, E. 1996. 'Development, Displacement and Rehabilitation: Locating Gender', *Economic and Political Weekly* 31(24): 1500–1503.

Tirtosudarmo, R. 2001. 'Demography and Security: Transmigration Policy in Indonesia', in M. Weiner and S.S. Russell (eds), *Demography and National Security.* New York and Oxford: Berghahn Books.

*Tobin, G.A. and L.M. Whiteford. 2002. 'Community Resilience and Volcano Hazard: The Eruption of Tungurahua and Evacuation of the Faldas in Ecuador', *Disasters* 26(1): 28–48.

Toussaint, E. 2004. 'IMF and WB: The Destruction of Indonesia's Sovereignty', CADTM. Retrieved 2 October 2008. http://www.cadtm.org/imprimer.php3?id_article=821.

Traufetter, G. 2007. 'The Age of Climate Refugees?', *Der Speigel Online*, http://www.spiegel.de/international/world/0,1518,476062,00.html.

Traynor, I. 2008. 'EU Told to Prepare for Floods of Climate Change Migrants', *The Guardian*, 10 March, London.

Tucker, C.J., H.E. Dregne and W.W. Newcombe. 1991. 'Expansion and Contraction of the Sahara Desert from 1980 to 1990', *Science* 253: 299–301.

Turton, D. 2003a. 'Conceptualising Forced Migration', *RSC Working Paper Series*, No. 12, Oxford: Refugee Studies Centre.

Turton, D. 2003b. 'Refugees and "Other Forced Migrants"', *RSC Working Paper Series*, No.13, Oxford: Refugee Studies Centre.

Turton, D. and P. Turton. 1984. 'Spontaneous Resettlement After Drought: A Mursi Case Study', *Disasters* 8(3): 178–189.

*Tushman, M. and P. Anderson. 1997. *Managing Strategic Innovation and Change.* Oxford: Oxford University Press.

*UK Government. 2007. House of Commons, International Development Committee, Humanitarian Response to Natural Disasters: Government Response to the Committee's Seventh Report of Session 2005–2006; Second Special Report of Session 2006–2007. London: The Stationery Office.

UNHCR. 1996, 1998. Compilation and Analysis of Legal Norms (Part I.), and Legal Aspects Relating to the Protection against Arbitrary Displacement (Part II.), Report of the Representative of the Secretary-General on

Internally Displaced Persons, Francis M. Deng, UN Docs. E/CN.4/1996/52/Add.2 and E/CN.4/1998/53/Add.1.

UNHCR. 2006. *The State of the World's Refugees.* Oxford: Oxford University Press.

UNHCR. 2007a. Policy Framework and Corporate Strategy: UNHCR's Role in Support of an Enhanced Inter-agency Response to the Protection of Internally Displaced Persons, 30 January, Geneva. Retrieved 3 March 2007 fromhttp://www.internal-displacement.org/8025708F004CFA06/ (httpKeyDocumentsByCategory./F5A6FBA6A5097460C125726F004A8B96 /$file/UNHCRIDPPolicy&Strategy22january.pdf.

UNHCR. 2007b. Statement by Mr. António Guterres, United Nations High Commissioner for Refugees, to the Third Committee of the United Nations General Assembly, 62nd Session, New York, 8 November. http://www.unhcr.org/476132d84.html

UN Office for the Coordination of Humanitarian Affairs. 1998. Guiding Principles on Internal Displacement. http://www.reliefweb.int/ocha_ol/pub/idp_gp/idp.html.

UN Office for the Coordination of Humanitarian Affairs. 1999. Handbook for Applying the Guiding Principles on Internal Displacement. http://www.unhcr.org/refworld/docid/3d52a6432.html.

* UN Office for the Coordination of Humanitarian Affairs. 2003. *No Refuge: The Challenge of Internal Displacement.* New York and Geneva: United Nations.

UN Office for the Coordination of Humanitarian Affairs. 2004. *The Guiding Principles on Internal Displacement.* New York and Geneva: United Nations.

United Nations Security Council. 2006. Transcript of 5476th Meeting. 28 June, New York.

United Nations University (UNU). 2007. *Re-thinking Policies to Cope with Desertification,* A Policy Brief based on The Joint International Conference: 'Desertification and the International Policy Imperative', Algiers, Algeria, 17–19 December, 2006, UNU.

Van Aalst, M. 2006. 'The Impact of Climate Change in the Risk of Natural Disasters', *Disasters* 30(1): 5–18.

Van Hear, N. 1998. *New Diasporas.* London: University College London Press.

Van Hear, N. 2006. 'I Went as Far as My Money Would Take Me': Conflict, Forced Migration and Class', in F. Crepeau et al. (eds), *Forced Migration and Global Processes: A View from Forced Migration Studies.* Lanham, MA: Lexington/Rowman and Littlefield, pp. 125–158.

*WCD (World Commission on Dams). 2000. *Dams and Development: A New Framework for Decision Making.* London and Sterling, VA: Earthscan Publications Ltd.

Webster, P.J., G.J. Holland, J.A. Curry and H.R. Chang. 2005. 'Changes in Tropical Cyclone Number, Duration, and Intensity in a Warming Environment', *Science* 309: 1844–1846.

*Wood, W. 2001. 'Ecomigration: Linkages between Environmental Change and Migration', A. Zolberg and P. Benda (eds), *Global Migrants, Global Refugees.* New York and Oxford: Berghahn Books.

*Woube, M. 2005. *Effects of Resettlement Schemes on the Biophysical and Human Environments: The Case of the Gambela Region, Ethiopia.* Boca Raton: Universal Publishers.

Wyndham, E. 2006. 'A Developing Trend: Laws and Policies on Internal Displacement,' *Human Rights Brief,* American University: American University Washington College of Law.

Yagura, K. 2005. 'Why Illness Causes More Serious Economic Damage than Crop Failure in Rural Cambodia', *Development and Change* 36(4): 759–783.

*Zaman, M.Q. 1989. 'The Social and Political Context of Adjacent to Riverbank Erosion Hazard and Population Resettlement in Bangladesh', *Human Organisation* 48(3): 196–205.

Web Resources

Protection of Internally Displaced Persons in Situations of Natural Disasters, A Working Visit to Asia by the Representative of the United Nations Secretary-General on the Human Rights of IDPs, 27 February to 5 March 2005, Office of the United Nations High Commissioner for Human Rights, http://www.brookings.edu/fp/projects/idp/20050227_Tsunami.pdf.

The Hyogo Framework of Action 2005–2015: Building the Resilience of Nations and Communities of Disasters, World Conference on Disaster Reduction, 18–22 January 2005, Kobe, Hyogo, Japan, http://www.unisdr.org/wcdr/intergover/official-doc/L-docs/Hyogo-framework-for-action-english.pdf.

The Hyogo Declaration, World Conference on Disaster Reduction, 18–22 January 2005, Kobe, Hyogo, Japan. http://www.unisdr.org/wcdr/intergover/official-doc/L-docs/Hyogo-declaration-english.pdf.

Yokohama Strategy and Plan of Action for a Safer World, Guidelines for Natural Disaster Prevention, Preparedness and Mitigation, World Conference on Natural Disaster Reduction. Yokohama, Japan, 23–27 May 1994, http://www.unisdr.org/eng/about_isdr/bd-yokohama-strat-eng.htm.

International Federation of the Red Cross and Red Crescent Societies – IFRC, http://www.ifrc.org/.

United Nations Environment Programme – UNEP, http://www.unep.org/.

Center for Research on the Epidemiology of Disasters. Since 1998, the CRED has maintained EM-DAT, a worldwide database on disasters. It contains essential core data on the occurrence and effects of over 14,000 disasters in the world from 1999 to the present. http://www.cred.be/.

Living Space for Environmental Refugees – LISER FOUNDATION, http://www.liser.org/.

Provention Consortium. Global coalition of governments, international organisations, academic institutions, the private sector and civil society organisations dedicated to increasing the safety of vulnerable communities and to reducing the impact of disasters in developing countries, http://www.proventionconsortium.org/.

Index